Palgrave Studies in Political Leadership

Series Editors
Ludger Helms, University of Innsbruck, Innsbruck, Austria
Gillian Peele, Department of Politics and International Relations,
University of Oxford, Oxford, UK
Bert A. Rockman, Department of Political Science, Purdue University,
West Lafayette, IN, USA

Palgrave Studies in Political Leadership seeks to gather some of the best work on political leadership broadly defined, stretching from classical areas such as executive, legislative and party leadership to understudied manifestations of political leadership beyond the state. Edited by an international board of distinguished leadership scholars from the United States, Europe and Asia, the series publishes cutting-edge research that reaches out to a global readership. The editors are gratefully supported by an advisory board comprising of: Takashi Inoguchi (University of Tokyo, Japan), R.A.W Rhodes (University of Southampton, UK) and Ferdinand Müller-Rommel (University of Luneburg, Germany).

More information about this series at
http://www.palgrave.com/gp/series/14602

Donatella Campus · Niko Switek ·
Marco Valbruzzi

Collective Leadership and Divided Power in West European Parties

palgrave
macmillan

Donatella Campus
University of Bergamo
Bergamo, Italy

Marco Valbruzzi
University of Naples Federico II
Naples, Italy

Niko Switek
Department of Political Science
Henry M. Jackson School for International Studies
University of Washington
Seattle, WA, USA

Palgrave Studies in Political Leadership
ISBN 978-3-030-75254-5   ISBN 978-3-030-75255-2 (eBook)
https://doi.org/10.1007/978-3-030-75255-2

© The Editor(s) (if applicable) and The Author(s), under exclusive license to Springer Nature Switzerland AG 2021
This work is subject to copyright. All rights are solely and exclusively licensed by the Publisher, whether the whole or part of the material is concerned, specifically the rights of translation, reprinting, reuse of illustrations, recitation, broadcasting, reproduction on microfilms or in any other physical way, and transmission or information storage and retrieval, electronic adaptation, computer software, or by similar or dissimilar methodology now known or hereafter developed.
The use of general descriptive names, registered names, trademarks, service marks, etc. in this publication does not imply, even in the absence of a specific statement, that such names are exempt from the relevant protective laws and regulations and therefore free for general use.
The publisher, the authors and the editors are safe to assume that the advice and information in this book are believed to be true and accurate at the date of publication. Neither the publisher nor the authors or the editors give a warranty, expressed or implied, with respect to the material contained herein or for any errors or omissions that may have been made. The publisher remains neutral with regard to jurisdictional claims in published maps and institutional affiliations.

Cover image: © Brain light/Alamy Stock Photo

This Palgrave Macmillan imprint is published by the registered company Springer Nature Switzerland AG
The registered company address is: Gewerbestrasse 11, 6330 Cham, Switzerland

Acknowledgments

This book originated from the paper, "Not only solitary leaders at the top: the experience of sharing party leadership", which Donatella Campus and Marco Valbruzzi prepared for the ECPR General Conference in Wrocław, Poland, from 4 to 7 September 2019. Then, in November 2019, Donatella Campus presented the research topic at one of the Jean Blondel Tuesday Seminars in Political Science at the Centre for the Study of Political Change (CIRCaP) at The University of Siena, Italy. We are grateful to the participants for the comments and reflections that were advanced on those occasions.

We are grateful to the series editors and the anonymous referee for their useful comments and suggestions. We would like to thank Ambra Finotello, who believed in this project from the very beginning and worked with us, and Arun Kumar Anbalagan at Palgrave Macmillan. Niko would like to thank Jamie Mayerfeld, Elizabeth Scrofano and Nicholas Wittstock for their helpful comments. Marco would like to thank Fabio Bordignon.

The book is the outcome of a joint, collaborative enterprise in which the three authors examined and thoroughly discussed all the issues together. Donatella Campus wrote Chapters 2 and 3; Niko Switek Chapters 4 and 5; Marco Valbruzzi Chapter 6. Donatella Campus and Marco Valbruzzi co-authored the introduction (Chapter 1); Donatella Campus, Niko Switek and Marco Valbruzzi the conclusions (Chapter 7).

All quotations originally written in foreign languages have been translated by the authors, except where there is an explicit reference to an edition in English.

Contents

1	Introduction	1
2	Not Only Solitary Leaders: Concepts and Theories	15
3	Birth, Life and End of Collective Leadership	33
4	The German Greens: Established Collective Leadership	63
5	Alternative for Germany: From Multimember to Dual Leadership	103
6	Five Star Movement: From Dual to Multimember Leadership	133
7	Conclusion	181
Author Index		209
Subject Index		217

List of Figures

Fig. 4.1	The electoral performance of the Greens at state, federal and European levels, 1979–2020 (%, mean for state level)	76
Fig. 4.2	Popularity of leading green politicians with Green Party voters/sympathizers (%)	87
Fig. 4.3	Number of articles mentioning the party chairs of the Greens in three German newspapers, 1993–2020	94
Fig. 5.1	The electoral performance of the AfD at the state, federal and European level, 2013–2020 (%)	112
Fig. 5.2	Popularity of leading AfD politicians with AfD voters/sympathizers (%)	118
Fig. 5.3	Number of articles mentioning the party chairs of the AfD in three German newspapers, 2013–2020	123
Fig. 6.1	Preferred leaders of the M5S voters/sympathizers (%)	158
Fig. 6.2	The electoral performance of the M5S at the regional, European and national elections, 2010–2020 (% list vote on the total valid votes cast)	159
Fig. 6.3	Number of interviews given by the main leaders of the M5S in Italian newspapers, 2009–2020	166
Fig. 6.4	Number of articles mentioning the main leaders of the M5S in Italian newspapers, 2005–2020	166

List of Tables

Table 4.1	Most significant events in the organizational evolution of the Greens/Alliance 90/The Greens (1980–2020)	66
Table 4.2	The organizational evolution of the Greens/Alliance 90/The Greens	70
Table 4.3	Type of leadership in the German Green Party 1979 to 2020	81
Table 4.4	Characteristics of the leadership structure in the phases of the Greens/Alliance 90/The Greens	93
Table 5.1	Most significant events in the organizational evolution of the Alternative for Germany (2013–2020)	107
Table 5.2	The organizational evolution of the AfD	113
Table 5.3	Type of leadership in the AfD 2013 to 2020	114
Table 5.4	Characteristics of the leadership structure in the phase of the AfD	130
Table 6.1	Most significant events in the organizational evolution of the M5S (2005–2021)	144
Table 6.2	The organizational evolution of the M5S	150
Table 6.3	Type of leadership in the M5S from 2005 to the present	161
Table 6.4	Characteristics of the leadership structure in the four phases of the M5S	171

CHAPTER 1

Introduction

1.1 Collective Party Leadership: A Largely Unexplored Phenomenon

Especially in recent times, political scientists have recognized the centrality of party leaders and their individual characteristics (Blondel & Thiébault, 2010; Cross & Pilet, 2015; Cross et al., 2018; Musella, 2018). As a consequence of the rise of some 'personal' parties controlled by their founders, (from Berlusconi's *Forza Italia* to Macron's *La République En Marche!*), and of the increasing discussion regarding the personalization of election campaigns and media coverage, attention has been especially directed toward individual leadership, which implies just one leader at the top, rather than toward cases of leadership duos or teams.

However, one-chief leadership is not the only existing model of party governance and some recent developments seem to have put forms of plural leadership into the spotlight. The team leadership of the Five Star Movement (M5S) in Italy and the co-leadership of the German Green Party can be considered examples of alternative models of leadership. Both parties have recently achieved remarkable electoral results. The former obtained the highest share of votes in both of the first two parliamentary elections (2013 and 2018) in which it competed. The latter happened to be the second largest party in the 2019 European elections,

© The Author(s), under exclusive license to Springer Nature Switzerland AG 2021
D. Campus et al., *Collective Leadership and Divided Power in West European Parties*, Palgrave Studies in Political Leadership, https://doi.org/10.1007/978-3-030-75255-2_1

surpassing even the Social Democrats (*Sozialdemokratische Partei Deutschlands*, SPD). Their positive achievements indicate that a single leader in charge of an organization that tries to compensate citizens' disaffection with traditional parties through a personal appeal is not the only path to success.[1] It should be clear that in the past powers and responsibilities in some prominent parties have been shared between different individuals—see, for instance, the exemplary case of the Christian Democratic Party in Italy. However, not only has this been the feature of several newly formed parties like the already mentioned Five Star Movement and *Alternative für Deutschland* (Alternative for Germany, AfD), but also of parties that had plural leadership in informal arrangements before deciding to adopt formal co-chairs, like the German SPD. As we will describe in further detail in Chapter 3, during the 1960s and 1970s, the SPD was governed by the so-called Troika, formed of three senior figures. However, there was always only one formal chairperson until 2019 when a reform established dual leadership.

In light of all this, we believe that addressing forms of party leadership involving more than just one leader is now particularly timely and useful. Therefore, this book calls for a deep and systematic analysis of all cases of parties in which powers and responsibilities appear to be shared among different individuals rather than being concentrated in the hands of just one leader.

As observed, most of the growing body of literature regarding political leadership has focused on single leaders and omitted cases of collective leadership from the analysis. The latter have been approached with the aim of identifying a real leader who concentrates more power than others in his or her hands (Pilet & Cross, 2014: 225–226). Indeed, all parties that do not fit into the category of the 'solo' leader are treated as a "further complication" (Pilet & Cross, 2014: 225) which makes comparisons unfeasible or more complicated. In other words, forms of collective leadership are considered as being a disturbing noise within the mainstream literature on leadership selection or deselection. The *a priori* assumption

---

[1] It should be noted that the empirical evidence indicating that elections are influenced by voters' assessments of party leaders is not uncontroversial. Authors such as King (2002) are skeptical about the decisive influence of leaders' personalities while others, like Bittner (2011), Garzia (2014), Lobo and Curtice (2015), argue that leaders have an impact on the electoral outcomes. For supporters of the 'conditionality' thesis, such as Barisione (2009) and Mughan (2015), research should determine the conditions that influence the extent of leaders' influence.

of this strand of studies is that political parties adopt a monocratic leadership structure, in which a single, almighty individual concentrates all main prerogatives, roles and functions on himself/herself. On the other hand, even if we intend to make the case for taking collective leadership seriously, it cannot be denied that in some, perhaps most, circumstances, "while the party could have a very complex organization, it is very easy to recognize the effective party leader at its head", namely, "the person in charge of guiding the party organization, defining its main political strategies and managing its relationship with the general public" (Musella, 2018: 12).

Collective leadership is also not taken into explicit consideration by the literature on intraparty politics (Belloni & Beller, 1978; Boucek, 2012; Duverger, 1954; Hine, 1982; Katz & Mair, 1994). Studies on the dynamics of groups of party members tend, instead, to adhere to a view of individual leaders engaged in a negotiation with party factions (Ceron, 2019; Greene & Haber, 2015; Harmel et al., 1995). Similarly, studies on the personalization processes tend to relate this phenomenon to individual leadership and to a top-down 'centralized' orientation, whereby "a single individual becomes increasingly prominent while her 'team' is decreasing in prominence" (Rahat & Kenig, 2018: 118). Some scholars, however, have not excluded that personalization may sometimes also involve a plurality of party actors in a sort of, 'bottom-up' or 'decentralized personalization' (Balmas et al., 2014). Thus, cases of collective leadership are not necessarily at odds with the process of personalization but can be, on the contrary, considered as elements "expressing decentralized personalization" (Rahat & Kenig, 2018: 226). Moreover, it is worth noting, however, that a large part of the studies on personalization concerns electoral campaigns and media coverage.[2] As a consequence, the object of such analyses is often presidential or top party candidates. As we argue, it may occur that collective leaderships are based on a division of labor in which a leader is the electoral candidate, while other individuals are in charge of other aspects. Hence, plural party leadership should not be trivially considered as a counter-trend in the ongoing process of party

---

[2] Actually political personalization is a multidimensional phenomenon that, as explained by Rahat and Kenig (2018), includes at least three facets: institutional personalization, media personalization, behavioral personalization. Reviews of research on electoral campaigns and media coverage can be found in Ohr (2011) and Rahat and Kenig (2018).

personalization. Indeed, in some circumstances, it may play a role in that process, albeit in a different or unexpected way.

If it is true that collective leadership has never been central in the literature on political leadership, nevertheless, there are authors who have argued for not overemphasizing individual, strong leaders and who have discussed alternative models. For example, in an impassioned criticism of the myth of the strong leader, Archie Brown (2014) argues in favor of a collegial style of leadership. He cautions against those leaders who try to dominate decision-making, bypassing ministers and the machinery of government, and he reminds us that important policy advancements were achieved through a collective effort. In a similar vein, Anthony King takes Switzerland as an example of a 'leader-proofed' democracy in which the government does not rely on strong leaders for its long-term success. In particular, he supports collegiality as a better form when compared to individuality, being a defense against potential harm done by a single person, especially those strong leaders that he defines as "high-risk individuals" (King, 2016: 135).

In particular, King focuses on the institutional devices that prevent a leader from acquiring too much power. Also Jean Blondel (1984) deals with the issue of collective leadership by concentrating on institutional actors and the power balance among them. He defines this as "a system where two, and only two, persons share the general matters of government formally, actually and consciously" (Blondel, 1984: 75). He refers to separating the position of the head of state from that of the head of government. Historically, an arrangement emerged for different reasons, "in particular because monarchs needed help in political and administrative fields; this is also why 'shared' leadership has frequently been instituted, recently, especially in the Third World" (Blondel, 1987: 156). In parliamentary democracy, the relationship between the head of state and the prime minister has been sometimes described as a duality, if not expressively as a dual leadership. The social prestige that encompasses the symbolic leadership of the head of state, (monarch, president of the republic, etc.), goes hand in hand with the operative leadership of the prime minister. Still in parliamentary regimes, "another form of dual leadership has emerged in many Western European cabinets, as a result of the part played by the minister of finance alongside the heads of government" (Larrson, 1993: 207). To some extent, "the minister of finance can even be regarded as a second prime minister, since no other minister is involved in all the aspects of the life of the cabinet in the way the minister of finance is" (207–208).

Finally, in semi-presidential systems, the roles of presidents and prime ministers together have been described as a "dual executive" (Elgie, 1999; Shugart, 2005; Shugart & Carey, 1992) or a "dual authority structure" (Sartori, 1994). In fact, the president is often predominant, and the prime minister is weaker and replaceable. Nevertheless, in cases of cohabitation, the prime minister gains greater autonomy and their dual leadership may become a form of competition/coordination. In other words, in the case of a unified government, the dual executive turns out to be a "duet" in which the voice of the president prevails over the prime minister. By contrast, in case of a divided government, the dual leadership becomes a "duel", that is, an overt competition between the two leaders (Pasquino, 1996).

Although such institutional facets are obviously related to the analyses of our book, our interest is actually on broader dynamics also involving a variety of psychological, cultural and organizational aspects. In this sense, the approach of this book is closer to the research design adopted by Strangio et al. (2015), who examined cases of political tandems, i.e., two individuals who concentrate authority in their hands and collaborate to provide policy directions. The authors analyze duos composed of a prime minister and an influential minister, working together to perform substantive policy reforms. Even if our concern regards a different context, with more of a focus on the party arena than on the executive arena, Strangio et al. (2015) can be considered to be an example of a fruitful application of concepts and analyses from organization theory and corporate governance literature to the political field. As we aim to illustrate, this is the path we intend to tread in our book.

In sum, with respect to most existing literature on political parties, this book intends to fill a gap and carry out a more realistic and less stylized analysis of leadership. We believe that party leadership cannot always be regarded as a monocratic structure that leaves little room for other influential actors, but it should be conceived of as a more flexible and inclusive arrangement. To do so, we need to develop an appropriate theoretical framework. Let us introduce the reader now to how we intend to proceed, by describing our research design and the selection of case studies.

1.2 Research Design and Case Selection

As has been argued, the object of this book consists of an issue that, until now, has not been extensively explored by political scientists. Nevertheless, the existence of parties whose governance appears different from the traditional 'one leader at the top' poses research questions to be answered and requires an appropriate theoretical framework to be developed. In particular, the evidence offered by some parties of recent formation or older parties that have recently adopted a form of collective leadership suggests that, in some cases, neglecting such arrangements could mean reaching only partial understanding of their nature and functioning.

In order to fill this gap, we will draw on the literature on leadership from organization and management theory, which, in contrast, has directed conspicuous attention to collective leadership. In the following chapters, we will review several contributions that have offered useful insights. A book by Alvarez and Svejenova (2005) has been particularly influential since it focuses on duos and small groups of leaders and deals with the mechanisms of their formation and maintenance at the top. Along a similar line, we intend to classify forms of collective leadership in the political field and analyze factors that affect their genesis and functioning.

A solid and well-articulated theoretical framework is needed, first, as an instrument to distinguish apparent from real collective leadership. Indeed, if in some cases the sharing of power and responsibilities is already evident in formal organizational structures, in others, only an in-depth analysis, carried out with appropriate conceptualization, allows us to ascertain if we are examining a collective leadership, either in the form of *dual* leadership (i.e., two co-leaders) or *multimember* leadership (i.e., more than two partners). Then, it is also crucial to identify some dimensions for attempting the classification of cases, such as the distinction between sharing positions and sharing power, or the presence of a division of labor and a complementarity among leaders. Finally, we will also try to identify some factors that may influence the emergence and the sustenance of collective leadership. Most of them are related to political, institutional and cultural contexts; thus, for this latter part of the analysis, we will rely on insights from theories of intraparty politics and party organizations.

Therefore, the first theoretical chapters of the book will be devoted to an effort of theory building that is meant to provide us with the tools for proceeding with the analysis of the case studies in the second part of the book. We expect that the outcome of such an empirical analysis will produce useful feedback to develop and refine our theoretical framework as well as generate some heuristic hypotheses that could be further tested on a larger number of cases in future research.

Having said that, it is clear that, in order to maximize the effectiveness of our research design, the selection of cases appears to be an especially important task. Indeed, it should be stressed that case selection follows different strategies on the basis of the specific goal of the researcher. Given the scope of our research, which has an inherently exploratory nature aiming at generating heuristic hypotheses (Gerring, 2006), the strategy for the selection of cases that we have followed has mainly attempted to maximize the variation of the variable at the center of our investigation, namely, the type of collective leadership. Moreover, in this exploratory study of a topic that has received thus far little attention by party scholars, the type of collective leadership is treated both as a dependent and an independent variable. More precisely, we are interested in generating and testing hypotheses on both the conditions explaining the emergence of collective leadership within political parties and, at the same time, on the effects that these specific configurations of party leadership may have on either the performance or the maintenance of the organization.

Consequently, our case selection strategy has aimed at maximizing variation within the category of those parties adopting some forms of collective leadership. More specifically, this maximization strategy has been based on three distinct criteria: (a) the separation between dual and multimember leadership; (b) the distinction between power-sharing and position-sharing arrangements in the distribution of power; and (c) the existence of a structural trait in the formation/establishment of collective leadership. Let us discuss each criterion in turn.

The first criterion relates to the distinction within the composition of the leadership structure (i.e., dual vs. multimember). In this respect, the three selected parties, (i.e., the German Greens, Alternative for Germany and the Five Star Movement in Italy), show significant variation both across cases and over time. In other words, patterns of dual leadership are the norm in the German Greens as well as in Alternative for Germany. In fact, both parties were founded with a multimember leadership structure but subsequently decided to reduce the chair-positions to two (in AfD a three-person leadership is still an option in the party statutes). Although they adopted this specific structure for very different reasons, that will be explored in-depth in the second part of the volume, both the Greens and AfD relied on a pair of co-leaders most of the time.

In contrast, the Five Star Movement has gradually moved from the initial dual leadership of the two party founders to a multimember configuration in which multiple leaders control a portion of intraparty power. Hence, as we have previously observed, variation in the type of collective leadership does not occur exclusively across the three parties/cases but also longitudinally within them, which is an aspect that, to some extent, expands the reach of our research and provides a more solid ground for the theoretical insights that can be drawn from it.

The second criterion, as specified above, concerns the specific arrangement used for distributing leadership among different actors (power-sharing vs. position-sharing arrangements). In this regard, the three cases that we have analyzed exhibit a great deal of variation. In fact, in its party statute, AfD set up a position-sharing arrangement according to which "two or three federal spokespersons" are responsible for the activity and the organization of the party. Similarly, in the German Greens the federal leadership of the party is formally distributed among two leaders/chairpersons, respecting the principle of gender balance ("at least one of whom shall be a woman", according to the party statute), and acting as representatives of the party both inside and outside the organization.

Although the two German cases present a situation in which power is shared by leaders occupying the same formal position within the party, as the case studies developed in Chapters 4 and 5 will show, there have been circumstances, especially in the Greens, in which other actors have played a leading role in the party's activity even though they have no formal position in the organizational chart of the party.

Unlike the Greens and AfD, in which a position-sharing arrangement for the party leadership has been the norm, the case of the Five Star Movement represents the opposite scenario, in which power is distributed among a team of leaders whose formal position within the party organization is unclear, unspecified or not even contemplated. Only in the last stage of the organizational development of the Five Star Movement was a position-sharing arrangement introduced, however, the party still presents many elements of division of power that are more in line with a power-sharing approach.

Finally, the third criterion used for case selection deals with a specific feature of collective party leadership. In particular, we have decided to focus on those cases in which collective leadership is not simply based on a temporary 'special relationship' between two or more individuals but, conversely, it can be considered as a structural feature of the party organization. In fact, all three of our cases have relied upon a form of collective leadership that, due to its durability over time and the alternation of different leaders, has become a structural, recurring pattern in the organization and also in the formal statute of the party.

The last additional criterion, that is to say, the selection of the cases in which the collective leadership is a lasting feature, contributes to explaining the choice of the German Greens, the AfD and the Five Star Movement. However, a final note about the cases that are, consequently, excluded is in order. This criterion led us to discard typical duos or tandems of leaders that represent excellent examples of many features of collective leadership. Indeed, there have been several relationships of specific presidents, premiers and formal party leaders with their deputies, vice or other senior colleagues that might be regarded as instances of dual leadership. Some of these cases, like Tony Blair and Gordon Brown in UK Labour party or Felipe González and Alfonso Guerra in Spanish PSOE, are, therefore, mentioned and discussed in the following chapters. However, albeit ideal examples to analyze the impact of personal bonds on leadership, such couples are less fitting for reconstructing an evolutionary path over time. These experiences may be, for instance, short term or a *unicum* in a context of individual leadership. Or they may present some ambiguities regarding the effective degree of hierarchy within the relationship. For all these reasons, considering that the nature of this book is to present an exploratory analysis, we have chosen to concentrate our attention on a different type of case study. Nevertheless, we consider this type of tandem as an important part of the phenomenon of collective leadership, certainly worthy of further research.

1.3 Outline of the Book

The first part of the book, composed of two chapters, is devoted to a conceptualization of plural leadership and to the design of a theoretical framework that will guide the analysis of the cases. The second chapter, *Not only solitary leaders: concepts and theories*, begins with a review of the literature of organization and management theory as inspiration for a classification of collective leadership types. Drawing on such contributions, we will distinguish between *dual* leadership (involving two people) and *multimember* leadership (involving a small group). The chapter intends to identify the main dimensions through which we will analyze the selected cases. A fundamental dimension to be taken into consideration is the distinction between experiences of co-leaders holding the same position (*position-sharing*) and experiences of co-leaders not holding the same position, but sharing in any case power and influence (*power sharing*). Another crucial dimension is the division of labor among leadership partners. Division of labor concerns any type of task distribution, but in several cases it is related to the degree and type of *complementarity* among leaders. Based on insights from organization theory and management studies, we will examine several forms of complementarity concerning roles, tasks and leadership styles. An especially useful concept is the distinction between *expressive* (relation-oriented) and *instrumental* (task-oriented) leadership functions, as theorized by authors like Verba (1961) and Etzioni (1965), and more recently developed by Rucht (2012).

On the basis of contributions from organization studies (Alvarez & Svejenova, 2005; Sally, 2002) and party theory literature, the third chapter, *Birth, life and end of collective leadership*, will discuss issues concerning the emergence and the sustenance of collective leadership. The chapter is organized around a number of questions. It starts by asking how collective leaderships are formed and if there are recurrent paths that lead to their adoption. We will discuss, among the other things, factors such as ideological predispositions and the need to merge different bodies together or to simply maintain unity among different factions. Then, the chapter proceeds by dealing with the nature of the relationship between leadership partners. Does the existence of close personal bonds, such as family ties or friendship, favor the formation of a plural leadership? Finally, the chapter analyzes those factors which may increase durability and stability or, in contrast, make a plural leadership fragile and exposed to dissolution. There are a number of circumstances that encourage partners to stay together despite tensions and conflicts: institutional and psychological factors, the existence of mutual benefits and the existence of a strong affective bond.

The second part of the book applies the theoretical framework described in Chapter 2 and discusses the issues raised in Chapter 3 through the analysis of three political parties, each of them analyzed in an individual chapter. More precisely, the fourth chapter is dedicated to the analysis of the German Green Party (*Bündnis 90/Die Grünen*, German Alliance 90/The Greens), from its foundation in the early 1980s to the recent electoral success obtained in the 2019 European elections. In particular, the chapter will provide a detailed overview of the transformations that occurred in the leadership structure of the German Greens, from its original multimember composition to the establishment of a dual leadership based on the principle of gender equality through the introduction of a position-sharing arrangement.

In Chapter 5, we remain in Germany but the analytical focus will be moved to a new political party that has emerged in the wake of the economic and migration crises that severely hit European countries in the early 2010s. In fact, Alternative for Germany was officially born in 2013, originally offering political representation to several smaller groups and organizations that had risen up in opposition to the European Union with its single currency, then moving the target of their criticism toward the migration and asylum policies adopted by the government headed by Angela Merkel. Formed as an anti-Euro party, the AfD has become a more 'traditional' far-right party with a peculiar mix of Euroscepticism, welfare chauvinism and nativism. Unlike the Greens, in the case of the AfD, the decision to establish a form of collective leadership was not inspired by some principles of participatory democracy or gender balance. To the contrary, the collective leadership introduced by the party founders was a nod to the various groups the party was based on, but it was perhaps more a concession than a conscious choice. This did not help to curb the high level of conflict, especially when the continuous electoral successes in state elections drew new actors into the party. In this case, after a short two-year period in which the party was led by a multimember body, a pair of co-leaders who share the same position within the party has been the norm.

In Chapter 6, we will investigate a different type of collective leadership, based primarily on a power-sharing arrangement between different and changing leaders. Arguably, the case of the Italian *Movimento 5 Stelle* (Five Star Movement, M5S) is one of the most peculiar, characterized by an analysis of plural party leadership. Founded in 2009 from the intuition of two web gurus (Beppe Grillo and Gianroberto Casaleggio), the M5S has rapidly become the largest party in Italy and, from 2018, it is the major partner in two consecutive coalition governments. In contrast to the experience of the two German cases (the Greens and AfD), the M5S party was co-founded as a political start-up by the duo Grillo-Casaleggio and controlled by a dual leadership up to 2014. At that time a group of leaders, both inside and outside of the formal boundaries of the party organization, has finally prevailed.

In the concluding chapter, we will summarize the main findings that have emerged from the empirical analyses conducted on the three selected political parties (Greens, AfD and M5S), and we will assess how the theoretical framework, designed in the first part of the book, can offer a better understanding into the functioning of those parties which have decided to not rely on a single, individual leadership. We expect that the suggestions deriving from the empirical analysis can help us to refine our theory, building and making it a more solid and useful tool for further research. In addition, the concluding remarks will focus on the conditions that can explain better performance of collective leadership or, to the contrary, those specific configurations that may hinder the organizational persistence or the electoral sustainability of the party. Finally, we will discuss how to improve and expand the scope of our research in a wider comparative perspective with the ambition to develop a realistic map of party leadership in Western Europe.

References

Alvarez, J. L., & Svejenova, S. (2005). *Sharing executive power: Roles and relationships at the top.* Cambridge University Press.

Balmas, M., Rahat, G., Sheafer, T., & Shenhav, S. (2014). Two routes to personalized politics: Centralized and decentralized personalization. *Party Politics, 20*(1), 37–51.

Barisione, M. (2009). So, what difference do leaders make? Candidates' images and the 'conditionality' of leader effects on voting. *Journal of Elections, Public Opinion and Parties, 19*(4), 473–500.

Belloni, F. P., & Beller, D. C. (Eds.). (1978). *Faction politics: Political parties and factionalism in comparative perspectives.* Santa Barbara, CA: ABC-Clio.

Bittner, A. (2011). *Platform and personality? The role of party leaders in elections.* Oxford University Press.

Blondel, J. (1984). Dual leadership in the contemporary world. In D. Kavanagh & G. Peele (Eds.), *Comparative government and politics* (pp. 73–91). Heinemann.

Blondel, J. (1987). *Political leadership. Towards a general analysis.* Sage.

Blondel, J., & Thiébault, J.-L. (Eds.). (2010). *Political leadership, parties and citizens: The personalization of leadership.* Routledge.

Boucek, F. (2012). *Factional politics: How dominant parties implode or stabilize.* Palgrave Macmillan.

Brown, A. (2014). *The myth of the strong leader. Political leadership in the modern age*. Bodley Head.

Ceron, A. (2019). *Leaders, factions and the game of intra-party politics*. Routledge.

Cross, W. P., & Pilet, J.-B. (Eds.). (2015). *The politics of party leadership: A cross-national perspective*. Oxford University Press.

Cross, W. P., Katz, R. S., & Pruysers, S. (Eds.). (2018). *The personalization of democratic politics and the challenge for political parties*. Rowman & Littlefield.

Duverger, M. (1954). *Political parties*. Wiley.

Elgie, R. (1999). *Semi-Presidentialism in Europe*. Oxford University Press.

Etzioni, A. (1965). Dual leadership in complex organizations. *American Sociological Review, 30*(5), 688–698.

Garzia, D. (2014). *Personalization of politics and electoral change*. Palgrave.

Gerring, J. (2006). *Case study research. Principles and practices*. Cambridge University Press.

Greene, Z., & Haber, M. (2015). The consequences of appearing divided: An analysis of party evaluations and vote choice. *Electoral Studies, 37*(1), 15–27.

Harmel, R., Heo, U., Tan, A., & Janda, K. (1995). Performance, leadership, factions and party change: An empirical analysis. *West European Politics, 18*(1), 1–33.

Hine, D. (1982). Factionalism in West European parties: A framework for analysis. *West European Politics, 5*(1), 36–53.

Katz, R. S., & Mair, P. (Eds.). (1994). *How parties organize: Change and adaptation*. Sage.

King, A. (2002). Conclusions and implications. In A. King (Ed.), *Leaders' personalities and the outcomes of democratic elections* (pp. 210–221). Oxford University Press.

King, A. (2016). In favor of "leader proofing." *Daedalus, 145*(3), 124–137.

Larsson, T. (1993). The role and position of ministers of finance. In J. Blondel & F. Müller Rommel (Eds.), *Governing together: The extent and limits of joint decision-making in Western European cabinets* (pp. 207–222). Palgrave.

Lobo, M. C., & Curtice, J. (Eds.). (2015). *Personality politics? The role of leader evaluations in democratic elections*. Oxford University Press.

Mughan, A. (2015). Parties, conditionality and leader effects in parliamentary elections. *Party Politics, 21*(1), 28–39.

Musella, F. (2018). *Political leaders beyond party politics*. Palgrave Macmillan.

Pasquino, G. (1996). Duetti e duelli: l'adattabilità dei semipresidenzialismi. In S. Ceccanti, O. Massari, & G. Pasquino (Eds.), *Semipresidenzialismo. Analisi delle esperienze europee* (pp. 99–148). Il Mulino.

Ohr, D. (2011). Changing patterns in political communication. In K. Aarts, A. Blais, & H. Schmitt (Eds.), *Political leaders and democratic elections* (pp. 11–34). Oxford University Press.

Pilet, J.-B., & Cross, W. P. (Eds.). (2014). *The selection of political party leaders in contemporary parliamentary democracies. A comparative study*. Routledge.

Rahat, G., & Kenig, O. (2018). *From party politics to personalized politics? Party change and political personalization in democracies*. Oxford University Press.

Rucht, D. (2012). Leadership in social and political movements: A comparative exploration. In L. Helms (Ed.), *Comparative political leadership* (pp. 99–118). Palgrave Macmillan.

Sally, D. (2002). Co-leadership. Lessons from Republican Rome. *California Review Management*, *44*(4), 84–99.

Sartori, G. (1994). *Comparative constitutional engineering: An inquiry into structures, incentives and outcomes*. New York University Press..

Shugart, M. S., & Carey, J. M. (1992). *Presidents and assemblies*. Cambridge University Press.

Shugart, M. S. (2005). Semi-presidential systems: Dual executive and mixed authority patterns. *French Politics*, *3*(3), 323–351.

Strangio, P., t'Hart, P., & Walter, J. (2015). Leadership of reforming governments: The role of political tandems. In D. Alexander & J. M. Lewis (Eds.), *Making public policy decisions: Expertise, skills, and experience* (pp. 166–184). Routledge.

Verba, S. (1961). *Small groups and political behavior*. Princeton University Press.

CHAPTER 2

Not Only Solitary Leaders: Concepts and Theories

2.1 How to Study Plurality at the Top: Insights from Organization Theory and Management Studies

Research in organization theory and management studies has devoted increasing attention to models of collective leadership challenging the idea of the single leader, alone at the top. One of the most fertile concepts in the field is that of "shared leadership," presented here in the classical formulation by Pearce and Conger (2003: 1): "a dynamic, interactive influence process among individuals in groups for which the objective is to lead one another to the achievement of group or organizational goals or both. This influence process involves peer, or lateral, influence and at other times involves upward or downward hierarchical influence. The key distinction between shared leadership and traditional models of leadership is that the influence process involves more than just downward influence on subordinates by an appointed or elected leader."

As a research framework, shared leadership appears actually "fragmented" in "a variety of conceptualizations and operationalizations" (Zhu et al., 2018: 834). The concept has been applied to different domains, especially healthcare and education (Kocolowski 2010). How does shared leadership relate to our analysis of party leaders? In general terms, if shared leadership may be regarded as a form of "horizontal leadership displayed by team members vs. hierarchical leader-focused view" (Zhu et al., 2018: tab. 3, 839), consequently, pairs and small teams of leaders at the top can be seen as a sort of special case of shared leadership. Indeed, Pearce and Conger themselves define co-leadership as a possible "two-person case" of shared leadership (2003, 8).

As argued by de Voogt and Hommes (2007: 1), shared leadership takes place either when co-leaders have equal rank or when, although involved in a hierarchical relationship, they actually share the lead. Both cases are relevant to the sphere of political leadership. In particular, it should be observed that the latter situation is more frequent than commonly supposed. In fact, in some cases, collective leaderships are formally recognizable, but in many other cases there are informal arrangements, such as O'Toole et al. (2002: 67) point out, "when the facts are fully assembled, even the most fabled 'solitary' leaders are found to have been supported by a team of other effective leaders." A note of caution, however, is in order: the boundaries between the role of a right-hand man (or woman) and that of a leadership partner are quite blurred. An accurate analysis of each single case is needed, then, in order to classify it properly as a case of co-leadership.

To restate the point, the concept of shared leadership is primarily relevant for our analysis of party leadership because, as observed before, it is—by definition—also comprehensive of couples or teams of leaders. Moreover, there is another interesting aspect, highlighted by Day et al. (2004: 875), that is the perspective of distributed leadership (a term they have used interchangeably with that of shared leadership) considers couples, pairs, or small groups in holistic terms by focusing on "joint work units and the properties of the relations between the unit members." In other words, it encourages extending the analysis beyond the personal characteristics of leaders and directing attention to the nature of the bond between them and to the dynamics of collective decision-making.

If it is true that research on shared leadership may provide inspiration for our analysis, on the other hand, it should be stressed that such an approach is ultimately projected to make sense of influences or roles that are dispersed across team members (Zhu et al., 2018: 837). In contrast, we concentrate our attention exclusively at what happens at the top of a party organization. Along this line, an especially influential book for our work is Alvarez and Svejenova (2005) on corporate power structures. The authors explicitly differentiate their approach from the paradigm of shared leadership by stressing that they are not dealing with the "leadership distribution across the organization" (14), but are rather focusing on duos and executive "constellations" of leaders. Analogously, in all the political organizations that we intend to analyze, we will assume that collective leadership is a centralized phenomenon that involves two or a small group of individuals jointly sharing power. In the vast world of studies on "leadership in the plural" as labeled in the most comprehensive way by Denis et al. (2012: 213), our study might be inscribed in the stream of scholarship that they refer to as "pooling leadership capacities at the top to direct others."

Small teams of leaders have been accurately analyzed by management theory as well, in particular, by studies on strategic leadership. "The study of executive leadership from a strategic choice perspective, or more concisely, strategic leadership, focuses on the executives who have overall responsibility for an organization — their characteristics, what they do, how they do it, and particularly, how they affect organizational outcomes" (Finkelstein et al., 2009: 4). "The prevailing conception of leadership generally considers the individual executive. In contemporary organizations, this particularly means chief executive officers (CEOs) and business unit heads. However, strategic leadership can also consider the small group of top executives, or the 'top management team (TMT)'" (9). In spite of the many differences between the world of business and that of politics, scholars of party organization have much to gain from exploring this literature. First of all, it may help political scientists to reflect on operational definitions. Starting from the premise that the distribution of power at the apex of an organization is not always equal, a key question is to identify which top executives are the most influential and who should be regarded as the members of the "top management team" (128–129). Similarly, in the study of party leadership, the main challenge is to understand the distribution and the sources of power in order to identify those actors who actually participate in collective leadership. A related aspect is that, even if members of top management teams share overall responsibility, they may have differing amounts of power. Furthermore, "some executives may have much more say than others" (Hambrick, 2007: 336), and, in addition, some political leaders may be more influential than others. In short, in spite of the differences, the logic of leading a large company and that of leading a political party are not totally diverse.

Second, the literature on strategic management highlights that top management groups are not always integrated teams, but may also be collections of competitive players (Finkelstein et al., 2009: 126). Hambrick (2007: 336) observes that "they often consist of semiautonomous 'barons', each engaging in bilateral relations with the CEO but having little to do with each other and hardly constituting a team." Analogously, in political parties, we may find actors who share power but are not able to cooperate or develop a common vision. Such dynamics depend on how and why a political party has arrived at adopting collective leadership. In any case, the existence of a group of leaders is not to be taken for granted as an indicator of cohesion and integration. This aspect cannot be ignored since the distribution of leadership may not necessarily be associated with idealist beliefs of internal democratization and cooperation. In fact, this is not always the case since collective leadership may sometimes derive from conflictual relationships.

Another seminal line of research in organization theory that has proven to be a fruitful source of inspiration for political scientists is centered on the concept of the dominant coalition. Drawing on the analysis of the role of coalitions within organizations by Cyert and March (1963), scholars such as Thompson (1967: 129 and ff.) and others have then elaborated the concept in different areas of organizational studies.[1] As for the political domain, one of the most influential applications, and certainly the most relevant to our analysis, is that of Angelo Panebianco in *Political Parties: Organization and Power* (1988). Panebianco argues that parties' power structures cannot be understood without considering that the leader is at the center of a coalition of actors with whom he/she needs to negotiate. Thus, dominant coalitions appear as alliances between leaders (national, local, and leaders of external organizations that are closely related to the party). The dominant coalition controls de facto party resources and their distribution. Although this concept is useful for interpreting some cases of collective leadership—see, for example, Panebianco's description of the relationship between the UK Labour Party's leaders and the Trade Unions' leaders—and highlights how power is actually negotiated among different actors with multiple goals, nonetheless, the definition of dominant coalition is too broad to capture the phenomenon we analyze in the following chapters. In fact, the dominant coalition may well not coincide with the limited group of people who are in charge of governing a political party, which is the object

---

[1] For a survey, see Stevenson et al. (1985).

of our study. Neither does the notion of Duverger's "inner circle" (1969) appear more appropriate, which evokes an oligarchic structure that may actually be compatible with an individual leader, around whom a group of people aggregate and prosper. Indeed, leaders are often surrounded by cliques that are based on members' attachment to a dominant chief. In only the type of oligarchy that Duverger labels as "teams of leaders" (152) is a horizontal relationship among partners assumed. However, the scope and influence of the cases he describes are quite different from the top executive level which we aim to analyze.

2.2 DUAL AND MULTIMEMBER PARTY LEADERSHIP

We agree with Gronn (1999: 58) when he says that "there are circumstances in which the appropriate unit of analysis is the stand-alone, *solo* performer leader, but equally there are many other occasions in which the unit of analysis is some kinds of collective form of leadership. A helpful starting point here might be to devise a spectrum or a template of possible leadership types and their distinguishing criteria against which to more accurately define cases and contexts nominated by commentators for scrutiny." With this goal in mind, we now proceed by categorizing possible leadership types found in party organizations.

Following Alvarez and Svejenova (2005), and also taking into consideration the specific characteristics of the political domain, we will differentiate cases of collective leadership involving two people from cases involving a small numbers of people (three or more). Precious insights also come from the analysis by Hodgson et al. (1965) of types of constellations—i.e., units that are "made up of a varying number of people performing certain roles that are interrelated in a number of different ways" (485)—and their distinction between dyads, triads and larger executive groups.

More precisely, we will refer to:

- *individual leadership* whenever the leadership stems from a single leader, usually a formally appointed leader, who is supposed to exert influence and authority over all other members of the party organization.

- *dual leadership* whenever the role of leadership is divided between two people.[2] This definition implies all types of dyads and pairs regardless whether co-leaders hold the same position or share power by performing different roles or functions.
- *multimember leadership* whenever the power is distributed among a small team of leaders.[3] This group may coincide with an appointed governing body or rather consists of a team of actors holding different positions. In order to qualify as a case of multimember leadership, there should be a horizontal and a reciprocal influence among the group members, who, at the same time, exert a top-down influence on the rest of the organization.

In this book, the last two types of leadership—dual and multimember—will be indistinctively addressed as forms of plural or collective leadership (we use the two terms interchangeably). Within each category, single cases can be classified according to specific dimensions. A valuable suggestion comes from de Voogt and Hommes (2007), who assume that the two key elements that characterize forms of shared leadership are: *formal hierarchy* (if co-leaders have the same rank or not) and *division of labor* (if they perform overlapping or separate tasks). Also Alvarez and Svejenova (2005, 119–120) have directed attention to the rank of leaders, by differentiating *hierarchical pairs* (when there are clear authority lines of superordination and subordination) from *partnership* (when two executives have equal power by design, such as formal co-leaders).

Drawing on such accounts, the two dimensions that will serve in the analysis of cases of political party collective leadership are, first, the distinction between position sharing vs. power sharing and, second, the existence of a division of labor. Let us proceed by examining each of them in more detail.

1. *Position sharing vs. Power sharing*

---

[2] De Voogt and Hommes (2007) employ the term dual leadership. However, they use it in a more restrictive way, mainly referring to cases of equal relationships between leaders who perform separate tasks.

[3] Strangio et al. (2015: 167) refer to "multimember leadership configurations" in a general sense. Instead, we are using the term multimember to include only cases of units with more than two people.

In cases of position sharing, all leaders hold the same position (for instance, they are party co-chairs or co-spokespersons). Here there is no hierarchical differentiation. They have the same rank. This arrangement may involve two or more people even if position sharing is more frequent in the case of dual leadership.

In cases of power sharing, leaders do not hold the same position; however, they share power and influence. They may have completely different positions with no formal hierarchical relationship between them (for instance, a prime minister and a majority party leader), or there can be a formal hierarchical relationship (for instance a prime minister and a very powerful minister).

It is worth noting that power sharing between two people who are in a hierarchical relationship where one is superior and the other is a subordinate, may be difficult to assess. In this case, the requirements for being considered a true instance of dual leadership depend on the autonomy and the concrete amount of power of both partners. In this regard, the scholars' interpretation can be more or less extensive. In a seminal book on co-leadership, Heenan and Bennis (1999) included in their case studies also deputy leaders or lieutenants who, although outstanding, could not be considered more than second in command. In the field of politics, for example, they offered an in-depth account of the relationship between President Bill Clinton and Vice President Al Gore. Gronn (1999) deals with "leadership couples" whose members do not have the same rank and one is in a superior position. Although these hierarchical relationships are often crucial for the good performance of an organization, not all cases can be ascribed to the dual or multimember leadership categories as we interpret them. Rather, we believe that an operational definition and some criteria should be established with the single aim of distinguishing proper cases of shared leadership from those of close and fruitful collaboration between a leader and his/her close subordinates. We following Gronn (1999) in assuming that key dimensions of leadership couples are the partners' dependence on each other and the discretionary power enjoyed by the subordinate. However, our inclination is to add further, more selective criteria to the list of requirements. In particular, we suggest considering primarily those cases of dual leadership in which partners have a sufficient amount of power that prevents one from prevailing upon the other. This means that, for instance, the formal leader cannot replace or break up with the other leader without compromising his/her capacities and jeopardizing his/her position. Or, in the best of possible cases, the superior pays a high price for the possibility of turning aside the subordinate.

We are aware that, in assessing the relationship of duos, in particular, it may be difficult to draw a clear line without a great deal of evidence and a detailed reconstruction of events. In some cases, the existence of a substantial parity in the relationship is evident. For instance, Gordon Brown, who was Chancellor of the Exchequer in the Blair governments, was not only one of the founders of the New Labour, but he also acquired so much credit and power that he became "unsackable" (Smith 2005: 160). In other cases, in contrast, a deputy leader may appear influential and powerful, but does not actually have an autonomous decision-making capacity or, even more revealing, can be replaced without great consequences if a strong disagreement with the superior arises. Therefore, even if such dual relationships are not the primary object of our study, we believe that this issue should be discussed much more thoroughly in a stream of literature that, up to now, has still been too focused on only a few charismatic leaders rather than on all the actors around them who are actually assuming leadership responsibilities.

2.3 Division of Labor

In dual and multimember leaderships, leaders may undertake the same or different tasks. For example, Spillane (2006: 39 and ff.) suggests differentiating the cases characterized by a *division of labor* according to which leaders perform different tasks separately from the cases in which multiple leaders perform the same tasks in a collaborative fashion (*co-performance*) or the same tasks in different contexts (*parallel performance*).

It is likely that a division of labor is present in cases of power sharing, where different positions are usually related to different tasks (even if there can be overlapping spheres of action, especially if a deputy leader happens to act on behalf of the formal leader and assume most of his/her responsibilities). Conversely, position sharing does not always coincide with the same allocation of tasks, but can be operationalized through a certain degree of division of labor, which also stems from the different expertise and competences of the two leaders. We might expect that the more the partners are complementary in their attitudes and skills the more the division of labor is pronounced. Due to its crucial importance for our study, the issue of complementarity will be elaborated more extensively in the next section.

It should be observed that a division of labor may be established by design, that is to say, different roles and related tasks are assigned to different people, or may emerge through a spontaneous process. Based on their studies of school systems, Leithwood and his colleagues[4] (Leithwood et al., 2009) developed a typology of leadership functions that can be applied to many other fields, including political leadership. They differentiated the following four configurations, each of which is associated with a cluster of values and beliefs: planful alignments, spontaneous alignments, spontaneous misalignments, and anarchic alignments (Leithwood et al., 2009: 225–227).

Planful alignments occur when leadership tasks and functions are distributed as the result of a discussion and an agreement among the organizational members. This configuration is inspired by the belief that cooperation is better than competition and supported by a mutual trust in other partners' motives and capacities. It is not to be taken for granted that a planned distribution of responsibilities and tasks always results in the optimal solution. However, Leithwood and colleagues seem to believe that this sort of planning increases the chance for a productive pattern of leadership distribution.

Spontaneous alignments occur when leadership tasks and functions are distributed with little or no planning. Even this configuration is possible if there are mutual trust and willingness to cooperate. In addition, there should be an underlying conviction that intuitions about who is better equipped to perform a task may govern the organization tacitly and effectively. If this does not happen, and the outcome of such spontaneous arrangements is unsatisfactory, then the organization may end up assuming the third possible configuration, *spontaneous misalignment*. In other words, the two arrangements—spontaneous alignment and spontaneous misalignment—originate from similar processes but differ from the point of view of their performance. In contrast, *anarchic misalignments* are based on the idea that competition is better than cooperation. Thus, this fourth configuration occurs when leaders act independently. In this case, commitment is to the individual or to the unit, but not to the goals of the whole organization.

---

[4] For a presentation and discussion of this typology, see also Anderson et al. (2009) and Bolden (2011).

As said before, Leithwood and colleagues' typology was elaborated with reference to another organizational field, but the analysis of our case studies in the following chapters will show just how much a reflection on the aspects of planning and cooperation is also crucial in order to assess instances of political plural leadership. On the other hand, it should be stressed that the existence of unplanned distributions of leadership responsibilities is a feature of many social movements that adopt forms of collective leadership. As Rucht (2012: 114) observes, "in especially larger and more enduring social movement groups, we find several leaders, usually specialized in one major task, who co-exist and work in an implicit division of labor. In most cases, such a division is not based on conscious decision-making. Rather it is a kind of organic and gradual recruitment process in which those individuals assume one of several leadership positions and (a) invest much time and energy for a movement or a SMO and (b) possess or gradually develop the necessary qualities to serve as a key organizer and/or perform other leadership functions."

Having discussed the possible configurations of leadership distribution of responsibilities and tasks, what areas of action may, in particular, be the object of the division of labor among political leaders? What are the practices and the functions they must perform? According to Hartley and Benington (2011), political leadership operates in a range of arenas (210). "Arenas are not only about physical spaces, though some (but not all) may be geographically identifiable, such as Parliament. Arenas can be conceptualized as social processes of mutual influence between a variety of stakeholders and the political leadership. Arenas can be thought of as spaces and flows of people, ideas, problems, legitimacy and resources. This requires thinking about political leadership as dynamic not static, and as contested between different groups in a dialectical space of ideas, values, processes and actions" (211).

What are the particular arenas in which party leaders exercise their power? Useful suggestions may come from the description of the three faces of party organizations by Katz and Mair (1994: 354): *party in public office*, e.g., in parliament or government; *party on the ground*, e.g., the members or activists; and *party in central office*, e.g., the national leadership. Those who become party leaders are expected to deal with all three levels since they are involved in internal party politics, but also need to maintain the support of the party on the ground and build enough consensus to win elections in order to remain in office. In order to perform all these functions, leaders face a formidable challenge that may require sharing or, at least, a certain degree of delegation of power. Different types of division of labor may be observed at the level of the bureaucratic organization with a distribution of tasks within the party executive élite. Different leaders may be in charge of separate tasks; for example, a leader may compete for a popular mandate while others deal with the party machinery. One may be the chief communicator who stays in the limelight while others take the back seat.

Depending on the institutional and political systems, party leaders play different roles in executive cabinets. In two-party systems, the majority leader becomes the prime minister and exerts greater influence than the prime ministers in multiparty systems, who have less opportunity to stand out above the leaders of the coalition parties (Blondel, 1987: 177). As discussed in the introduction, however, both scenarios can give rise to forms of collective leadership. In the first case, some types of tandems could be found within the executive, composed of the prime minister and another minister who enjoys a level of authority superior to the other colleagues (Strangio et al., 2015). Also, the possibility is not to be excluded that, once the party leader has become head of the government, he/she concentrates his/her attention on the executive functions and allows a formal deputy party leader to become the informal party leader.

In the second category, which includes multiparty systems and coalition governments, other possible configurations of collective leadership exist. For instance, in a cabinet where the prime minister is a "primus inter pares" (Sartori, 1994: 102), he/she may be the negotiator while others, namely the party leaders who are outside of the cabinet, set the agenda, thus giving birth to a form of power sharing. Or party leaders may enter the cabinet and hold ministerial posts. Moreover, an overview of party leadership across European parties shows that there are powerful party leaders who are able to accumulate functions, resources and powers, but there are also other less hierarchical arrangements, as will be seen in the following chapters.

2.4 COMPLEMENTARITY

We have discussed how collective leadership offers an opportunity for a division of labor that may help any type of organization face the complexity of today's environment (Kocolowski, 2010). We have assumed that it may be difficult for just one leader to deal with multiple tasks. We have detailed the many functions a party leader must perform, which is a long list that makes the case for some form of division of labor. But is the increase in the number of leaders a sufficient answer to the complexity? Is plurality at the top a guarantee of effective outcomes?

Complexity may require different backgrounds and skills; then, complementarity of expertise, experience and skills also becomes a resource (Hogdson et al., 1965; Gronn, 1999). O'Toole et al. (2002: 74) argue that shared leadership is more likely to succeed when the actors involved play complementary roles. Along the same lines, Alvarez and Svejenova (2005: 117) highlight that a partnership works well when the two people involved not only have common backgrounds, values and experience (a condition referred to as *commonality*), but also *complementary* skills, styles and social capital. In a subsequent article (Alvarez et al., 2007), they illustrate this list of necessary qualities for successful cooperation among leadership partners as follows: complementarity, compatibility and commitment (as manifested by a common vision). Strangio et al. (2015) include complementarity within the essential characteristics that qualify a political tandem and make it effective. In other words, the outstanding individual skills of leaders may not suffice for the formation of a good team, if co-leaders are not able to complement each other.

There can be different forms of complementarity. Miles and Watkins (2007) distinguish four of them: *task complementarity*—to manage complexity, leaders take responsibility for different blocks of tasks; *expertise complementarity*—leaders are trained and develop competences in different areas; *cognitive complementarity*—leaders have different cognitive characteristics that lead them to perform different functions: for instance, one has vision and the other has a great capacity for achieving goals; *role complementarity*—they assume different social roles, for instance, one is loved and the other is feared.

A basic form of complementarity is dual leadership as described in early studies (Etzioni, 1965; Verba, 1961). Starting from the assumption that there may be several leadership functions and that they can be assumed either by the same person or by different individuals (Verba, 1961: 121), Verba argues that leaders have at least two main tasks: first, securing a satisfactory affective tone and social relationship within the group; second, maintaining an effective group structure that will guarantee the accomplishment of the expected goals (123). Therefore, he distinguishes between an *expressive* and an *instrumental* dimension. This model of dual leadership explains very well the functioning of small experimental groups in which a bifurcation of the two roles with the emergence of two leaders has been observed (143). Starting from the assumption that the relationship between affective and instrumental functions is a central issue in the study of leadership, Verba offers some reflections on dual leadership in political systems and organizations as well (184). In these contexts, however, he seems more inclined to think that there are alternative mechanisms to deal with the duality of instrumental and expressive relationships. Indeed, the legitimation of an appointed office, the exercise of control by impersonal rules, the greater distance with followers allow the leader to make decisions on instrumental grounds and to be less dependent on the affective response of followers. In contrast to what happens in the experimental groups, "in on-going situations, the responsibility for instrumental acts is projected onto the demands of the situation or the group norms" (180). Nevertheless, also in such cases, under some circumstances, "the need for positive affective outputs is best satisfied by the development of a dual leadership structure" (180). Thus, functional differentiations, (such as the delegation of unpopular acts or duties to a 'scapegoat' subordinate leader), might be a useful means of solving the conflict caused by the negative affective reactions of followers (182).

While Verba's focus is on small groups, Etzioni (1965) analyzes complex organizations and argues that both *expressive* (relations-oriented) and *instrumental* (task-oriented) leadership functions are needed for providing effective leadership. The two roles may be performed by different leaders and each organization gives priority to the diverse functions (and the people who incarnate them) depending on its organizational characteristics and goals. Similarly, Hodgson et al. (1965) found that the members of the executive triad of their study "were involved in both the instrumental-adaptive and the expressive-integrative aspects of administration" (…), but each man specialized "to emphasize certain functions and to minimize or neglect others that were in turn given more emphasis by his co-executives" (70). Such an instrumental/expressive duality has been substantially validated also by more recent analyses, for instance, O'Toole et al. (2002: 74) claims that a match of an *emotional* leader with a *task* leader may produce the best arrangement for dual leadership.

In the conceptualization of what is the expressive function of leadership developed in early accounts, the prevailing focus has been on the internal relationship between the leader and the adherents to the group or the organization. Verba, for instance, distinguishes internal and external group tasks and assigns to the leader the key role of communicating with the external environment (153); however, regarding the expressive side of leadership, he seems to consider it primarily as the capacity to maintain an emotionally satisfying relationship within the group. In fact, he argues that the distance between the leader and the followers, as may occur in complex organizations, is a way of insulating the leader from the affective reactions of the group, which may decrease his/her instrumental effectiveness (176).

However, if we shift the attention to a political organization such as a party, it is likely that the leaders' affective skills are not limited to exerting an influence within the organization, but are also projected outside to impress the public and build consensus. In complex political systems, the ties between leaders and followers are no longer personal in a physical sense. But this virtual relationship is, nonetheless, quite important in establishing emotional bonds. The mechanism at work is a form of intimacy between celebrities and their audience that is produced through media interactions (Meyrowitz, 1985; Thompson, 1995). As Pels points out: "A politics of personal style may generate democratic effects, by expanding the forms of popular appeal and emotional identification that cut through technocratic smoke-screens and institutional inertia. A performative politics foregrounds the politician as an actor, whose performance on the public stage is continuously judged in terms of authenticity, honesty and 'character'" (Pels, 2003: 9–10). Therefore, the expressive functions of leadership should be definitively extended to include the capacity of a leader to express empathy and establish affective bonds with citizens through a media-savvy propaganda. This aspect has been vastly explored in relationship to individual leadership,[5] but is worth being further elaborated within the framework of plural leadership as well.

In light of all this, it is appropriate to differentiate between the capability of a leader to be relations-oriented, supportive and informal toward members of his/her organization and the capability of inspiring admiration and affect in more distant followers. In this regard, Dieter Rucht (2012: 110–111) appropriately introduced a double level in his analysis of

---

[5] For instance, Joseph Nye (2008), in his well-known definition of soft power, combines emotional intelligence, which implies an orientation toward relations, with the capability of persuading near and distant followers. However, these different functions are discussed in relation to the skills and styles of individual leaders.

the leadership of social and political movements. He proposes to cross the instrumental/expressive dimension with the spatial dimension of internal (influence on members and activists)/external (influence on the public). The outcome is a typology including four core functions corresponding to four profiles of leadership:

1. The *organizer* "is basically a manager of internal resources"; "may maintain a low-profile but is still fairly influential for the internal functioning of the movement"; he/she may serve "as mediator or broker between different internal units of strands of the movement."
2. The *motivator* has the role of motivating members and activists to take action. "His basic means are agitation, persuasion, enthusiasm."
3. The *strategist* "has a clear idea about what directions to go in and how to ultimately reach the stated goals." Here the locus of enacted leadership is external to the movement and the target is increasing consensus. The strategist "must not necessarily be known as the leader from an outside perspective."
4. The *president* is the "face of the movement for the outer world." He/she is the speaker, the symbol and has the task of impressing the public.

According to Rucht, some leaders may combine several functions together. However, in other cases, we may observe that various people specialize in different functions. Therefore, there could be a differentiation between those leaders who appear as an icon for the outer world and those who are in charge of the organization and the strategies of the party. In a similar vein, Duverger (1969: 215) observed that, if in many political parties formal and real leaders coincide, it should not be taken for granted that all power is exclusively in the hands of the apparent or "titular" leaders. Furthermore, the expressive functions (toward the internal and toward the external) are likely to be assumed by the same person but could also be incarnated by different individuals, as Rucht's distinction between the two figures of the motivator and the president seems to suggest.

In sum, theoretical reflections on the multiplicity of leadership functions suggest that the need to perform several roles should be regarded, if not as a sufficient condition, at least as an incentive to collective leadership. If there are more leaders, mutual support between them becomes very important for producing effective leadership (Etzioni, 1965). The complementarity between different leaders in its several manifestations, from their cognitive propensities to the social roles they perform is, therefore, a crucial lens through which to analyze instances of dual and multimember leadership as we will carry out for the three case studies in the second part of this book.

References

Alvarez, J. L., & Svejenova, S. (2005). *Sharing executive power: Roles and relationships at the top*. Cambridge University Press.

Alvarez J. L., Svejenova, S., & Vives, L. (2007). Leading in Pairs. *MIT Sloane Management Review*, https://sloanreview.mit.edu/article/leading-in-pairs/. Accessed on 5 January 2021.

Anderson, S., Moore, S., & Sun, J. (2009). Positioning the principals in patterns of school leadership distribution. In K. Leithwood, B. Mascall, & T. Strauss (Eds.), *Distributed leadership according to the evidence* (pp. 111–136). Routledge.

Blondel, J. (1987). *Political leadership. Towards a general analysis*. Sage.

Bolden, R. (2011). Distributed leadership in organizations. A review of theory and research. *International Journal of Management Reviews, 13*(3), 251–269.

Cyert, R. M., & March, J. (1963). *A behavioral theory of the firm*. Prentice Hall.

Day, D., Gronn, P., & Salas, E. (2004). Leadership capacity in teams. *The Leadership Quarterly, 15*(6), 857–880.

de Voogt, A., & Hommes, K. (2007). The signature of leadership—Artistic freedom in shared leadership practice. *The John Ben Sheppard Journal of Practical Leadership, 1*(2), 1–5.

Denis, J.-L., Langley, A., & Sergi, V. (2012). Leadership in the plural. *The Academy of Management Annals, 6*(1), 211–283.

Duverger, M. (1969). Oligarchy in leadership. In J. Blondel (Ed.), *Comparative government* (pp. 105–111). Palgrave Macmillan.

Etzioni, A. (1965). Dual leadership in complex organizations. *American Sociological Review, 30*(5), 688–698.

Finkelstein, S., Hambrick, D., & Cannella, B. (2009). *Strategic leadership: Theory and research on executives. Top management teams, and boards*. Oxford University Press.

Gronn, P. (1999). Substituting for leadership: The neglected role of the leadership couple. *The Leadership Quarterly, 10*(1), 141–162.

Hambrick, D. (2007). Upper echelons theory: An update. *The Academy of Management Review, 32*(2), 334–343.

Hartley, J., & Benington, J. (2011). Political Leadership. In A. Bryman, D. Collison, K. Grint, B. Johnson, & M. Uhl-Bien (Eds.), *The Sage handbook of leadership* (pp. 203–214). Sage.

Heenan, D. A., & Bennis, W. (1999). *Co-Leaders: The power of great partnerships*. Wiley.

Hodgson, R., Levison, D., & Zaleznik, A. (1965). *The executive role constellation. An analysis of personality and role relations in management*. Harvard University—Division of Research Graduate School of Business Administration.

Katz, R. S., & Mair, P. (Eds.). (1994). *How parties organize: Change and adaptation*. Sage.

Kocolowski, M. (2010). Shared leadership: Is it time for change? *Emerging Leadership Journeys*, 3(1), 22–32.

Leithwood, K., Mascall, B., Strauss, T., Memon, N., & Yashkina, A. (2009). Distributing leadership to make schools smarter: Taking the ego out of the system. In K. Leithwood, B. Mascall, & T. Strauss (Eds.), *Distributed leadership according to the evidence* (pp. 223–251). Routledge.

Meyrowitz, J. (1985). *No sense of place. The impact of electronic media on social behavior*. Oxford University Press.

Miles, S., & Watkins, M. (2007). The leadership team: Complementary strengths or conflicting agendas? *Harvard Business Review*. https://hbr.org/2007/04/the-leadership-team-complementary-strengths-or-conflicting-agendas. Accessed on 5 January 2021.

Nye, J. S. (2008). *The power to lead*. Oxford University Press.

O'Toole, J., Galbraith, J., & Lawler, E. (2002). When two (or more) heads are better than one: The promise and pitfalls of shared leadership. *California Review Management*, 44(4), 65–83.

Panebianco, A. (1988). *Political parties: Organization and power*. Cambridge University Press.

Pearce, C., & Conger, J. (2003). All those years ago: The historically underpinnings of shared leadership. In C. Pearce & J. Conger (Eds.), *Shared leadership* (pp. 1–18). Sage.

Pels, D. (2003). Aesthetic representation and political style: Rebalancing identity and difference in media democracy. In J. Corner & D. Pels (Eds.), *Media and the restyling of politics* (pp. 41–66). Sage.

Rucht, D. (2012). Leadership in social and political movements: A comparative exploration. In L. Helms (Ed.), *Comparative political leadership* (pp. 99–118). Palgrave Macmillan.

Sartori, G. (1994). *Comparative constitutional engineering: An inquiry into structures, incentives and outcomes*. New York University Press.

Smith, D. (2005). The Treasury and economic policy. In A. Seldon & D. Kavanagh (Eds.), *The Blair Effect 2001–5* (pp. 139–183). Cambridge University Press.

Spillane, J. P. (2006). *Distributed leadership*. Jossey-Bass.
Stevenson, W., Pearce, J., & Porter, L. (1985). The concept of "coalition" in organization theory and research. *Academy of Management Review, 10*(2), 256–268.
Strangio, P., t'Hart, P., & Walter, J. (2015). Leadership of reforming governments: The role of political tandems. In D. Alexander & J. M. Lewis (Eds.), *Making public policy decisions: Expertise, skills, and experience* (pp. 166–184). Routledge.
Thompson, J. G. (1967). *Organizations in action*. McGraw-Hill.
Thompson, J. (1995). *The media and modernity*. Polity Press.
Verba, S. (1961). *Small groups and political behavior*. Princeton University Press.
Zhu, J., Liao, Z., Yam, K., & Johnson, R. (2018). Shared leadership: A state-of-the-art review and future research agenda. *Journal Organizational Behavior, 39*(7), 834–852.

CHAPTER 3

Birth, Life and End of Collective Leadership

3.1 Pathways to Collective Leadership

What are the paths leading to parties' adoption of a form of collective leadership? How are dual and multimember leaderships developed? Our hypothesis is that there are at least *four* types of contexts that encourage their emergence. The list is not exhaustive, but we consider it to be an initial analytical categorization that may be enriched and improved by further research on case studies.

The first reason why collective leadership emerges is that it helps to preserve unity and manage internal party divisions. In fact, two or more leaders can be jointly appointed with a view toward representing different wings or viewpoints within the party.

In the founding phase of a new party, this type of arrangement can derive from the previous history of the party members. For instance, in case of a merger between two already existing parties, the adoption of a duo of leaders rather than just one may be a way of including and recognizing the different founding units of the newly created party. Let us consider the case of German *Linke*, which in 2007 adopted a dual leadership. Created by merging two different party organizations—the post-socialist *Partei des Demokratischen Sozialismus* (PDS) and the splinter social-democratic faction, the WASG (*Wahlalternative Soziale Gerechtigkeit*)—the new left-wing party needed a mechanism for ensuring

© The Author(s), under exclusive license to Springer Nature Switzerland AG 2021
D. Campus et al., *Collective Leadership and Divided Power in West European Parties*, Palgrave Studies in Political Leadership, https://doi.org/10.1007/978-3-030-75255-2_3

equal treatment to both organizations. Among other instruments (quotas, special veto rights, etc.), the fusion of the two parties was accepted under the proviso of the appointment of two leaders, one from the former PDS and the other from the WASG (Patton, 2013: 221). Originally designed as a temporary solution, the dual leadership in the *Linke* is still in force as the party is currently led by two leaders a man (Detterbeck & Rohlfing, 2014; Olsen, 2018).

Generally, it should be stressed that parties are not unitary bodies. Indeed, they are often organized into factions that can have different natures. Giovanni Sartori's distinction between what he refers to as *fractions of principle* and *fractions of interests* highlights the plurality of reasons why a party may be internally divided along different ideological and value-driven viewpoints and/or competing claims for spoils and power shares (Sartori, 1976: 66–78). In this regard, abundant research has been devoted to the analysis of the so-called intra-party politics, which refers to the dynamics and power relations among groups of party members (Belloni & Beller, 1978; Boucek, 2012; Duverger, 1954; Harmel et al., 1995; Hine, 1982; Katz & Mair, 1994). In the line of research on intra-party politics, leaders are usually intended to be individual actors who negotiate with the different internal factions to preserve unity and establish their leadership on the basis of a spoils distribution (Cross & Blais, 2012; Pilet & Cross, 2014). Most studies focus on how leaders are selected and how they manage to survive and prosper in contexts of intra-party divisions (Müller & Meth-Cohn, 1991; Ennser-Jedenastik & Muller, 2015; Bynander & t'Hart, 2008). The party leader, on one hand, and the factions, on the other, are conceptualized as interacting actors embedded in a relationship that can be more or less autonomous depending on how much the former is dependent on the latter's intentions (Ceron, 2019).

However, at least in some cases, the relationship between leaders and factions could be also interpreted through the perspective of collective leadership. The leaders that Ceron (2019: 159) refers to as "non-autonomous", that is to say, leaders who are "nothing more than the outcome of an inter-factional agreement" and "whose discretional behaviour can produce dissatisfaction and can be cause of leader removal", might be reconceptualized as actors actually involved in a structure of plural leadership in which the power is actually shared by a group of people. This interpretation is appropriate for describing the case of the Italian Christian Democracy (DC), the largest Italian political party from the birth of the Republic to the beginning of the 1990s. The DC has been usually described as a "confusing mélange of mutually-overlapping factions gravitating around coalitions of leading personalities" (Zariski, 1965: 20). More specifically, the organization of the party was based on the constantly precarious balance of power between competitive oligarchies, each of which were represented by a distinct set of leaders or leading personalities. Even Alcide de Gasperi, the leader who gave the largest contribution to the party's structuring and consolidation shortly after World War II and who may be reputed to have been the center of the DC's "dominant coalition", was never in full control of it (Panebianco, 1988: 125). Moreover, the history of the party was characterized, with only a few exceptions (Pasquino, 2007), by the separation of powers and roles between the leadership of the party (Secretary) and the premiership of the cabinet (President of the Council). And the harmony within the party as well as the stability of the government depended upon the cohabitation of the party chairman and the prime minister, appointed by the same party.

In sum, it may be argued that there is a blurred area between those situations in which the appointed party leader negotiates with factional leaders to maintain an internal equilibrium that may guarantee his/her survival and those situations of open and clearly evident plural leadership where there are appointed co-leaders who represent different factions. In this area, one may find instances of collective leadership in which the appointed leader appears as just one of the organizational actors who performs vital functions for the party, as a sort of *primus inter pares*. Therefore, looking at the phenomenon from this point of view, collective leadership may be seen as a possible way of handling party factionalism.

The second path leading to collective leadership is that it originates from some initial characteristics of the party. For example, collective leadership is likely to be found in the genes of those parties that originally developed from a social movement. It should be stressed that movements can be organized differently and some of them have a strong individual leader from the very beginning. However, examples of distribution of leadership are quite common. Such arrangements are characterized by a specialization and a division of labor among different individuals who invest time and energy in the movement and gradually become in charge of some leadership functions (Rucht, 2012: 114). Furthermore, forms of plural leadership have the advantage of appearing more acceptable to adherents who value internal democracy and who could feel expropriated by a hierarchy that is too vertical. This is especially true for those parties that come into existence through a process of "territorial diffusion" (Panebianco, 1988: 50–51), according to which local party associations are integrated or federated into a national organization. In other words, the genetic model can explain the structure/nature of future party leadership.

As a consequence of this imprinting, a movement in the process of transforming itself into a party may maintain collective leadership in its organizational structure. This has been the case of the Five Star Movement, which will be extensively described in Chapter 6. However, it should be stressed that although the presence of collective leadership in the genetic model is a potential characteristic, it may not be a determinant of what happens in a subsequent phase. In 1911, Roberto Michels advanced the thesis that the evolution of parties points inevitably to the establishment of oligarchic executives at the expense of grassroots politics. Accordingly, the reinforcement of central leadership could be seen as the correct approach for avoiding fragmentation. In principle, the achievement of this goal should not necessarily imply the appointment of a 'solo' leader as it may also be compatible with a duo or a team of leaders. In practice, the process of institutionalization produces the emergence of a single leader in several cases. This happened to the Hungarian Fidesz, which shifted from an initial collective leadership to Victor Orbàn's strong individual leadership (Ilonszki & Vàrnagy, 2014). Another interesting evolutionary process occurred in the Spanish Podemos. The current leader, Pablo Iglesias, was initially selected as the face of the movement because of the television appearances that made him popular (Iglesias, 2015), however, he did not have a special predominant position among the other founders. Instead, he was a member of a sort of "*triumvirate*" formed of two other academics also, Inigo Errejòn and Carlos Monedero, who were surrounded by other influential members (Kioupkiolis, 2016). When, in 2014, the discussion was addressed as to what organizational model should be adopted, Podemos' affiliates preferred Iglesias' proposal, "centred on the Citizen Council (*Concejo Ciudadano*), the highest party body between assemblies, together with a party leader with great powers in order to ensure unity of action and coherent political discourse" (Lisi, 2019). At that time, Iglesias was elected as party leader by a large majority, while Podemos moved toward a less decentralized organization (Fittipaldi, 2017).

The third reason why a party adopts collective leadership is that the distribution of power represents an explicit ideological choice. Indeed, in some movements and parties, adherents believe that there should be no hierarchies and there should certainly not be a single person in charge. As Rucht (2012: 102) points out, "groups embracing individual freedom, equality, and 'horizontality' may be sceptical towards the very existence of leaders and therefore only allow for low-profile leaders".

The preference for collective leadership is, for instance, quite pronounced in the family of Green parties, thus suggesting the existence of a direct connection between the organizational structures and their belief system. Indeed, as Burchell (2002: 104) argues, the Greens' distinctive organizational characteristics are a key component of the "new politics" and the post-materialist values associated with ecologist parties (Muller-Rommel & Poguntke, 1995, 2002). In general, European Green parties have embraced forms of direct participation of rank and file members and democratization of power, in which an emphasis on forms of collective leadership has been one of the many aspects (Rihoux, 2016).

Now dual leadership is, for instance, a regular feature of the German Greens, surely the most illuminating case, which will be extensively illustrated in Chapter 4. The Belgian Green party *Ecolo (Ecologistes Confederes pour l'Organisation de Luttes Originales)* opted for a system with five to eight co-leaders, which was gradually reduced to two (Wawreille & Pilet, 2016). The Austrian party (*Die Grünen – Die Grüne Alternative*) has always been run by a federal executive committee, however, up to 1992, there were also two federal party managers (while the 'face' of the party was the head of the parliamentary party). Then, after 1992, the party opted for a nominal party leader (Dolezal, 2016: 28). Analogously, in the pursuit of an ideal of internal democracy, British and Swedish Greens made their party convention the key decision-making body and rejected the figure of a single leader by, instead, appointing a number of chairs and/or spokespersons (Burchell, 2002, table 5.1: 108).

In France, the ecologist movements have always promoted collective leadership and ideals of grassroots democracy (Villalba, 2016: 105). It should be observed, however, that the need to select presidential candidates produced some "de facto leaders" who appeared as the most high-profile figures without being formal leaders (Burchell, 2002: 119). Nonetheless, the collective dimension of leadership has always remained a distinctive trait, since adherents have acknowledged the necessity of having some visible spokespersons who may convey their message, but who have also been concerned about not giving them too much independence (Faucher, 1999: 219).

Abundant evidence shows that an association exists between collective leadership and Green parties' values and beliefs. Throughout their history, several of these parties experienced different forms of plural leadership as they developed from situations in which leadership functions were shared among members of executive boards to forms of dual leadership, often composed of a male and a female leader (Rihoux, 2016: 305–306). The connection between collective leadership and parties with other ideological viewpoints is less evident. Surely, one may find instances of dual leadership in left-wing parties (see, for instance, the German SPD and Linke). Conversely, strong individual leadership is largely diffused among the radical right parties and, therefore, one may suppose that plural leadership is less suitable to that ideological camp. However, in the case of *Alternative für Deutschland*, extensively illustrated in Chapter 5, this seems to be the exception to the rule. In conclusion, we may advance the argument that sharing power is likely to be more compatible with values such as equality, and ideals such as participatory democracy, but nothing prevents its adoption by parties with other prevailing belief systems as well. By the way, it should be remembered that the adoption of pairs or teams of leaders does not necessarily imply a true distribution of leadership across an organization. Thus, the concentration of power in the hands of a few individuals, rather than a single leader, is not inconceivable in a hierarchical organization in which the loyalty of rank and file members does not depend on their involvement in decision-making.

The fourth argument for collective leadership is that it may be the answer to a state of crisis or a signal of change. When things get worse for any number of reasons (loss of electoral consensus, scandals damaging the image of the party and so on), the need for renewal at the highest levels may come out as a way of contrasting a negative wave. This argument is often advanced to explain the appointment of female leaders, sometimes made possible in troubled times (Campus, 2013), but which could be extended to the adoption of forms of collective leadership as well. The logic behind such choices is very similar—offering a novelty as an indicator of reform and change. By the way, the two instruments are often entangled since the adoption of dual leadership has sometimes been justified as the need for equal gender representation.

Two fairly recent cases deserve to be mentioned in this regard. The German SPD is an example of a party that has undergone a process of reform as a way of reacting to electoral setbacks. As Gauja (2016: 50 and ff.) points out, the need for improving electoral performance is usually regarded as essential for a party's organizational development. After two heavy electoral defeats, (in the 2017 parliamentary elections and in the 2019 European elections), the SPD changed the leadership selection procedures by including all party members and lowering the bar for candidates to be part of the consultation process (Jun & Jakobs, 2021). In particular, the party's executive committee has encouraged the candidacies of teams (composed of a woman and a man), even if single candidacies were also allowed.

It was observed that the proposal of having two co-chairs may have become popular because of the success of the Greens, which has long adhered to the same organizational model (Knight, 2019). In fact, it is worth noting that the SPD has a history of informal power-sharing arrangements. We are referring to the so-called Troika, which characterized the party governance in the 1960s and 1970s. The different skills of Willy Brandt, Helmut Schmidt and Herbert Wehner and their efficient division of labor are seen as a main reason for the strong electoral results and the ability of the party to enter and later lead the federal government. This model was not a consequence of party statutes but rather a joint and conscious decision by the protagonists to arrange positions as chancellor (candidate), party chair and head of parliamentary group in a specific, interlocking mode (even spanning federal levels at times) (Rupps, 2004). Despite problems and tensions at the end of the Troika in the 1980s (and a failed attempt to recreate it in the 1990s with a new set of actors), the memory of a successful phase may well have instilled sympathy toward the principle of power sharing.

In 2019, for the first time several teams competed in a first election round and the two most highly voted for went on to the second round, in which Norbert Walter-Borjans and Saskia Esken prevailed. The winning team was supposed to represent the moderate left wing of the party, while the losing team, composed of Olaf Scholz and Klara Geywitz, was regarded as the right wing. Therefore, in this case, co-leadership was not adopted with the aim of accommodating different viewpoints within the party, but each team of candidates represented a distinctive position. An attempt to unify the party, however, was partially accomplished through the election of Geywitz to one of the vice-chairs by party congress delegates (Jun & Jakobs, 2021).[1]

In the SPD, if a gender-balanced team of leaders becomes part of a renewal plan in a traditional party, the co-leadership of a woman and a man was meant to be an exemplary signal within a male-dominated political system, as in the case of the newly established Italian party, *Italia Viva*. In 2019, Matteo Renzi, who was the former party leader of the *Partito Democratico* (PD, Democratic Party), the primary center-left party, and who was also prime minister from 2014 to 2016, broke away from the PD and founded a new party, intending to launch a centrist and liberal project. Despite being quite unusual in the Italian political scenario in which women politicians at the top level are very rare, the new party was committed to nominating a man and a woman for each leadership role at both national and local levels. Therefore, two members of the new party, Teresa Bellanova and Ettore Rosato, both former PD parliamentarians, were first appointed as national coordinators and then, respectively, as national Chairwoman and Chairman. There is no doubt that Italia Viva's organizational structure is an innovative experiment in the pronounced attention to gender representation as stressed by Renzi himself in various interviews (Cerasa, 2019; Terragni, 2019). It should be highlighted, however, that he is the indisputable head of *Italia Viva*, as shown by his prominent role in defining the party's political strategies.[2] He also appears to be the "face" of the party, while the other appointed "titular leaders", according to Duverger's definition (1954: 146), seem to play primarily an organizing or administrative role according to the party statute. In this sense, they represent the *internal* face of the party organization, with the task of coordinating the activities of the 'party in public office' with the still rather limited 'party on the ground'. From this point of view, it is to be noted that in the national press Ettore Rosato is defined as "Renzi's deputy" (Conti, 2020), while Teresa Bellanova, the Minister of Agriculture in the Second Conte Government, has been described as the "strong voice of Matteo Renzi" within the cabinet (Martini, 2020).

---

[1] It is important to specify that the process of leadership election for the SPD formally ended with the vote of the delegates at the party congress (December 2019), in which the results of the vote among party members were ratified.

[2] For example, Renzi participated in the meeting to discuss the strategies (and a possible reshuffle) of Conte II's cabinet (Patta, 2020).

3.2 Personal Relationships: Do They Make Collective Leadership Easier?

As highlighted in the previous section, collective leadership may result as the outcome of different processes. Identifying such mechanisms, however, says little about the relationship among co-leaders. Alvarez and Svejenova (2005) highlight the role of a binding social relationship in the foundation of professional partnerships. Ruef et al. (2003), for instance, have shown that family ties are recurrent within entrepreneurial funding teams. Is it the same in politics? Does political dual leadership most likely arise in a family setting, such as, between spouses, siblings, parents and sons? Are groups of close friends a suitable environment for establishing forms of political entrepreneurship that are characterized by multimember leadership? Finally, does affection and familiarity between co-leaders make their relationship stronger and more lasting?

The issue is relevant and deserves to be analyzed. Let us begin by considering *family relationships*. As a sort of legacy of the hereditary model for the transmission of power, dynasties have remained in existence in contemporary democracies also, whenever members of the same family use the advantages of a 'brand name' to run for political offices. This path, by the way, appears to be one of the most frequent gateways to power for women (Campus, 2013). Thus, the range of women political leaders comprises several instances of wives who were pushed to enter politics after the tragic disappearance of their husbands (e.g., Violeta Chamorro in Venezuela and Cory Aquino in the Philippines) as well as daughters who inherited the legacy of their fathers (e.g., Indira Gandhi in India and Benazir Bhutto in Pakistan). Such a passing on of the mantle of leadership not only occurs in areas of the world where dynastic politics is a recurring phenomenon, such as Latin America and Asia. In Europe as well, Marine Le Pen succeeded her father as the head of the French National Front (*Front National*, now renamed as *Rassemblement National*).

Therefore, there are several instances of family bonds between political leaders, but how many of them are cases of co-leadership and not simply the transmission of power? Over the past centuries, the politics of marriage alliances among royal houses produced examples of powerful pairs of rulers, such as Henry II of England and Eleonor d'Aquitaine or Isabel of Castile and Ferdinand of Aragon. In the Middle Ages and during the Renaissance, it was quite common for rulers to ask their wives to replace them in government while they were away, during a war. For example, Bianca Maria Visconti was in charge of the Duchy of Milan when Francesco Sforza was fighting the Republic of Venetia (Santoro, 1992: 72) However, our interest here lies in the forms of co-leadership found in contemporary democracies. With this in mind, it should be observed that cases of office sharing are highly unlikely since it would be unusual for spouses to be elected simultaneously for the same office.

Instead, cases of dual leadership that are based on power sharing are more common. In several political parties, marriages or partnerships between politicians holding prominent positions can be found. Possible examples are Ségolene Royal and François Hollande in the French Socialist Party; then there is Oskar Lafontaine, founder of the German *Linke*, and his wife Sarah Wagenknecht; and finally, Pablo Iglesias and Irene Montero in Podemos. Although it is plausible that these people tend to support each other at several stages in their careers, this does not imply that they should be classified as cases of dual leadership. Only a detailed examination of family dynamics and political experiences allows us to distinguish between different arrangements.

Let us consider, perhaps, the most famous of these couples. François Hollande, whose life partner was Ségolène Royal (during their relationship—now dissolved—they had four children), was the leader of the French Socialist Party when Royal ran for President of the French Republic in 2007. Hollande himself defined his relationship with Royal as *"un couple, deux libertés"* (Malouines & Meus, 2007: 57), which is a formula that revealed the existence of an alliance, but one in which the two partners pursued their individual careers. Over the years it is likely that Royal and Hollande helped each other in reaching their own goals. In 2007, as party secretary, he was in the position of competing for the presidency; but, once he realized that she was more popular, he stepped aside and did not advance his own candidacy (Wall, 2014: 23–24). However, their political activities do not appear to be entwined enough to be defined as a true party co-leadership. In fact, Royal, who was a former minister in the Bérègovoy and Jospin Cabinets and then as President of the Region of Poitou–Charentes, entered the party primaries as an outsider with respect to other candidates belonging to the Socialist old guard. During the presidential campaign as well, she appeared rather detached from the party strategies (Matonti, 2007) and even Hollande was critical of her at times (Murray, 2009). Perhaps, if Royal had become president of the republic, then it would have been interesting to observe the political equilibrium between herself and her party, and consequently, between herself and Hollande. Based on what happened, however, we do not feel that this couple can be taken as a good example of co-leadership.

Sometimes the spouses of political leaders are not professional politicians, but are indeed in the position of exerting a great influence. However, the most politically engaged are also more likely to be precious advisors rather than true co-leaders. Since their power is usually derived from their spouse's office, their degree of autonomy is quite limited. Let us consider the case of Hillary Rodham Clinton, the American First Lady who came close to our definition of a co-leader, especially at the beginning of the first Clinton Administration. As Carl Berstein (2007, 306–307) observes, "no first lady had come to the White House with much substantive experience in government and politics... In Arkansas no major policy decisions had been made in contravention of Hillary's views". The relationship between the president and his wife was publicly stigmatized through the adoption of the nickname, 'Billary', which reflected a certain popular blame for the protagonism of the first lady (Schnoebelen 2009; Loizeau, 2015). After the failure of the health care reform proposal that she had championed, however, Hillary Clinton adopted a lower profile (Berstein, 2007). The campaign for her husband's re-election marked a complete change in that slogans like 'Buy one, get one free', which had characterized the 1992 narrative, disappeared as well as any references to Bill and Hillary as political partners (Loizeau, 2015: 5). Later, Hillary Clinton embarked on a political career on her own by running for Senator of the State of New York, in the elections of 2000. A few years later, it was Bill Clinton's turn to stand by his wife in a presidential campaign. In conclusion, as an indisputable power couple, the Clintons certainly supported each other in many stages of their careers, however, the Clinton administration cannot actually be considered a case a of co-presidency.

The case of Eva Peron, who was the first wife of the president of Argentina Juan Peron, is somehow different. It is commonly assumed that Eva Peron's symbolic function was fundamental in the ascent of Peronism. The First Lady was the 'face' of the movement; a sort of maternal icon (Taylor, 1979). Her large following among the Argentinian people was a personal one and partially autonomous from that of her husband. Eva Peron never had a formal role, even though, at a certain point, the possibility that she run as vice president was discussed.[3] Nonetheless, her impact on Argentinian politics was real. Indeed, her widespread influence is confirmed by the fact that, after her early and tragic death, Peron still needed to use her image in support of his political activity (Weir, 1993: 163).

Since the most common manifestation of dynastic politics is the intergenerational passage of power, sons and daughters become more frequently 'heirs' rather than co-leaders. Only a detailed analysis of each individual relationship can highlight whether, especially during the transitional phase, there may be a possibility for horizontal interaction and true co-optation within the pair. But it should be stressed that, in most cases, the heir becomes leader after his/her parent is no longer in power, thus denying any possibility of cohabitation. In contrast, a greater horizontality may take place in political dyads formed by siblings. The most famous example of a two-brother pair in politics is that of John and Robert Kennedy. The latter played an essential role in the former's ascent. It was Robert who ran his brother's campaigns for senator and for president. Then, once appointed as attorney general, he actually did much more than his job required. He vetted appointments, handled international crises, dealt with a large range of issues; in sum, "JFK gave his brother the broadest portfolio any president had given not just his attorney general, but any cabinet officer" (Tye, 2016: 184). Arthur Schlesinger, advisor to JFK, described his friend Bob Kennedy as "the man on whom the President relied for penetrating questions, for follow-up, for the protection of the presidential interest and objectives" (Schlesinger, 2002: 1551). According to all reports, the two brothers had a very close bond. In their case, mutual affection is supposed to have been capitalized as a political resource.

Another two siblings, in this case twins, can be taken as an exemplary case of dual leadership, Lech and Jaroslaw Kaczynski, who co-founded the Polish Law and Justice Party (PiS) in 2001. The two "founding brothers" (Jasiewicz, 2008: 12) had the party under their direct control and may be described as "a real tandem dictating the directions of the party development" (Hartlinski, 2019: 98). Their relationship appears to have been a joint political trajectory, albeit characterized by a division of labor in which Lech held more institutional positions including the presidency,

---

[3] For an analysis of the reasons of her missed candidacy see Zanatta (2009: ch. 11).

while Jaroslaw was more focused on the leadership of the party and its parliamentary activity (100). In 2006, the former nominated the latter as prime minister, an office he held for a year. After the tragic disappearance of Lech, victim of a plane accident in 2010, the symbolic narrative of the two twins in politics has remained alive, with Jaroslaw Kaczynski presented as "the brother who must do now the job for two" in order to promote the values both cared about (Sendyka, 2013: 129–130).

It cannot be taken for granted, however, that siblings always support each other. This hypothesis has been, for instance, disconfirmed by two brothers in politics, David and Ed Miliband. For years the younger Ed followed in the elder David's footsteps, first, at the same university and college, Corpus Christ at Oxford; then, a career in the Labour party in Parliament and in the government (Hansen & McIntyre, 2012). Ed entered the government in 2007, while at that time David was already an experienced politician having served in various ministerial posts under Tony Blair and been promoted to the prestigious position of Foreign Secretary in Brown's cabinet. When the 2010 elections resulted in a hung parliament, the Labour party lost the government and Brown resigned, while David was regarded as the front runner for the party leadership (Bale, 2015). Instead of playing Bob Kennedy's role and backing up his elder brother,[4] rather unexpectedly Ed challenged him. He was not stopped by fear of "ripping the family apart" (26); and the fraternal allegiance did not refrain his campaign staff from picturing David in "a ruthless way" as a Blairite unable to connect with the common people (24). In very tight competition, finally, Ed prevailed with 50.6 percent of the votes. His case shows that family ties are not enough for establishing a dual leadership when other important ingredients are missing. First, the two brothers were not committed to a common vision, Ed being more left-wing than David.[5] Second, their complementary skills were not well matched to the roles they were supposed to assume in the case of co-leadership. In fact, Ed had a propensity for personalized politics

---

[4] In the past, the Miliband brothers have been described as the Kennedys of British politics (Hansen & McIntyre, 2012). But, during the campaign for the party leadership, Ed stated his individuality by declaring, "We're brothers, not clones. We have different backgrounds" (Stratton & Wintour, 2010).

[5] During the campaign for Labour Party leadership, the media nicknamed him "Red Ed", since he represented the leftist wing and was supported by the trade unions (Gaffney & Lahel, 2013: 486).

and celebrity, as seen in the years of his party leadership,[6] which pushed him into the limelight—a position that is by definition the premier's prerogative.

While in the business world, family bonds are more frequently conducive to cases of dual or multimember leadership, we may conclude that evidence is not as abundant in politics. In contrast, other social bonds can be more relevant, like *friendship or closeness*. For instance, attending university together or working in the same place may offer two or more people the opportunity to exchange ideas and launch a political project. These types of relationships then may become the foundation for a future collective leadership.

As will be detailed in Chapter 6, the Italian Five Star Movement originates from the initiative of two friends, Beppe Grillo and Gianroberto Casaleggio, who had already worked together on other projects. In general, several political movements started from the initiative of a group of friends or acquaintances. We have already mentioned the Spanish party Podemos as an example of a movement that first adhered to a horizontal and leaderless organization, which then evolved into a more vertical leadership structure. But who are the main protagonists of the history of Podemos? And did their relationship matter? Launched in 2014, Podemos's first nucleus included a group of researchers from Complutense University of Madrid (UCM) together with militants from *Juventud sin Futuro* (Youth without a Future), student associations, *La Tuerka* and other political and social organizations, as well as alternative cultural projects and 15-M (Iglesias, 2015: 18). Specifically, the circle of academics is given credit to have played a key role. Among them, in particular, Pablo Iglesias, who then became the party leader, and Inigo Errejòn, who contributed a great deal to Podemos' electoral strategies with his elaboration of Laclau's discourse theory (Kioupkiolis, 2016). The close personal bond between Errejòn and Iglesias was an empowering force during the initial stage (Cué 2019), but did not prevent them from later embracing different views about the direction of the party (Lisi, 2019). Iglesias' line prevailed, and for some time Errejòn headed a faction within the party, but eventually they went their separate ways in 2019.

---

[6] Ed Miliband made extensive use of personalized politics by "bringing himself" center stage (Gaffney & Lahel, 2013: 497). He even became a sort of celebrity politician with a teenage girls' fanbase on social media (Dean, 2017).

As shown by the case of Podemos, university institutions are ideal places in which a political movement may be conceived of and develop. The Hungarian party Fidesz was also established as an independent youth organization founded by a group of university students. Among them there were some close friends that then took part in the party ruling elite (Lendvai, 2016, ch. 2 and 3). In both cases of Podemos and Fidesz, the academic institution was confirmed to be a suitable environment. Alvarez and Svejenova (2005: 129) pointed out that universities are "magnet places"[7] and mentioned examples of college buddies who co-founded new ventures and became successful entrepreneurs. Indeed, universities may provide their students and academic staff with resources, such as proximity, familiarity and often cultural turmoil. The same dynamics may well hold in politics as well. Initially, members of a network meet regularly, enjoy one another's company and talk about their vision of society. Then, one day, the group may decide that time has come to take political action. The emerging movement would have never been established without the propulsive force of that initial circle of friends or acquaintances.

A group composed of young socialists—many of them students—was formed in Seville in the early 1960s, giving rise to one of the most paradigmatic examples of political co-leadership, which involved Felipe González and Alfonso Guerra. Even in this case, the members of the group were bound by what Guerra himself defined as "good personal relationships" (quoted in Ortuno Anaya, 2002: 24). At that time, the Socialist Party (PSOE) was still a banned organization in Spain, (it would be legalized in 1977). In the meantime, in 1974, González was elected as General Secretary in the Congress of Suresnes. During that period, Alfonso Guerra first became the Secretary of Party Organization and, then, in 1979, became the Deputy party leader. The PSOE distanced itself from its Marxist components and moved toward more moderate positions, a process that was not easy,[8] however, "Felipe González and Alfonso Guerra were able to manage the party quite well and to enforce

---

[7] Alvarez and Svejenova (2005) adopted Farrell's (2001) notion of magnet places, originally describing the rise of collaborative circles in the world of art and literature, and applied it to the business world.

[8] In 1977 the PSOE took part in the general elections and became the second largest party. González's plans of rejecting Marxism, however, were initially contrasted at the party congress of 1979. He resigned, but in the same year he was then re-elected as party leader with a vast majority.

effective internal discipline and control" (Padrò-Solanet, 1996: 465). In 1982, the PSOE won the Spanish general election and remained in power for more than thirteen years, until 1996.

The two men represented a formidable dual leadership, cemented by a personal bond, and based on a complementarity, well synthetized by Guerra in an interview: "*Hicimos un buen dúo: él tenía un gran carisma aquí y yo conocía bien la organización.* (We formed a good duo: he had great charisma and I knew the organization well)" (Coca, 2019). Between them, there was a true "division of labor" (Bosco, 2005: 87). While González, a gifted communicator and strategist, was more focused on the external, (he was the electoral leader, the face of the party and the prime minister), Guerra's internal role as the "organizer" of the PSOE was essential for sustaining the party's achievements. He also participated in González's cabinets as vice president, a position he held until his resignation in 1991 due to his brother's involvement in political scandals. As evidence of the strength of their bond, it is worth noting that González initially defended Guerra by saying that, in case of Guerra's resignation, it would be 'two for one' since he would resign as well.[9] Then, the scandal escalated, Guerra left the government and their friendship and political partnership came to an end (El Plural, 2011).

People may be friends before entering politics, but friendship may also be formed among those who are already party members and activists. Joined by common views, such bonds may lead to the emergence of a collective leadership. Tony Blair and Gordon Brown, for example, met when they were both young representatives in Parliament (Allport, 2009: 62). From their relationship, the project of New Labour, a movement intended to renew the platform of the Labour party, branched out. As is well known, the vision of the duo Blair/Brown changed the direction of their party and, in general, of British politics. In 1994 Tony Blair was elected the Labour party leader and in 1997 became prime minister while Brown assumed the role of Chancellor of Exchequer. As already mentioned in Chapter 1, their collaboration may be seen as a form of dual leadership between two complementary partners. Rivalry between

---

[9] Specifically, in parliament González stated: "Si el vicepresidente del Gobierno sintiera la tentación de presentar su dimisión por el cuestionamiento que se hace de su honradez o le forzaran a ello, habrán ganado dos batallas por el esfuerzo de una, la dimisión de Alfonso Guerra y la de Felipe González" (Rosell, 2010). On this sentence, see also Alvarez and Svejenova (2005: 198).

them eventually took over; nevertheless, the duo has been described by Kavanagh (2005: 9) as "the most formidable partnership in modern British politics". As stated by a former collaborator, "they were better together than perhaps they were individually" (Curtis, 2010), a sentence that precisely captures the essence of their relationship, and of dual leadership as well.

Finally, a point that should be remembered is that relationships may evolve over time. Therefore, co-leaders who start out as almost strangers may become friends, while two good friends may end up becoming enemies. Moreover, some power equilibria change over time. Right hands may start in a subordinate position and gradually become so indispensable and necessary to the organizational structure that they can be considered as de facto co-leaders. As explained in Chapter 1, the boundaries between being a deputy leader and a true co-leader are often blurred. Since we opted for a quite restrictive definition of co-leadership, we assume there are different levels of involvement and that they may vary throughout the passage of time by transforming the status of each partner. In general, a pre-existing personal bond does not guarantee the success or the survival of plural leadership over time, but surely influences its evolution. It is not the only factor, however, as we are going to illustrate in the next section.

3.3 Factors Facilitating the Sustenance and the Stability of Collective Leadership

Thus far, we have analyzed some factors inducing the emergence of plural leaderships, ranging from the nature of the bonds among partners to the organizational characteristics of the party. Now we are going to discuss the factors that are likely to facilitate the sustenance of this type of leadership over time.

To begin with, we need to observe that, with few exceptions, political leaders, either individual or plural, usually hold a formal position. Leaders' positions, as Blondel points out (1987: 148 and ff.), are shaped by institutions and other arrangements. This book focuses mainly on party leadership, but in many different ways it also concerns other offices within the parties and cabinets, since our hypothesis is that collective leadership may also involve cases of power sharing in which the formal party leader is flanked by other actors, who are playing different roles. Moreover, party leaders may hold two positions simultaneously, i.e. when they win elections and become heads of the executive. As a consequence, even though an analysis of institutional resources is needed in order to understand individual leadership, the same effort of examining the potential impact of formal and institutional rules is required in order to understand how collective leadership functions and survives. It should be clear, however, that a well-grounded assessment of this impact is more than what can be presently achieved on the basis the small amount of research in the field. However, we intend to advance some hypotheses that may prompt a number of reflections and may, at least partially, be tested in the case analyses contained in the following chapters.

The first observation regarding the stability of collective leaderships concerns the existence of institutional and formal mechanisms preventing its break-up by making it impossible for a co-leader to ascend to a position of individual leadership. In listing the ten lessons that can be learnt from the Roman institution of consuls, Sally (2002) mentions the fact that when Rome was forced to appoint a dictator to face severe threats by enemies, no consul could be selected for that role, thus blocking any attempt of a consul to accumulate power and to prevail over the other. In cases of position sharing, such a preventive effect might be obtained by institutionalizing the dual structure. It is worth noting that this is not always enforced by the party statute, which in some cases, allows both individual and dual leadership, such as in the German SDP. But actually, this flexibility could tempt co-leaders to boycott the relationship, hoping to remain alone at the top. An alternative measure for achieving the same result—another suggestion originating from Roman wisdom—could be that of establishing fixed terms (Sally, 2002: 87). Without the possibility of being re-elected with a different partner, who may perhaps be more compliant or weaker, co-leaders are encouraged to collaborate. Neither of them is drawn to push the other toward an exit strategy if he/she will also be replaced at the time of the other's premature resignation.

In the case of power-sharing temptations to break alliances, these may stem from either internal party disagreements or from tensions that emerge between the executive and coalition parties. Some institutional arrangements hamper long-term stability more than others. For instance, in parliamentary systems, the government may be led by a prime minister who is not the leader of the majority party, neither the leader of the largest coalition party. This arrangement is likely to give rise to a dual or multi-member leadership that may enter into a crisis if the prime minister is too inclined to reaffirm the autonomy of his cabinet from coalition parties. On this basis, it can be argued that the stability of the pact between co-leaders, then, depends on elements that vary from country to country. In some national contexts, for instance, institutional procedures are designed to make it quite difficult to replace the prime minister and his/her cabinet. So, for instance, the constructive vote of no confidence works (Müller & Strøm, 2000). In contrast, in other contexts, such as in Italy, the cost of dissolving a government has always been quite low (Mershon, 2002). If a government may be easily dismantled and another formed with the same coalition parties (or just with some slight differences) but with a different prime minister, this condition poses a notable limitation on the sustenance of a plural leadership.

In general terms, it may prove be difficult to have a well-functioning and durable plural leadership when the chief executives are markedly constrained by the configuration of political forces in government. An interesting example of this sort is the first Prodi Government (1996–1998). In 1996, a center-left coalition, called "*Ulivo*" (The Olive Tree), won national elections and was headed by the Professor of Economics Romano Prodi. The coalition gathered together several parties, among them the main leftist party, the DS (Left Democrats) and the Catholic party *Partito Popolare* (Popular Party). The *Ulivo*'s arrangement could be interpreted as a case of multimember leadership, including the coalition leader (who did not have his own party) and the leaders of the main parties within the coalition (Pasquino, 2005). Once the government was formed, tensions surfaced between Prodi, who demanded autonomy, and the other partners, who instead decided to control the government's activity more closely. The situation was described as a struggle between the "*partito dell'Ulivo*" (the Olive Tree party, intended as a unitary political actor) and the "*Ulivo dei partiti*" (The Olive Tree of the parties) (Diamanti, 2005). Eventually, the government fell because of a vote of no confidence that followed the withdrawal of the *Rifondazione Comunista* (Communist Refoundation), a far-left party outside the government coalition which had previously given its external support. The party leaders within the *Ulivo*, then, took advantage: A new government was formed under the leadership of Massimo D'Alema (leader of the Left Democrats), while Prodi retired from politics for a period (he subsequently became President of the European Commission before returning as prime minister in 2006). Presumably, if the dissolution of Prodi's government would have necessarily led to new elections, all partners of the collective leadership had been encouraged to maintain the initial agreement in order to avoid the uncertainties of an early election.

In light of this, we could advance the hypothesis that the institutional or formal mechanisms provide a framework that affects the sustenance of plural leadership either when the arrangement involves just the sharing of party leadership or when it concerns the relationship between prime ministers and coalition party leaders. For these reasons, this category of factors is largely subject to a high degree of country to country variations. The scope and applicability of other factors, on the contrary, are more general and less context-dependent. Let us take into consideration, for instance, the role of leaders' personalities. Character traits are supposed to influence the style of a political leader (Barber, 1977; Etheredge, 1978; Steinberg, 2008). Thus, if we assume that plural leadership requires mutual collaboration, it is reasonable to think that co-leaders or members of a leadership team cannot be too dominant and domineering or their inclinations risk to jeopardize internal harmony and reciprocal respect. Indeed, for Sally (2002), another good practice among the lessons that can be learned by the experience of consuls in the Roman Republic is that co-leaders should show a certain degree of humility and not seek personal glory. Thus, should we think that Alpha males or females are unable to share power?

Although the incapability of limiting one's ego is certainly an obstacle to collective leadership, it is not said that assertive and ambitious leaders can never cohabit with others, especially if there is a certain degree of complementarity among them. As observed in Chapter 1, it is commonly believed that the individuals who exercise leadership should perform both instrumental and expressive roles. These roles can be performed by different individuals and, therefore, they can accommodate different personality profiles. For instance, authors who have reflected on how co-leaders work together seem to positively assess the existence of a complementarity of roles, such as, "the one is feared; the other is loved" (Miles & Watkins, 2007) or "good cop/bad cop" (Sally, 2002). Although the partners may decide to assume such roles interchangeably depending on circumstances, it is likely that the assignment of the role to be played actually reflects their psychological predispositions.

Another factor that may influence the functioning and the sustenance of collective leadership is leaders' motivation. Political psychologists have stressed the importance of motives in influencing leadership styles and actions (Winter, 1995; Renshon, 2005; Hermann, 2014). Among the several possible motives—such as an ideological commitment, the desire to solve a problem or to advance a cause, the need for approval, the urge to exert power over other people—in a context of plural leadership seeking status and public recognition may become a crucial issue. On the one hand, the presence of people who compete for status has been considered to be an obstacle to the emergence of shared leadership. Studies of the interpersonal dynamics within groups show that individuals actively seeking status behave in such a way to prevail over other members and so automatically create leadership differentials (Seers et al., 2003: 90). It is certainly true that too much personal ambition may be a deterrent; however, also in this case, it should be remembered that political organizations require different leadership functions. Some give leaders more visibility and external recognition; others are more low-profile but, nonetheless, provide power and influence. Thus, the craving for status and celebrity, which appears to be a distinctive trait of individual personalized leadership, can be accommodated in a plural structure as well. Agentic and perhaps also narcissistic leaders who need to be in the limelight can become "presidents", according to Rucht's typology, or at least be in charge of communication and external relations, while more discreet personalities may prefer to provide the party with structure and organization, and, sometimes, also with the political vision that their more visible partners are supposed to promote in public.

Finally, as observed in Chapter 1, in order to truly understand collective leadership, one should go beyond leaders' personal characteristics and, instead, focus attention on the nature of the bond between partners. This factor needs to be taken into consideration in assessing the stability of a plural leadership over time. Alvarez and Svejenova (2005: 172) urge to distinguish cases of time-bound commitment from long-term binding relationships that they refer to as "united careers". In such cases "there is a symbiosis in the professional and emotional domains, which is conducive to meaningful work trajectories and personal lives for each of the individuals involved, and to success for their joint enterprise" (173). Partners in these plural leaderships appear to be greatly dependent on each other, in the sense that "for the duration of the coupling the career motives, moves, decisions, and achievements of one individual cannot occur or be understood separately from those of the other individual(s)" (179). Alvarez and Svejenova's notion of united careers can be useful for interpreting some political experiences as well. When two or more people bind their political careers together, this obviously gives rise to a special form of plural leadership in which achievements and failures concern all of the partners. An electoral success, for instance, may open the door to executive offices or other forms of spoils distribution. A failure is a backlash for each of them.

In the cases described by Alvarez and Svejenova (2005) a likely feature of a united career seems to be the existence of an affective attachment among partners. In their examples, most couples are bound together by family or romantic ties or at least close friendships. Thus, the implication is that partners "care deeply" about the relationship and "try to reconcile their differences in amicable ways in order to perpetuate it" (194). In party politics, however, affection could matter less than convenience. Above all, the longevity of a united career could be enhanced by the high cost of breaking the relationship, if this implies pursuing an individual path alone without the support of a group or a faction. Understanding this may also lead people who do not really like each other, or that at a certain point have stopped liking each other, to maintain a close professional collaboration. The previously mentioned diarchy of Blair and Brown is a good example in that tensions among them are well known (Heffernan & Webb, 2005: 41; Helms, 2005: 85–86) and often reported by the press (Heffernan, 2006: 594). However, Brown remained chancellor until he did not have the opportunity of replacing Blair as prime minister.

In other words, the key point is that the sustenance of any kind of plural leadership largely depends on the partners' awareness that they could not achieve more alone or through another alliance. If, on the contrary, the co-leader is offered the right incentive, he/she can be motivated to end the relationship. Politics is a field in which breakups of even close collaborations, abandoning of benefactors and mentors by protegees, and other similar cases, are not unusual. There are examples of successful individual careers started when an individual had the capability of breaking bonds that had become problematic. For instance, when Helmut Kohl was implicated in a donations scandal, Angela Merkel distanced herself and publicly urged the party to get emancipated from him. The image of Marine Le Pen as a strong and autonomous leader was reinforced when she expelled her father from the *Front National*. The number of cases of political leaders who became political adversaries of their patrons is quite impressive, not only in authoritarian regimes, but also among democratic leaders (Ludwig, 2002, 95).[10] Thus, if breaking alliances and ending previously close relationships happen quite frequently and have even proven to be rewarding, what should be different in the case of a plural leadership?

Regarding this issue, it is quite hard to establish a rule, and perhaps, it is not even possible. Empirical evidence, however, suggests that it is not easy to dissolve a long-term dual leadership without paying a price and/or creating a *vulnus* in the organization. And this seems to hold also for the co-leader who is apparently the most advantaged by the break-up. As mentioned above, Gordon Brown succeeded in replacing Blair as prime minister in 2007, but he was not able to regenerate the New Labour project, partly because the project itself "was intertwined with his predecessor's personality" (Kettell & Kerr, 2008: 496). On the other hand, Brown could not reject the legacy of the Blair years as he himself, as Chancellor and de facto co-leader, had presided over the government action. As a 'solo' leader, Brown "ran up against a whole range of problems that typically handicap multi-term governments and that challenge 'tail-end' prime ministers following dominant and long serving predecessors" (Theakston, 2011: 97).[11] Finally, the 2010 elections ended with a hung parliament and paved the way for the return to power of the Tories. Strangio et al. (2015) narrate the dissolution of the successful tandem composed of the Australian prime minister Bob Hawke and his Treasurer, Paul Keating. After years of fruitful collaboration, which allowed the government to accomplish significant economic reforms, an increasingly frustrated Keating "tore the king down" (179). He became prime minister, but as an individual leader he was less effective in realizing his agenda (170–171). Finally, when the equilibrium is based on two

---

[10] The professor of Psychiatry, Arnold Ludwig (2002: 440), examined a sample of rulers and found high percentages of betrayal of mentors in most categories. The lowest one, that of democratic leaders, nonetheless, is about one-fourth.

[11] Foley (2009) argues that Brown was a victim of the model of leadership that the New Labour had promoted and that had worked well with Blair. We can add that he was also a victim of the division of labour that ruled their dual leadership, which allowed Brown a large room for maneuver in some policy areas, but invested Blair with the task of establishing clear authority as prime minister. In this sense, Blair had been a performer and interpreter of a "high exposure model of leadership" (510). In contrast, Brown, as prime minister, "became increasingly locked into a condition in which the more he attempted to comply with the imperatives of a leader-centred politics, the more he was exposed in a negative light" (511).

leaders' united careers, and this reaches an end, there may be negative consequences for the organization, as in the case of PSOE after the break-up of González and Guerra, with the establishment of two conflicting factions, "the *guerristas*" and "the *renovadores*", each supporting one of the former co-leaders (Bosco, 2005; Ruiza 2004).

One final observation is that plural leadership is not indissoluble and all types may be terminated for one reason or another. Those based on strong personal bonds do not make an exception. Indeed, it is worth noting that, within a duo or a group of leadership partners, there may be competitive dynamics that may be not easy to keep under control in the long-term, as seen in the cases of AfD and M5S, which will be detailed in the following chapters. In any case, it should be stressed that the emergence of some dysfunctionalities or the conclusion of the experience does not deny that plural leadership may be, at least for a certain length of time, the right answer to tame internal tensions and solve organizational problems. Some of the cases mentioned in this chapter help to show that, before their dissolution, some plural leaderships have lasted for long periods of time and proved to be rewarding both for the leaders involved and for their parties.

In conclusion, this chapter has highlighted a number of aspects relating to how a collective leadership emerges, is maintained over time and is dissolved. In the following chapters, the analysis of three case studies, in their variety, will illustrate some of these mechanisms at work. The German Green Party incarnates an example of a movement that has the distribution of power in its genes, while the AfD highlights how plural leadership may be useful for sustaining party unity. The latter also shows how competition between partners may break up specific arrangements without jeopardizing adherence to the principle of leadership sharing. Finally, the M5S epitomizes the great potential of a symbiotic relationship between two founders, and the difficulties that must be faced in order to evolve after their exit.

References

Allport, A. (2009). *Gordon Brown*. Infobase publishing.
Alvarez, J. L., & Svejenova, S. (2005). *Sharing executive power: Roles and relationships at the top*. Cambridge University Press.
Bale, T. (2015). *Five year mission. The Labour party under Ed Miliband*. Oxford University Press.

Barber, J.D. (1977). *The presidential character: Predicting performance in the White House*, II ed., Englewood Cliffs., Prentice Hall.
Belloni, F. P., & Beller, D. C. (Eds.) (1978). *Faction politics: political parties and factionalism in comparative perspectives.* ABC-Clio.
Berstein, C. (2007). *A woman in charge. The life of Hillary Rodham Clinton.* Alfred A. Knopt.
Blondel, J. (1987). *Political leadership. Towards a general analysis.* Sage.
Bosco, A. (2005). *Da Franco a Zapatero. La Spagna dalla periferia al cuore dell'Europa.* Il Mulino.
Boucek, F. (2012). *Factional politics: How dominant parties implode or stabilize.* Palgrave Macmillan.
Burchell, J. (2002). *The evolution of green politics.* Earthscan Publications.
Bynander, F., & t Hart, P. . (2008). The Art of handing over: (Mis) Managing party leadership successions. *Government and Opposition, 43*(3), 385–404.
Campus, D. (2013). *Women political leaders and the media.* Palgrave Macmillan.
Cerasa, C. (2019, September 30) Manifesto per un governo vivo, *Il Foglio*, p. 1 &14.
Ceron, A. (2019). *Leaders, Factions and the Game of Intra-Party Politics.* Routledge.
Coca, C. (2019, Apr 9). Alfonso Guerra: «Mi madre decía de mí: 'Este nos va a sacar de la pobreza'». https://www.diariosur.es/nacional/alfonso-guerra-madre-20190408152310-nt.html. Accessed on January 6, 2021.
Conti, M. (2020, August 9). Serve un'inchiesta parlamentare. E basta pieni poteri, *Il Messaggero*, p. 3.
Cross, W., & Blais, A. (2012). Who selects the party leader? *Party Politics, 18*(2), 127–150.
Cué, C., Marcos, A. and Marcos, J. (2019, January 29). Podemos: el partido en el que no caben dos amigos. https://elpais.com/politica/2019/01/19/actualidad/1547925666_294597.html. Accessed on January 6, 2021.
Curtis, P. (2010, September 1). Tony Blair's memoirs. Gordon Brown holds fire over old rival's criticisms. https://www.theguardian.com/politics/2010/sep/01/tony-blair-gordon-brown-reaction. Accessed on January 6, 2021.
Dean, J. (2017). Politicising fandom. *The British Journal of Politics and International Relations, 19*(2), 408–424.
Detterbeck, B., & Rohlfing, I. (2014). Party leader selection in Germany. In J-B. Pilet, & W. Cross (Eds.), *The selection of political party leaders in parliamentary democracies. A comparative study* (pp. 77–92). Routledge.
Diamanti, I. (2005). Confusi e infelici. Dal partito dell'Ulivo all'Unione dei partiti. *Il Mulino, 5*, 863–871.
Dolezal, M. (2016). The Greens in Austria and Switzerland: Two successful opposition parties. In E. van Haute (Ed.), *Green parties in Europe* (pp. 15–41). Routledge.

Duverger, M. (1954). *Political parties*. John Wiley and Sons.

El Plural (2011, November 3) González y Guerra, historia de una amistad, una ruptura y una reconciliación... más o menos. https://www.elplural.com/politica/gonzález-y-guerra-historia-de-una-amistad-una-ruptura-y-una-reconciliacion-mas-o-menos_70935102. Accessed on January 6, 2021.

Ennser, L., & Muller, W. (2015). Intra-party democracy, political performance and the survival of party leaders: Austria 1945–2011. *Party Politics, 21*(6), 930–943.

Etheredge, L. S. (1978). Personality effects on American foreign policy, 1898–1968: A test of interpersonal generalization theory. *The American Political Science Review, 72*(2), 434–451.

Farrell, M. (2001). *Collaborative circles: Friendship dynamics and creative work*. University of Chicago Press.

Faucher, F. (1999). *Les habits verts de la politique*. Presses de Sciences Po.

Fittipaldi, R. (2017). Alla ricerca di una nuova grammatica politica: Podemos e gli scenari di una nuova impresa. *Quaderni Di Scienza Politica, 24*(1), 37–61.

Foley, M. (2009). Gordon Brown and the role of compounded crisis in the pathology of leadership decline. *British Politics, 4*(4), 498–513.

Gaffney, J., & Lahel, A. (2013). Political performance and leadership persona: The UK Labour party conference of 2012. *Government and Opposition, 48*(4), 481–505.

Gauja, A. (2016). *Party reform. The causes, challenges, and consequences of organizational change*. Oxford University Press.

Hansen, J., & McIntyre, J. (2012). *The Milibands and the making of a Labour leader*. Biteback publishing.

Harmel, R., Heo, U. K., Tan, A., & Janda, K. (1995). Performance, leadership, factions and party change: An empirical analysis. *West European Politics, 18*(1), 1–33.

Hartlinski, M. (2019). Twins in power. Jaroslaw Kaczynski and Lech Kaczynski as leaders of Law and justice. *Polish Political Science Review, 7*(1), 96–106.

Heffernan, R. (2006). The Prime Minister and the news media: Political communication as a leadership resource. *Parliamentary Affairs, 59*(4), 582–598.

Heffernan, R., & Webb, P. (2005). The British Prime minister: much more than «first among equals». In T. Poguntke & P. Webb (Eds.), *The presidentialization of politics: A comparative study of modern democracy* (pp. 20–62). Oxford University Press.

Helms, L. (2005), *Presidents, prime ministers, chancellors*. Palgrave Macmillan.

Hermann, M. (2014) *Political psychology*. In R. Rhodes & P.'t Hart, *The Oxford handbook of political leadership* (pp. 117–131). Oxford University Press.

Hine, D. (1982). Factionalism in West European parties: A framework for analysis. *West European Politics, 5*(1), 36–53.

Iglesias, P. (2015). Understanding Podemos. *New Left Review*, 93 (May-June), 7–22.
Ilonszki, G. and Várnagy, R. (2014). Stable leadership in the context of party change. The Hungarian case. In J-B Pilet. & W. Cross (Eds.), *The selection of political party leaders in contemporary parliamentary democracies* (pp. 156–170). Routledge.
Jasiewicz, K. (2008). The new populism in Poland: The usual suspects? *Problems of Post-Communism.*, 55(3), 7–25.
Jun, U., & Jakobs, S. (2021). The selection of party leaders in Germany. In N. Aylott & N. Bolin (Eds.), *Managing leader selection in European political parties* (pp. 73–94). Palgrave Macmillan.
Katz, R. S., & Mair, P. (Eds.). (1994). *How parties organize: change and adaptation.* Sage.
Kavanagh, D. (2005). The Blair premiership. In A. Seldon & D. Kavanagh (Eds.), *The Blair effect 2001–5* (pp. 3–19). Cambridge University Press.
Kettell, S., & Kerr, P. (2008). One year on: The decline and fall of Gordon Brown. *British Politics*, 3(4), 490–510.
Kioupkiolis, A. (2016). Podemos: the ambiguous promises of left-wing populism in contemporary Spain. *Journal of Political Ideologies*, 21(2), 99–120.
Knight, B. (2019, June 24). German Social democrats adopt gender parity leadership, DW. https://www.dw.com/en/german-social-democrats-adopt-gender-parity-leadership-model/a-49335395. Accessed on January 6, 2021.
Lendvai, P. (2016). *Orbàn. Europe's new strongman.* Oxford University Press.
Lisi, M. (2019). Party innovation, hybridization and the crisis: the case of Podemos. *Italian Political Science Review/Rivista Italiana Di Scienza Politica*, 49(3), 245–262.
Loizeau, P-M. (2015). "First lady but second fiddle" or the rise and rejection of the political couple in the White House: 1933-today. *European Journal of American Studies*, 10(1). https://doi.org/10.4000/ejas.10525.
Ludwig, A. (2002). *King of the mountain. The nature of political leadership.* The University Press of Kentucky.
Malouines, M., & Meus, C. (2007). *Ségolène Royal, l'insoumise.* Fayard.
Martini, F. (2020, September 27). Sbagliato chiudere le scuole e tradire i commercianti. Il paternalismo fa solo danni, *La Stampa*, p. 1&3.
Matonti, F. (2007). La singularité française: La campagne présidentielle de Ségolène Royal. *French Politics, Culture & Society*, 25(3), 86–101.
Mershon, C. (2002). *The costs of coalition.* Stanford University Press.
Michels, R. (1911). *Zur soziologie des parteiwesens in der modern demokratie.* Verlag von W. Leipzig.
Miles, S., & Watkins, M. (2007, April). The leadership team: Complementary strengths or conflicting agendas? *Harvard Business Review.* https://hbr.org/

2007/04/the-leadership-team-complementary-strengths-or-conflicting-agendas.
Müller, W. C., & Meth-Cohn, D. (1991). The selection of party chairmen in Austria: A study of intra-party decision-making. *European Journal of Political Research, 20*(1), 39–65.
Müller, W. G., & Strøm, K. (Eds.). (2000). *Coalition governments in Western Europe*. Oxford University Press.
Müller-Rommel, F. & Poguntke, T. (Eds.) (1995). *New politics*. Dartmouth.
Müller-Rommel, F., & Poguntke, T. (Eds.). (2002). *Green parties in national governments*. Routledge.
Murray, R. (2009). Was 2007 a landmark or a let-down for women's political representation in France? *Representation, 45*(1), 29–38.
Olsen, J. (2018). The Left party in the 2017 German federal election. *German Politics, 27*(1), 131–135.
Ortuño Anaya, P. (2002). *European socialists and Spain. The transition to democracy, 1959–77*. Palgrave Macmillan.
Padrò-Solanet, A. (1996). Political parties in Spain: A review of literature since the democratic transition. *European Journal of Political Research, 29*(4), 451–475.
Panebianco, A. (1988). *Political parties: organization and power*. Cambridge University Press.
Pasquino, G. (2005). Too many chiefs and not enough indians: the leadership of the centre-left. *Modern Italy, 10*(1), 95–108.
Pasquino, G. (2007). Capi di partito e capi di governo: lezioni per il Partito democratico. *Il Mulino, 57*(3), 409–420.
Patta, E. (2020, November 4). Per Italia Viva fa l'esordio in campo Renzi, *Sole 24 Ore*, p. 9.
Patton, D. F. (2013). The Left party at six: The PDS–WASG merger in comparative perspective. *Germany Politics, 22*(3), 219–234.
Pilet, J.-B., & Cross, W. P. (Eds.). (2014). *The selection of political party leaders in contemporary parliamentary democracies. A comparative study*. Routledge.
Renshon, S. (2005). Psychanalytic assessment of character and performance in presidents and candidate: some observations on theory and method. In J. Post (Ed.), *The psychological assessment of political leaders* (pp. 105–134). The University of Michigan Press.
Rihoux, B. (2016). Green party organisations: The difficult path from amateur-activist to professional-electoral logic. In E. van Haute (Ed.), *Green parties in Europe* (pp. 298–314). Routledge.
Rosell, F. (2010). 20 anos del "dos por el precio de uno". https://www.elmundo.es/suplementos/cronica/2010/746/1264892401.html. Accessed on January 6, 2021.

Rucht, D. (2012). Leadership in social and political movements: A comparative exploration. In L. Helms (Ed.), *Comparative Political Leadership* (pp. 99–118). Palgrave Macmillan.

Ruef, M., Aldrich, H. & Carter, N. (2003). The Structure of founding teams: Homophily, strong ties, and isolation among U.S. entrepreneurs, *American Sociological Review*, 68(2), 195–222.

Ruiza, M., Fernández, T. & Tamaro, E. (2004). Biografia de Alfonso Guerra. *Biografías y Vidas. La enciclopedia biográfica en línea*. Barcelona https://www.biografiasyvidas.com/biografia/g/guerra_alfonso.htm. Accessed on January 6, 2021.

Rupps, M. (2004). *Troika wider Willen: wie Brandt, Wehner und Schmidt die Republik regierten*. Propyläen.

Sally, D. (2002). Co-leadership. Lessons from Republican Rome. *California Review Management*, 44(4), 84–99.

Santoro, C. (1992). *Gli Sforza*. Corbaccio.

Sartori, G. (1976). *Parties and party systems: A framework for analysis*. Cambridge University Press.

Schlesinger, A., Jr. (2002). *Robert Kennedy and his times*. A Mariner book, Houghton Mifflin Company.

Schnoebelen, J, Carlin, D. & Warner B. (2009). Hillary, you can't go home again. The entrapment of the First Lady role. In T. Sheckels (Ed.), *Cracked but not shattered. Hillary Rodham Clinton's unsuccessful campaign for the presidency* (pp. 45–68). Rowman & Littlefield.

Seers, A., Keller, T., & Wilkerson, J. (2003). Can team members share leadership? Foundation in research and theory. In C. Pearce & J. Conger (Eds.), *Shared Leadership* (pp. 77–102). Sage.

Sendyka, P. (2013). The mythical journey of a dead president and how it is used in politics. *Zeszyty Etnologii Wrocławskiej*, 19(2), 119–132.

Steinberg, B. (2008). *Women in power: The personality and leadership styles of Indira Gandhi, Golda Meir, and Margaret Thatcher*. McGill's Queens University Press.

Strangio, P., t Hart, P., & Walter, J. (2015). Leadership of reforming governments: The role of political tandems. In D. Alexander & J. M. Lewis (Eds.), *Making public policy decisions: Expertise, skills, and experience* (pp. 166–184). Routledge.

Stratton, A. & Wintour, P. (2010, May 21). Ed Miliband. "We are brothers, not clones. We are different from David". https://www.theguardian.com/politics/2010/may/21/ed-miliband-interview. Accessed on January 6, 2021.

Taylor, J. (1979). *Eva Peron. The myth of a woman*. Chicago University Press.

Terragni, M. (2019, September 25) La svolta rosa del rottamatore, *Quotidiano Nazionale*, p. 5.

Theakston, K. (2011). Gordon Brown as prime minister: Political skills and leadership style. *British Politics*, 6(1), 78–100.

Tye, L. (2016). *Bobby Kennedy. The making of a liberal icon*. Random House.

Villalba, B. (2016). From the Greens to Europe Ecology -The Greens: Renaissance or more of the same? In E. van Haute (Ed.), *Green parties in Europe* (pp. 92–111). Routledge.

Wall, I. (2014). *France votes. The election of François Hollande*. Palgrave Macmillan.

Wawreille, M.-C., & Pilet, J.-B. (2016). The Greens in Belgium's federal landscape: Divergent fates. In E. van Haute (Ed.), *Green parties in Europe* (pp. 42–58). Routledge.

Weir, S. (1993). Peronisma: Isabel Peron and the politics of Argentina. In M. Genovese (Ed.), *Women as national leaders* (pp. 161–176). Sage.

Winter, D. G. (1995). Presidential psychology and governing styles: A comparative analysis of the 1992 presidential candidates, in S. Renshon (ed.) *The Clinton presidency: campaigning, governing, and the psychology of political leadership* (pp.113–134). Westview.

Zanatta, L. (2009). *Eva Peron. Una biografia politica*. Rubbettino.

Zariski, R. (1965). Intra-Party conflict in a dominant party: The experience of Italian Christian Democracy. *The Journal of Politics*, 27(1), 3–34.

CHAPTER 4

The German Greens: Established Collective Leadership

4.1 From Anti-party-party to Established and Successful Actor in the Party System

The German Alliance 90/The Greens resemble a prototype of collective leadership. The German Greens are part of the larger Green Party family that emerged from new social movements in the 1970s and 1980s in most Western European countries (Kitschelt, 2006). With their roots in social movements, a self-declared goal was to keep the party organization closely linked to its activist base. This led to several specific innovations in setting up the statutes of the many new Green Parties in Western Europe, one of them being the implementation of collective leadership (Burchell, 2001). This was to prevent the emergence of a strong party leadership, or party elite, that might prioritize its career objectives over the policy goals of the party. Additionally, the idea of a strong, central leadership was alien to the new party, which perfectly follows Panebianco's definition of territorial diffusion (Panebianco, 1988): Green actors and groups originated from movements; organized local and regional lists which only over time converged into an actual center. While many of the organizational characteristics (e.g., term limits and rotation of mandates, separation of office and mandate, caps on salaries) came under pressure as the party converged with its more established competitors and evolved into a somewhat regular actor in the party system, collective (i.e., dual) leadership is still the norm within the German Green Party, for the party central office and for the party in public office, on the national as well as the subnational level.

The Greens were the first party in Germany to install a model of formal position sharing, but the existing German parties were no strangers to informal power-sharing arrangements. This is less the case for the Christian Democrats, where there was typically one strong leader, whose position was further emboldened by merging the offices of chancellor and party leader or party leader and head of parliamentary group. This reduced the relevance of shared leadership. However, we already mentioned the case of the Social Democratic Party, which, in the 1960s and 1970s, was dominated by a "Troika," a collective leadership made up of Willy Brandt, Helmut Schmidt and Herbert Wehner (Rupps, 2004). This model was not based on the party statutes but rather implied an agreement of three protagonists regarding their distinct leadership positions in the party and in public office. Wehner provided discipline among the older socialist party cadres, Schmidt calmed the ideology-free pragmatists and Brandt appealed to the young idealists (Walter, 2000: 248). Despite complications toward the end, the "Troika" was judged to be a successful model of integrating the three most influential actors in the SPD, ultimately increasing the electoral appeal and bringing the party into the federal government. Tensions existed and there were phases that were more harmonious than others, but all three understood that only together they could lead the country and act as the three most powerful individuals in Germany (Rupps, 2004).

After the Greens this model was adapted by other German parties, indicating its sustained attractiveness: When the PDS, the successor of the former East German state party SED, merged with the small Social Democratic splinter party WASG, the conglomeration opted for a dual leadership structure (Patton, 2013: 221). This was a convenient way to have both parties, and thereby both parts of Germany, represented. Likewise, the Alternative for Germany (AfD), the most recent addition to the German party system, implemented a model of collective leadership (see Chapter 5). This is somewhat surprising, as right-wing populist parties with their affiliation for authoritarianism tend to form around strong, individual leaders (Heinisch & Mazzoleni, 2016). Finally, in 2019 the German Social Democratic Party, the oldest party with a close to 160-year history, introduced the option of dual leadership (Jun & Jakobs, 2021). The positive associations of the original "Troika" (the failed attempt to revive this model in the 1990s is seen as less inspiring) help to explain the appeal of reforming leadership in this direction. Alongside a direct intra-party election of the two chairpersons, this was one of the answers to a perceived prolonged crisis, after multiple significant electoral defeats and several leadership turnovers (see Chapter 3 for details).

German parties are heavily regulated and need to conform to the parties act to compete in elections and to receive federal subsidies (Merten, 2013). The act requires parties to be organized in a way that guarantees members an adequate role in political opinion formation. The party chair and the executive committee have to be elected by a party congress. While parties organize this with delegates from regional or local branches, an assembly of all party members is not ruled out. For instance, the AfD, with its calls for more direct democracy, at first organized several national congresses inviting the whole party on the ground. The regulations in the political parties act, in theory, secure a clear-cut democratic accountability of leadership to the assembly, however, in practice, "… competitive leadership contests have been rather rare. There are strong efforts within German parties to reach a consensus on a single candidate prior to the formal election; he/she is then presented to the conference delegates and usually 'coronated' by very large margins" (Detterbeck & Rohlfing, 2014).

4.2 The Continuous Evolution of Leadership in the Green Party

The German Greens look back on a forty-year life span in which the party has experienced successes and defeats (see Table 4.1). Specifically, because of its novel and experimental character the party drew a lot of scientific attention in its founding phase (Poguntke, 1993; Raschke, 1993; van Hüllen, 1990). Throughout its history the party changed, programmatically and organizationally. The different stages have been extensively researched and retraced (Mende, 2011; Probst, 2018; Probst, 2013; Raschke & Hurrelmann, 2001; Switek, 2015). There are competing approaches to determining phases of Green Party evolution, but with the focus of this analysis primarily on collective leadership, we structure our analysis into four stages: the foundation stage, where the party set up its formal organization and experienced its first successes with parliamentary representation (1980–1990); the reform phase, where a heavy electoral loss in the first federal elections in a reunited Germany

Table 4.1 Most significant events in the organizational evolution of the Greens/Alliance 90/The Greens (1980–2020)

Date	Event
Foundation stage	
7 October 1979	First green electoral list (*Bremer Grüne Liste*) enters a state parliament
7–10 June 1979	Participation in European elections as *SPV/Die Grünen* (3.2%)
12–13 January 1980	Founding party congress in Karlsruhe
21–23 March 1980	Adoption of basic program at party congress in Saarbrücken
5 October 1980	First participation in a federal election (1%)
28 February 1981	Anti-nuclear protest with 100.000 participants
6 March 1983	The Greens receive 5.6% in the federal election, they are the first new parliamentary group in Bundestag since 1957
1984	All female leadership of parliamentary group (*Feminat*)
12 December 1985	First government participation on the state level in coalition with Social Democrats in Hesse (collapses 1987)
15–19 May 1986	Party congress in Hannover adopts gender parity requirements for all party bodies and electoral lists
2 December 1990	Greens miss the electoral threshold (4.8%) in the first election in a reunited Germany, only Alliance 90 and East German Greens represented in parliament
Reform stage	
14 October 1990	Novel coalition government of SPD, Greens and Liberals in Brandenburg
26–28 April 1991	Party congress in Neumünster adopts organizational reforms, switches to dual leadership; party redefines itself as 'ecological reform party'
14–16 May 1993	Party congress in Leipzig confirms merger of Alliance 90 and Greens
16 October 1994	Greens re-enter the parliament (7.3%)
27 September 1998	First participation in a federal government in a coalition with the SPD (ministers A. Fischer, J. Fischer, Trittin)
Coalition stage	
1999	The engagement of the German military in the Kosovo-Conflict threatens to split the party
12 January 2001	Party chair Künast replaces A. Fischer as a minister and takes over the portfolio of agriculture, food, and consumer protection
2001	The engagement of the German military in Afghanistan poses another crucial test for the party

(continued)

Table 4.1 (continued)

Date	Event
17 March 2002	A party congress in Berlin ratifies the second basic program "The future is green"
22 September 2002	The Greens receive their best result on the federal level (8.6%)
May 2003	To resolve a conflict about the separation of party office and public mandate, the party conducts an intra-party direct vote; 67% vote for a relaxation of the strict incompatibility (2 of 6 executive committee members can hold a mandate)
2005	SPD-Chancellor Schröder loses a vote of confidence in parliament, in the snap-elections SPD and Greens lose their majority, and CDU/CSU and SPD form a grand coalition
Fall and stabilization stage	
April 2008	First CDU-Green coalition is formed in Hamburg
September 2009	First CDU-Liberal-Green ('Jamaica') coalition in Saarland
2009	Green New Deal: attempt to merge economic and ecological questions
March 2011	In state elections in Baden-Württemberg the Greens (24.2%) surpass the SPD (23.1%), handing them the first Green prime minister Kretschmann
November 2013	Leading candidates (Göring-Eckart, Trittin) and top priorities for federal election campaign are determined by an intra-party vote
November 2014	After experiments with coalitions with CDU and Liberals, the Greens form the first state government with Left party and SPD in Thuringia
March 2016	The Greens improve their result in Baden-Württemberg (30.6%) and form a coalition with the CDU; Kretschmann stays in office
January 2017	Again, leading candidates (Göring-Eckart, Özdemir) and top priorities for the federal election campaign are determined by an intra-party vote
October–November 2017	After the 2017 federal election the Greens negotiate with CDU/CSU and Liberals about forming a coalition; the talks end with the FDP walking away from the table
23–26 May 2019	The Greens (20.5%) surpass the SPD (15.8%) in the European elections
22 November 2020	A digital party congress ratifies the third basic program

Source Authors' own compilation from literature

in 1990 provoked extensive organizational reforms (1990–1998); the federal government phase, where the decision to enter a coalition government led by the Social Democrats elevated the party into the executive sphere and provided a severe reality check for Green programmatic demands (1998–2005); finally, as the party had to come to terms with its government participation it embarked on a strategy of opening up to other coalition models, in combination with a push for professionalization and moderation (2005–2020). This last phase was the first that exhibited multiple segments of effective leadership originating from the formal chairs of the party, emblematized by the current popular leadership of Annalena Baerbock and Robert Habeck (Probst, 2020).

If we align this chronological segmentation with the phases of movement-parties developed by Hopper (1950), the first phase corresponds to the popular phase, where the Greens—still as an extraparliamentary force—attracted a lot of publicity and attention and the party relied extensively on voluntary work and enthusiasm of its members. The second stage aligns with the formal stage, where the party reformed itself to comply with the requirements of parliamentary realities in the German political system. With government participation, the Greens reached the institutional stage, even if there was a strong imbalance between the influence and visibility of the Green ministers and the party leadership. While the end of the SPD-Green federal government was a shock, the party recovered and is now a recognized and established part of the party system. This is especially visible through the many different state coalition governments in which the Greens are members.

4.2.1 Foundation Phase: From Movement to Party (1980–1990)

The foundation of the Greens in Germany in the 1980s cannot be seen isolated from a larger societal shift occurring in all industrialized Western countries. Inglehart (1971) was the first to identify the appearance of a new societal cleavage between materialistic and post-materialistic groups. The stability and economic growth in the post-war years coupled with the extension of the welfare state created a base for societal groups to push for novel quality of life and environmental issues. These issues triggered and mobilized different movements (e.g., university students, feminists, pacifists, new left), which embraced activist politics and extra-parliamentary action to generate change. Despite the strong political engagement of these groups, they shunned established parties, which were seen as ignorant or disparaging concerning these new demands. While these larger trends were similar in most West European states, some specific conditions in Germany created additional support. Kitschelt (1989) argues that two factors were crucial in the ascent and establishment of the German green party: First, the prominence of the anti-nuclear movement, which German state institutions countered with strong repression, prompted further mobilization and banded activists strongly together against a common adversary (Rucht, 2008). Second, in the 1970s and early 1980s the Social Democratic Party was in government in Germany, and therefore less able and willing to react to new policy demands.

Yet, there was an extensive debate in the various groups and movements about whether the path forward should include the foundation of a political party at all. Critics assumed that this would inevitably discourage activists and lead to a detachment from the original movements (Poguntke, 1993). The European election in 1979, the first direct election of the European parliament, was helpful, in a sense. Under German electoral rules, this election could be contested as a *Sonstige Politische Vereinigung* (miscellaneous political organization). With this label, the formal foundation of a political party could be sidestepped for the time being. Nevertheless, the first cautious move in that direction had been made, and this predecessor organization already featured a multimember leadership. Accordingly, the first Green Party organization in 1980 was built on top of these rudimentary structures. This is an interesting qualification of Pedersen's declaration and authorization stage. The Greens only reluctantly entered the electoral arena, unsure what role prospective mandates should play in the overall strategy (see Table 4.2).

In engineering a party statute, a vital factor was preserving the roots in the social movements. As one of four founding principles, the Greens stressed *Basisdemokratie* (grassroots democracy) (Raschke, 1993). This encompassed general demands for the German society and political institutions to become more participatory, democratic, and decentralized, but also influenced the set-up of the party organization itself. The Greens accordingly labeled themselves as an *Anti-Parteien-Partei* (anti-party-party). The decision to implement collective leadership was therefore strongly related to core issues of party identity (Poguntke, 1993). There were specific conceptions about the role of party leadership which significantly deviated from the way this was set-up in other parties: Installing a multimember leadership was supposed to impede the establishment of a

Table 4.2 The organizational evolution of the Greens/Alliance 90/The Greens

	Foundation stage	Reform stage	Federal government stage	Fall and reconstruction
Period	1980–1990	1990–1998	1998–2005	2005–2020
Party Lifespan Threshold	Authorization and Representation	Representation	Executive Power	
Party Central Office	1980–1981 Kelly, Haußleitner, Mann 1981–1982 Kelly, Maren-Grisebach, Burgmann 1982–1983 Maren-Grisebach, Knabe, Trampert 1983–1984 Schmidt, Knabe, Trampert 1984–1987 Ditfurth, Beckmann, Trampert 1987–1988 Ditfurth, Michalik, Schmidt 1989–1990 Hammerbacher, Krieger, Fücks	1990–1991 Damus, Rühle, Ströbele 1991–1993 Weiske, Volmer 1993–1994 Birthler, Volmer 1994–1996 Sager, Trittin 1996–1998 Röstel, Trittin	1998–2000 Radcke, Röstel 2000–2001 Künast, Kuhn 2001–2002 Roth, Kuhn 2002–2004 Beer, Bütikofer	2004–2008 Roth, Bütikofer 2008–2013 Roth, Özdemir 2013–2018 Peter, Özdemir 2018–2020 Baerbock, Habeck
Party in Public Office	1980: 10 MdL 1985: 27 MdB, 55 MdL, 7 MdEP	1990: 8 MdB, 114 MdL, 7 MdEP 1995: 49 MdB, 155 MdL, 12 MdEP	2000: 47 MdB, 131 MdL, 7 MDEP 2005: 51 MdB, 125 MdL, 13 MdEP	2010: 68 MdB, 164 MdL, 14 MdEP 2015: 63 MdB, 244 MdL, 11 MdEP 2020: 67 MdB, 264 MdL, 21 MdEP
Party on the Ground	1980: 21.000 1985: 37.000	1990: 41.316 1995: 46.410	2000: 46.631 2005: 45.105	2010: 52.991 2015: 59.418 2020: 100.000

Note MdB—member of the federal parliament; MdL—member of a subnational parliament; MdEP—member of the European parliament

Source Authors' own compilation. Data for party central office from https://cms.gruene.de/uploads/documents/GRUENE_Chronik_1979-2019.pdf; party in public office—https://de.wikipedia.org/wiki/Liste_der_Wahlergebnisse_und_Regierungsbeteiligungen_von_B%C3%BCndnis_90/Die_Gr%C3%BCnen; for party on the ground from Niedermayer (2020)

political elite or oligarchy, and to keep the links to the movements alive. The three-person leadership of the new party organization was given the mandate to execute the will of the base and not engage in strong leadership itself. Their official title was "spokesperson" and not "chairperson." Unsurprisingly, Green party leaders did not command extensive authority in the party and found themselves in weak positions. As a consequence, prominent Green party politicians showed reluctance to take on these roles, resulting in significant fluctuation in these positions (see Table 4.2).

As an unintended consequence, the multiple leadership roles (first in the party organization, subsequently in the party in public office) allowed for representation of different intra-party groups and factions (Raschke, 1993: 488)—indicating a close relationship between factionalism and collective leadership. The multiple groups engaged in the foundation phase, as well as other actors joining later, attracted by the preliminary success, implied a high degree of heterogeneity in the new party (Mende, 2011). A second consequence was the extensive informal structuration of the party. Factions, wings and sub-groups played an important role in determining the party platform and strategy, as they countered and corrected certain formal dysfunctionalities (Klein & Falter, 2003: 52–71; Nishida, 2005).

The party structures were based on extensive theoretical reflections on organizational politics, but they soon proved to complicate political action and routines. "The reform process was identified as a recognition that the alternative organisational structures created by the Greens could not function effectively within the current structures of competitive European party systems" (Burchell, 2001: 114). Elected representatives struggled to align the requirements of parliamentary work with the complex party rules, which imposed sweeping constraints on their behavior. As parliamentary groups commanded extensive resources, in combination with the intentional separation of party organization and party in public office, the groups soon outmatched and outperformed the party. Ultimately, their earnest and continuous parliamentary work set the party on a path of normalization and de-radicalization (Hölscher et al., 2015).

The history of the German Greens is a history of organizational reform, as its unique instruments and procedures came under pressure through the party's evolution into an established element of the German party system (Probst, 2018; Switek, 2015).

4.2.2 Reform Phase: Shock of Missing the Electoral Threshold (1990–1998)

Over time, most of the organizational instruments derived from grass-roots democracy were modified or abolished. A particular turning point in this respect was the federal election in 1990, the first in a reunited Germany, where the West German Greens failed to pass the five percent electoral threshold. They lost their full parliamentary group, which had existed since 1983 (only the East German Green Party was represented from 1990 to 1994, with 8 deputies). In the wake of this electoral defeat, the following party congress in the town of Neumünster in 1991 cleared the path for organizational reforms, causing the most radical faction to exit the party (KleinFalter, 2003: 87–98). An element of this reform was the reduction of the number of spokespersons to two (see Table 4.2). As with the previous multimember leadership, the two leaders were formally equal and both simultaneously represented the party. Yet, how they organized their work and how they cooperated depended on the individual personalities and the specific context.

The Greens officially merged with the East German Greens and Alliance 90 (a group of opposition members and anti-regime activists—giving the party its current twofold name) in 1993. Despite a programmatic overlap, the actors brought in very different experiences. Katrin Göring-Eckart remembers misunderstandings, mistakes, and shows of force, while the chair Marianne Birthler references the diverging origins of political engagement: "In the German Democratic Republic we stood unified against a strong adversary and had learned to read between the lines. In contrast, the Greens to my mind were very loud, very confrontational" (quoted in Bündnis 90/Die Grünen, 2019: 47).

In the original founding phase, the multiple intra-party factions disagreed on how to incorporate parliamentary representation into their overall strategy (Siegert, 1986): Should it be merely a theater stage to advertise their agenda to a larger public? Or should this be seen as a forum to earnestly engage to influence law-making? In contrast, the reform phase was dominated by questions about the if and why of government participation on the state level (*Bundesländer*). Specifically, the pragmatic groups and the parliamentarians developed a certain taste for working within the system and valued the additional leverage being offered by government participation (Thaa et al., 1994). This sparked heavy intra-party conflicts about decisions to join governments with the

Social Democrats. For instance, the Greens insisted on holding coalition negotiations in Hesse in public, so the party base would not be excluded from the process (Johnsen, 1988). However, coalitions with the Social Democratic Party became more frequent and evolved into an accepted model within the Green Party (Lees, 2000; Switek, 2015). Government participation added another layer of influential actors to the equation; ministers in elevated positions are typically seen as representatives of the party by the wider public. Their statements in practice often command more weight than those of the party leadership (Raschke & Hurrelmann, 2001). Additionally, they were gaining and expanding their expertise in their respective policy fields. Finally, within the federal setting of Germany, the second chamber on the national level (*Bundesrat*) is comprised of delegates from the state governments, in a way integrating Green ministers into policy making on the national level (Jungjohann, 2018).

While a cautious and slow process of professionalization played out in this phase which helped to strengthen the position of the party leaders, the increasing number of state coalition governments with ministers from the Green party, in part, counterbalanced this development.

4.2.3   *Federal Government Phase (1998–2005)*

The previous phase illustrated that parliamentary representation integrated the party into the institutions and fostered willingness to compromise and engage in earnest legislative behavior. In addition, a second major influence on the party organization, and therefore its leadership, was the government status. Through multiple experiences with coalition governments at the state level, the attractiveness of this option grew substantially within the party. This process culminated in 1998 with the Greens joining the federal government as a junior partner of the Social Democratic Party for the first time (Raschke & Hurrelmann, 2001). This red-green coalition held on to their majority in the subsequent election in 2002 and governed until 2005 (a decision by SPD-chancellor Gerhard Schröder to call for snap-elections cut the original four-year term short).

The potentially diverging priorities of the various faces of parties are typically counterbalanced through merging leadership positions. In Germany, the chancellor (i.e., prime minister) will generally chair his or her party organization; for parties not included in government the head of their parliamentary group tends to also head the party organization

(Forkmann & Schlieben, 2005). This was one reason why the SPD politician Olaf Scholz, finance minister and vice-chancellor in 2019 vied for the position of SPD-chairperson. Green Party statutes originally prohibited this strategy, again to prevent the creation of a strong elite and a misguided oligarchy (Poguntke, 1993). Therefore, Green politicians, as members of government on state and federal levels, never formally participated in the national or subnational party leadership. However, the consequences of this set-up were detrimental: Because of the weak party leadership and the separation of the extra-parliamentary and parliamentary face of the party, members of government with visible and high-profile offices wielded extreme influence in the party as a whole. The mechanism in the federal government with its three Green ministers was similar to the subnational level, where the limelight rested primarily on the Green ministers Joschka Fischer, Jürgen Trittin and Andrea Fischer (replaced by Renate Künast in 2001). The Green Party organization itself remained invisible, following in the footsteps of the policies shaped by the government (Raschke & Hurrelmann, 2001). The significant policy questions were decided in government, where the Greens as junior-partner had to push hard to realize at least parts of their electoral pledges. Reaching the party lifespan threshold of executive power had far-reaching consequences for the Greens (see Table 4.2).

The SPD-Green government without a doubt pursued a progressive agenda that realized demands of the Green party platform, e.g., reforming the citizenship law or introducing a same-sex civil union (Egle et al., 2003). One signature issue was the decision to phase out nuclear energy in Germany, which was realized in 2002 (Jahn & Korolczuk, 2012). The Green minister Jürgen Trittin (a former party leader and head of the left *Fundi* faction) headed the negotiations with the nuclear industry. The unquestionably historic compromise was met with frustration in the Green party though (Switek, 2012). The remaining run-times granted to the nuclear power plants were seen as too generous, the party on the ground had hoped for a speedy and immediate phasing-out. A similar example was the field of foreign policy, where the red-green government was the first German government that supported a military intervention in the Balkans, an absolute line in the sand for Green members with pacifist roots (Bukow, 2016). While the party leadership worked tirelessly behind the scenes to foster a compromise that would let the Green Party stay in government, it was foreign minister Joschka Fischer who dominated the public debate about this issue (and he was the one who held the fiery speech on the decisive party congress in Bielefeld in 1999).

In the shadow of these grand national policy debates, which strained the programmatic positions of the Greens, there were additional tentative organizational reforms, driving a further professionalization of the leadership structures (Frankland, 2006). For the first time, there was a competitive salary for party leaders, increasing the attractiveness of this office. This phase also saw the first so-called dream team of chairpersons, Fritz Kuhn and Renate Künast, who both came from the pragmatic faction (*Realos*) (Richter, 2005). This facilitated easier cooperation and reduced the tension between the two leadership positions. Kuhn and Künast strengthened the party headquarters and marked the beginning of a trend of lower fluctuation in office (Künast's leadership talent was recognized when, after a shakeup in government, she became minister of agriculture, food and consumer protection in 2001).

In this period, there was another attempt to reform one of the rules connected to the founding principles: the separation of party office and public mandate. The ability for members of the executive committee to become members of parliament was supposed to enhance communications between group and party. Despite Claudia Roth's popularity as party chair, a party congress came short of the two-third majority necessary for a statute reform (Switek, 2012). Roth had to resign and this question was put to an intra-party vote to resolve the gridlock. Here a simple majority was sufficient and the large support for the reform in this vote (67% of the members voted for the change) showed that the party on the ground was more pragmatic and moderate than activists and middle-level elites. This was only a partial loosening of the rule though: Two of the six members of the executive committee (including the two party chairs) could be members of parliament, and they could not be head of the group, minister or member of the European commission.[1]

---

[1] Even with the renunciation of a principal incongruity this rule is not irrelevant. For the federal election 2013 four of the committee members ran for a seat in the parliament (Özdemir, Roth, Lemke, Spitz), three were successful. The observer Astrid Rothe-Beinlich was already a member of the subnational parliament in Thuringia. Independent of the consequences of the disappointing election result, the committee would have been forced to change its composition.

4.2.4 Fall and Stabilization Stage (2005–2020)

After the end of the red-green coalition on the federal level, the Green Party entered a difficult period. Government participation had exhausted the party. The membership slightly declined. Even if the national and European election results remained on a similar level (see Fig. 4.1) there was a series of weak election results in the states. Over the course of the next years, the Greens lost all their government participation in the states (Switek, 2019). Similar to the loss of parliamentary representation in 1990, this marked a particular turning point in Green Party history. One major reorientation was the willingness to pursue a centrist and moderate

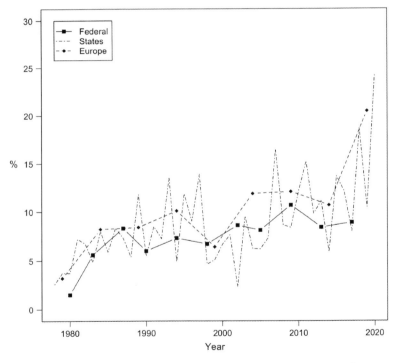

Fig. 4.1 The electoral performance of the Greens at state, federal and European levels, 1979–2020 (%, mean for state level) (*Source* Authors' own figure with data from https://de.wikipedia.org/wiki/Liste_der_Wahlergebnisse_und_Regierungsbeteiligungen_von_B%C3%BCndnis_90/Die_Gr%C3%BCnen)

position in the German party system. This was typified by a coalition strategy which embraced the pursuit of new coalition models beyond the accepted cooperation with the SPD (Gross & Niendorf, 2017; Switek, 2015). The pragmatic *Realo* wing primarily pushed for this strategy and the left *Fundi* faction reluctantly followed along. This was not based on a single decision but rather an incremental process, driven through motions in party conferences and coalition experiments in the states. While the national party leaders at times offered benevolent or critical statements, depending on their factional affiliation, this was not a purposeful strategy and resembled a bottom-up process. The long-term strategy of broadening coalition options almost paid off after the federal election in 2017, when the Greens came close to building a novel federal government coalition with the Christian Democratic Party (CDU/CSU) and the Liberal Party (FDP) (Faas & Klingelhöfer, 2019).

Since the beginning, the chairpersons of the German Greens held equal rights and standing. Under the current statutes, they are part of an executive committee made up of six persons (the secretary general, the treasurer and two observers). The executive committee represents the federal party inwards and outwards and conducts the daily business on the basis of the decisions of the party congress. All members of the executive committee are elected every two years by the party congress, with a gender quota. There are no ex officio memberships. The secretary general, referred to as political director in the statutes, is directly elected by the congress, without formal approval of the chairpersons, giving him or her a unique and independent position.[2] The secretary general sometimes complements the external presentation of the party; however, her or his work is typically directed into the party organization. The position is responsible for organizing federal election campaigns. While in the early years there was a strict incompatibility rule, the separation of party office and public office is looser today: two of the six executive committee members are allowed to hold a public office.

---

[2] Occasionally, this independence led to tensions. For instance, the relationship between the party leaders Özdemir and Roth and political director Steffi Lemke was strained in the summer of 2012, leading the former to push for a resolution taking away Lemke's staff responsibility inside the party central office and transferring this to the treasurer. "One year before the federal elections the party leadership is at war with the most important campaign manager" (Beste, 2011: 28).

In addition to the executive committee there is the position of organizational director, focused on administrative tasks for the party organization. The party leaders nominate a person who is voted on by the party congress. For this position, there were never any rotation rules, allowing for a high continuity. The high fluctuation of chairpersons was compensated for through this position. Even if the position is somewhat detached from political competition, it is an important role in organizing and steering the party. When the position had to be filled in 2012, there were competing proposals coming out of the committee (Gathmann, 2012).

The organizational infrastructure and main power resource are the party headquarters in the German capital Berlin. In the early days of the party, the headquarters received only limited funds: "[...] in the mid 1990s there was a discussion, why do we need a party central office at all" (employee of the party headquarters, quoted in Bukow, 2013: 193). As late as 2001 observers saw a vacuum on national level: "There is no effective federal party" (Raschke & Hurrelmann, 2001: 324). This sparked repeated discussions in the party regarding how the executive committee could be turned into an efficiently working institution and, respecting the grassroots preferences of Green Party members, how influential persons in the party could be assembled here.

The two chairpersons and the secretary general command their own offices with staff (Baerbock and Habeck for the first time merged their previously independent offices). The subtle upgrading and extension of the party headquarters provoked a professionalization (Bukow, 2013). In 2006, a central membership management system was introduced which allowed for novel instruments of member recruitment and support. Since then, the central office can address all members through email (Probst, 2009: 258).

Overall, the influence of the party central office within the Green Party organization is smaller than often assumed. The few staffers (most of whom are tasked primarily with organizational issues) are confronted with a resource-strong parliamentary group (Bukow, 2013). This is reinforced if the party is part of a coalition government and influential ministers are part of the equation. Additionally, there is a strong federal element to the party, through which the full-time professional staff is distributed across the different levels. The largest share of personnel works for regional branches, districts or local chapters, which hire staff themselves and guard their autonomy (Niclauß, 2002: 170).

There is one very crucial area though, where the chairpersons find themselves in powerful positions: coalition negotiations (Switek, 2012). Preliminary talks and coalition negotiations are the exclusive responsibility of the party leaders; they head the core negotiation team, and they sign the coalition agreement. The parliamentary group supplies expertise, and the leaders of the group (and the leading candidates) are typically part of the delegation as well. While members of parliament are trained in compromise-building, focused on the feasible, and oriented toward the electorate at large, the party usually positions itself as guardian over the policy platform. Coalition governments with the Social Democratic Party are well practiced for the Greens, and there is no resistance from the party base (Lees, 2000). However, other coalition constellations are eyed with more suspicion. It is the responsibility of the leadership to convince the base that a new coalition model will be a beneficial strategy for the party as a whole. The chairs are required to communicate heavily into the party, integrating factions and levels.

One clear indicator of the growing authority and stability of the party central office in this stage is the low fluctuation in party leadership. Yet, parallel to the higher stability there was a pronounced element of factional politics in leader selection. This did not automatically lead to tension between the chairpersons, but rather personal characteristics determined how well the leadership duos could work together. This phase saw an alternation of complementary and confrontational pairs. Since 2018 there has been another dream team of Annalena Baerbock and Robert Habeck (Probst, 2020). Both subscribe to the idea of collective leadership and present an integrative and coordinated style of sharing power. This led to a resurgence in the polls and very strong electoral results on all levels (see Fig. 4.1). This has created a situation in which Greens are competing with Social Democrats for second place in the party system. This gain in prestige clearly increased the leadership capital of Baerbock and Habeck.

While the Green party eliminated many organizational particularities over time, the notion of collective leadership continues to be the dominant norm in leadership of the party central office, and party in public office on the federal level, as well as for regional branches, with very few exceptions. Organizational reforms concerning the role and shape of party leadership have always been contested (Burchell, 2001; Frankland, 2006). Even if leading candidates are picked for elections, this position is typically twofold (Träger, 2015). Though this personalization strategy is meant to lend distinct faces to the campaign, in practice it extends the scope of leadership even more. Prominent exceptions are the rather informal leading role of foreign minister Joschka Fischer in 2002, a consequence of his enormous popularity, and the nomination of party chair Annalena Baerbock as a single leading candidate for the federal election 2021. The latter confirms the unusually high authority the current party leadership commands, as there was virtually no criticism from the party base or intraparty factions. This is even more surprising because for the first time this position represents more than a campaign instrument. With the Greens polling close to the Christian Democrats and significantly above Social Democrats and Liberals there is a chance that they end up as the largest party in a coalition after the election, what would hand them the office of chancellor. It is difficult to isolate effects from the organizational reforms and the simultaneous process of overall moderation. However, there is a clear trend when looking at leadership fluctuation in the Green Party over time (see Table 4.3): From 1979 to 1990, 17 different individuals represented the party (three positions). From 1991 to 2000, there were a total of ten chairpersons that made up the dual leadership. From 2001 to 2010, this number dropped down to seven and since 2011 the party only saw five different individuals as chairpersons.

4.3 The Configuration of Leadership in the Different Phases

4.3.1 Organizational Experiments (1980–1990)

The concept of collective leadership is deeply embedded in the party identity of the German Greens. Green-alternative parties as a new party family cannot be understood without the previous emergence of the new social movements in the 1970s (Kitschelt, 1989). To keep the links to the movements intact, the Greens experimented with different organizational instruments, deviating strongly from existing party organizations. One of these elements was collective leadership, which activists saw as a measure to prevent the establishment of single influential leaders, who might put their interest over that of the party (Poguntke, 1993). Following Panebianco (1988) this has left an indelible mark on the organizational culture of the party that extends beyond the actual implementation in the statutes. Not only does collective leadership continue to exist today, but it influences the perceptions and positions of the party members, which tend

Table 4.3 Type of leadership in the German Green Party 1979 to 2020

Period	Type	Leaders
1980–1981	Multimember Leadership	Petra Kelly, August Haußleiter, Norbert Mann
1981–1982		Petra Kelly, Manon Maren-Grisebach, Dieter Burgmann,
1982–1983		Manon Maren-Grisebach, Wilhelm Knabe, Rainer Trampert
1983–1984		Rebekka Schmidt, Wilhelm Knabe, Rainer Trampert
1984–1987		Jutta Ditfurth, Lukas Beckmann, Rainer Trampert
1987–1988		Jutta Ditfurth, Regina Michalik, Christian Schmidt
1989–1990		Ruth Hammerbacher, Verena Krieger, Ralf Fücks
1990–1991		Renate Damus, Heide Rühle, Hans-Christian Ströbele
1991–1993	Dual Leadership	Christine Weiske, Ludger Volmer
1993–1994		Marianne Birthler, Ludger Volmer
1994–1996		Krista Sager, Jürgen Trittin
1996–1998		Gunda Röstel, Jürgen Trittin
1998–2000		Antje Radcke, Gunda Röstel
2000–2001		Renate Künast, Fritz Kuhn
2001–2002		Claudia Roth, Fritz Kuhn
2002–2004		Angelika Beer, Reinhard Bütikofer
2004–2008		Claudia Roth, Reinhard Bütikofer
2008–2013		Claudia Roth, Cem Özdemir
2013–2018		Simone Peter, Cem Özdemir
Since 2018		AnnaLena Baerbock, Robert Habeck

Source Data from https://cms.gruene.de/uploads/documents/GRUENE_Chronik_1979-2019.pdf

to be more critical and skeptical of party elites and leadership (Switek, 2012).

Linking the foundation stage of the party and the reasons for deviating from existing models of party organizations in Germany with research on collective leadership, this refers to two different explanations: First, with the new social movements as a base of the new party, the idea of the equality of all party members, the repudiation of hierarchies and the criticism of the other parties as self-interested oligarchies was ingrained in the genes of the first-hour activists. Second, at the same time the development of this leadership model was an explicit ideological choice. The

Basisdemokratie as one of the four core principles fueled the strong belief that hierarchies are unavoidably flawed and for this reason there should not be a single leader at the top of an organization (Raschke, 1993).

Coincidently, the multiplication of leadership positions, which was meant to weaken leadership, was utilized to represent the scope of groups involved in creating the new party. While research on collective leadership states that the parties are often motivated to opt for more than one chair to manage internal party divisions and preserve unity, for the German Greens this was less a dominant reason for choosing this model and more a side-effect, where experiments with new forms of leadership structures were based strongly on ideology.

One root of Green Parties is the Feminist movement, and calls for gender equality have been part of the party platform since its founding (Mende, 2011; van Hüllen, 1990; Ahrens et al., 2020), even if the explicit statute was only realized at a party congress in Hannover in 1986. Collective leadership—ultimately based on democratic ideals—was at the same time tied to questions of equal representation. The collective-, and later dual-leadership aligned nicely with the desire to implement gender quotas, meaning every chairperson-team had to be made up in half by women.

The early years of the German Green Party were characterized by heavy intra-party strife (Raschke, 1993). There was mistrust of the newly formed party and the party struggled with integrating and prioritizing the abundance of issues brought forward by members and supporters. Some observers pointed to the external impact of the five percent electoral threshold in German electoral law, which functions as a hurdle new parties have to overcome. This acted as an external brace keeping the party together, as individual sub-groups would have been too small to enter parliament by themselves (Nishida, 2005). Accordingly, in the first phase of the party's existence, leadership attempted to balance different group interests and facilitate some sort of equilibrium rather than to effectively develop and execute forward-looking strategies. In addition, there were frequent changes of chairpersons, as this office did not offer substantial prestige and the party base retained a healthy skepticism concerning longer tenures. The elevation of single party members into leading positions contradicted the egalitarian predispositions of the grassroots ideal. "The Greens at that time did not like celebs" (Volmer, 2009). As a consequence, it often fell to the party in public office (also headed by a dual leadership) to act as an engine moving the party forward (Bukow, 2016).

The duplication of leadership positions allowed for representation of the two major factions, but added the task of horizontal coordination between the leaders to the vertical coordination-exercises required in any (party) organization. It should be stressed that parties only in theory correspond to unitary actors. Instead, they are typically organized into sub-groups or factions that can be of different nature and position (Beller & Belloni, 1978; Doherty, 1992). In fact, two or more leaders can jointly be appointed with the view to represent wings, factions or networks within the party. In the line of research on intra-party politics, party leadership is typically understood as an individual leader, who negotiates with the internal factions to preserve unity and establish leadership on the basis of a spoils distribution (Cross & Blais, 2012; Pilet & Cross, 2014). In contrast, collective leadership allows for a way of handling party factionalism. However, in the German Green Party this reduced the need for the chairpersons to build and offer an integrating strategy for all groups in the party. The two dominant wings would see one of the chairpersons as their explicit representative and person of contact. This rather fueled than reconciled conflicts within the party and led to a routine co-performance of chairs.

The intentional weakening of the party leadership, organizationally realized through a strict separation of office and mandate, as well as the limited financial resources for the central office, meant that power of leadership initially rested primarily on a representation of Green ideological patterns (especially vis-à-vis parliamentary representatives) and less on organizational resources and rules (Switek, 2015). Not until 1987 did a party congress implement financial support for members of the executive committee. However, mistrust and skepticism against party leadership remained strong. One former board member recounts his frustration with this position: "I left the steering committee, because I did not want to be pushed around by everyone and having to constantly apologize for my leadership role" (quoted in Kitschelt, 1989: 140). This precarious and unpopular position became a transitional stage in individual career plans. "Typically people are interested in serving on the steering-committee to draw attention to themselves and prepare for a subsequent parliamentary mandate" (Tiefenbach, 1998: 40). In combination with rotation rules and term limits, this led to a high fluctuation in leadership positions.

The first phase of collective, multimember leadership in the Green Party, with ideological restrictions, as well as de facto limitations because of factional counterbalances, can be categorized as anarchic alignment

(Leithwood et al., 2009). While the Green's grassroots ideology is not synonymous with anarchy, there is quite some overlap in its repudiation of powerful actors. Along this shared ideology the collective leadership did not aspire to lead the party and they actively rejected influence from others about what they should be doing in their own sphere of influence. They behaved highly independently depending on their intra-party group of origin, pursuing different goals (e.g., achieving gender equality or organizing anti-nuclear protests). Their commitment was attached to their own specific group context rather than the whole organization's goals. This fits the unique characteristics of the Greens as a movement party. The stated idea was to keep the leadership weak and toothless. The party chairs remained invisible and did not fulfill any leadership roles. Tasks for building the organization, determining policy positions and developing a strategy were distributed across the whole range of actors, e.g., party congresses, parliamentary groups on different levels, and informal groups. There was clear position sharing in the formal multimember leadership of the party, but this coincided with a model of power sharing, where many other intra-party actors had a say in determining the direction of the party.

Because of these ideological roots, it was hard to criticize difficulties or aberrations. The party as a whole slowly started to recognize and reflect certain deficiencies and repeatedly engaged in correcting dysfunctional and impractical party statutes, inevitably setting the party on a path of convergence with established party organizations (Burchell, 2001; Frankland, 2006). The overall establishment and normalization of the Greens are mirrored in the increasing stability of roles and composition of leadership.

4.3.2 *Tentative Professionalization (1990–1998)*

In the first elections in a reunited Germany, the West German Greens scored 4.8%, narrowly missing the five percent electoral threshold. The electoral campaign had mostly ignored the issue of reunification which, for the voters, was a highly salient topic (Boll & Poguntke, 1992). This electoral shock generated pressure to reconsider policy positions and organizational characteristics. At the same time, the parliamentary arena was abruptly cut off, so that the attention of Green politicians turned back to the party organization. The crucial event was the party congress in Neumünster in 1991 (Frankland, 2006). There was an extensive debate about party reform and how the party organization could become more efficient. As a first step, the party leadership was reduced to a dual leadership. Another idea was to create a new body (*Parteirat*) that would assemble prominent and influential politicians and assist the small executive committee. The other parties in Germany typically elect a larger board, which then in turn creates a smaller executive committee (Niclauß, 2002). This met heavy resistance from fundamental groups in the party who believed this would be a sell-out of their original principles. There were extensive discussions about size, composition, and incompatibility for the new advisory board. The second crucial event was the merger with the East German party Alliance 90. This party was mainly made up of activists who were engaged in opposition to the East German regime and played a role in toppling the undemocratic government. With their background, they were more skeptical of socialism than some of the intra-party groups in the West German Greens. They embraced democracy and rule of law. They were less fundamentally critical of leadership, even if they understood themselves as an element of a larger opposition movement (Olivo, 2001). Somewhat naturally, the first chairperson combination represented the two distinct former parties, Alliance 90 and West German Greens (Poguntke, 1993). But as the influence of the East German activists in the party waned, this representation strategy was abandoned and the party returned to the framework of factional representation. This was paralleled, or even influenced, by the weak position of the East German regional branches of the party (Poguntke, 1993). The East German electorate did not share a post-materialist orientation and instead held economic topics as a clear priority, seeking a major transformation of the economic system. Facing a high number of foreclosures and rising unemployment, they found the Green Party platform less attractive.

Up until 1990, intra-party politics essentially revolved around three structural elements: the party itself, the group in the parliament and the factions. With the group non-existent in this phase, there was a considerable shift of power to the factions (Klein & Falter, 2003). While the strong factionalization in the first phase of the party had often resulted in dysfunctional gridlock, the organizational reforms of 1991 had led to the exit of one of the most radical left-ecological groups, spearheaded by the former party leader Jutta Ditfurth (Nishida, 2005). This eased tensions and established a dualism of two factions (the more moderate and centrist *Realos* vis-à-vis the more dogmatic and leftist *Fundis*) that helped to structure the party. Leadership capital was distributed by the factions and authority rested less with the formal leaders of the party.

One of the leaders of the left faction, Jürgen Trittin, in 1994 took over one of the chairperson positions, merging formal and informal leadership (see Table 4.3). Ultimately, this was in preparation for taking over a position in government on the national level in 1998. The most prominent Green leadership figure, Joschka Fischer, never formally led the party, but his influence was revealed through his indisputable entitlement to a minister position in the federal coalition (Hockenos, 2008). All the more, as it was his personal choice to take over the portfolio of foreign policy, which was not in any way central to the core of the Green Party platform. The figures about the perceived importance of politicians (see Fig. 4.2) impressively substantiate the dominance of Joschka Fischer, before and after taking over the position of foreign minister. For a time, he is the only Green politician on the list. Only since 1998, when the Greens gained importance through their government participation, have other influential Green party members joined this list. Furthermore, in 1997 over 40% of Green voters and sympathizers saw Fischer as one of the most important politicians. In 1998 this figure went up to 74%. The formal party leaders are dwarfed by Fischer, who never was in a formal leadership position for the party central office. "Large parts of the party decried this leadership they saw as illegitimate. But at this point it was the only possible way, in the face of party internal obstruction of leadership through the elected leadership" (Unfried, 2020).

As factions performed the main structuration of the party and heavily influenced internal debates, their representatives accordingly wielded high authority in the party (Nishida, 2005). In this sense, formal leadership roles were still misaligned in the party, but this was less based on structural conditions and more on the extent of informal factions. In some intermittent phases, the factional structuration aligned with the formal organization structures. Overall, this stabilized the role of the chairpersons, making them more influential inside the party and vis-à-vis the parliamentary group. We can therefore classify this phase as spontaneous misalignment (Leithwood et al., 2009). Despite the efforts made to build a more effective organizational structure, roles and profiles were distributed in an unplanned manner. The same tasks were co-performed simultaneously by different leaders, creating tensions and conflicts. A reduction to two chairpersons gave this phase more defined contours, but this was still supplemented by a model of power sharing and position sharing. The latter was less broadly distributed in the party at large though and primarily rested with the two dominant groups.

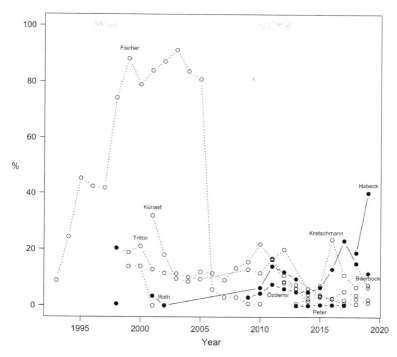

Fig. 4.2 Popularity of leading green politicians with Green Party voters/sympathizers (%) (*Note* Question: Who are currently the most important politicians in Germany? Mentions of Green politicians by respondents who intended to vote for the Greens, if there was a federal election next Sunday. *Source* Authors' own compilation with data from Jung, Matthias; Schroth, Yvonne; Wolf, Andrea: Politbarometer 1993–2019. GESIS Data Archive, Cologne. https://www.gesis.org/en/elections-home/politbarometer)

4.3.3 Push for Stronger Leadership (1998–2005)

Government participation in 1998 had a major impact on the party. The two key figures, and representatives of the dominant factions, Trittin and Fischer, advanced to positions of ministers in the coalition government. Their influence and standing became obvious when there was virtually no debate over handing them two of the three ministerial positions of the Green Party, which clearly violated the otherwise sacred gender quota (Ahrens et al., 2020). Government participation put stress on the party platform, specifically the challenges in foreign policy, but also the demands of tackling major policy issues, such as phasing out nuclear energy and reforming the German citizenship law. The party leadership went along with governmental policy rather than steering or coordinating it (Raschke & Hurrelmann, 2001). One of their main tasks at that time was drafting a new basic program, which was meant to update the original 1980 platform.

The combination of visibility, high prominence and support of his faction led Joschka Fischer to a bolder criticism of the party leadership made up by Gunda Röstel and Antje Radcke (again a West–East team), who he deemed insufficient (Radcke, 2001). His unparalleled popularity in the electorate at large and with Green voters and sympathizers increased his leadership capital and strengthened his authority vis-à-vis the party. The other two Green ministers, Andrea Fischer (succeeded in 2001 by Künast) and Trittin, came nowhere close to Joschka Fischer's levels (see Fig. 4.2). However, the former two still trumped the ascribed importance of Claudia Roth, who became party chair in 2001 and was the first Green actor in party central office on this list (Trittin moved from party chair to minister in 1998).

Fischer expected more loyal and efficient support from the party and pushed to install Fritz Kuhn and Renate Künast, both respected in the party and both from the *Realo* faction. Observers interpreted this new leadership taking over in 2000 as a first decisive shift of the role toward effectiveness and clout. The new chairpersons did not challenge the ministers, but engaged in an overall moderation. Further structural reforms and an increasing professionalization laid the groundwork for the successful tenure of Kuhn and Künast, whose work was lauded as efficient, smooth and successful (Richter, 2005: 198). They fulfilled very similar roles (organizer and strategist) and tasks (instrumental), but built effective routines in sharing these. Their successors built on this shift in leadership and managed, to a similar extent, to integrate the party. It helped that Reinhard Bütikofer started in the position of secretary general of the party, before he switched into the office of chairman. Here we see a clear complementarity between the emotional leader Claudia Roth, assuming expressive tasks, and the organizer and strategist Bütikofer, responsible for instrumental tasks: "With Reinhard Bütikofer a programmatically versed organizer took over leadership, who alongside the full-blood-politician Claudia Roth made a team, that could potentially integrate and unfurl a broad effect" (Richter, 2005: 123).

The pressure to professionalize the party headquarters grew alongside the need to organize election campaigns, which, in turn, sparked more general changes in the intra-party power balance. The campaigns became more important once the party was in government, as there was suddenly more to lose. As the rules for party funding prohibit the use of parliamentary group resources for campaigning, the leadership understood this as an opportunity to finally assert their authority. In the run-up to the federal election of 2002, the executive committee made an unprecedented claim over all campaign-related activities and stipulated that the direction and main themes of the campaign were to be decided in Berlin (Neuner-Duttenhofer, 2004: 75). The federal elections of 2002 and 2005 produced some major changes in the further centralization of the operational realm of campaigning, so that a small circle of persons was responsible for major campaign-related decisions. Another indicator of professionalization was that, for the first time, external public relations and public opinion polling agencies were brought in to help construct and define strategies (Probst, 2013: 112). Delegating tasks to an external actor was a clear-cut taboo before. External actors were commissioned and steered by the party headquarters, with party funding, limiting the influence the party in public office and party in government could exert.

Another distinct signal was the introduction of leading candidates for election campaigns. The idea was to mobilize voters with the elevation of specific prominent and popular Green politicians. Because of the Green organizational specifics, those Green Party politicians would often not be part of the formal leadership, but instead would seek out limited, campaign-focused positions as they proved more rewarding. The positions nevertheless adhered to the logic of collective leadership as they were made up of two persons, including requirements of equal gender representation (again the campaign in 2002, focusing strongly on the most popular Green politician, Joschka Fischer, was an exception). Because there were multiple and competing accentuated positions, this provided a useful way to concentrate the public attention on two frontrunners; on the other hand, this added yet another layer to the confusing tableau of leading Green figures.

As this personalization contradicted the core grassroots principles, and because leadership could not build a compromise itself, the party on the ground elected the candidates in an intra-party direct vote in 2013 (Träger, 2015), which was repeated in 2017. Resorting to this mechanism had its own risks though: In 2013, the party chair Claudia Roth ran for this position, but the members voted for two members of the parliamentary group instead, putting a dent in Roth's authority and leadership capital.

In the shadow of government participation, a substantial professionalization occurred. Influential ministers, and the small group of Green politicians who made up the circles of powers around ministers and factions, pushed for this. However, the succession of capable leaders, their complementarity, and their willingness to cooperate were factors as well. While there was a clearer leadership alignment, it still has to be classified as spontaneous, as it depended on the external support of other influential Green politicians who were not part of the executive committee. Leadership tasks and functions were still distributed with limited planning, but tacit and intuitive decisions about who should perform which leadership functions resulted in a fortuitous alignment of functions (Leithwood et al., 2009: 226). Leaders trusted their colleagues' motives and idealistic beliefs while remaining committed to shared organizational goals. The teams Künast and Kuhn, and Roth and Bütikofer agreed that cooperation rather than competition was the best way to promote a successful strategy for the Green Party. Again, formal position sharing extended into a power-sharing model between the two influential ministers, and leaders of the two factions. The chairpersons understood not to challenge them on their respective policy fields, but they nevertheless pushed for higher autonomy regarding organizational aspects of the party. The chairs were effective in dividing their tasks, but with the influential ministers, who also executed leadership, there was an overall parallel performance in two different arenas.

4.3.4 More Influential and Powerful Party Leadership (2005–2020)

Despite the progress in stabilizing the position of dual leadership and the authority of the party central office, the overall role of party leadership remained weak while the Greens governed on the federal level as part of a coalition with the larger Social Democratic Party, from 1998 and 2005, as well as during a phase of re-orientation afterward, where regional branches would, at times, challenge the national leadership (often because Greens would join governments on the state level) (Richter, 2005).

The fragile position of party leadership is in no way exclusive to the German Greens. In all democratically-structured parties, leaders struggle more or less to exert influence, considering the fragmentation and heterogeneity, which are integral elements of a voluntary party on the ground, and the character of an alliance of multiple sub-groups (Korte et al., 2018). Party leadership is only rarely able to exert broad top-down control over the regional branches or other intra-party groups, just as bottom-up subnational and local units are not able to directly influence the upper echelons of the party (Wiesendahl, 2006: 36).

Yet, both characteristics are even more than usually pronounced for the German Green Party. Chairpersons and board members exerted limited leadership and guidance; instead, they engaged in coordinating and connecting different segments of the party. For the Green Party, leadership positions were always challenged and had to be seen as part of a network of adjoining actors. In the party history, elites were surrounded by competing, strong, non-institutionalized power centers, which formed in factions first, then in the parliamentary group, later in government (Richter, 2005: 207).

Since 2018 the party has been chaired by a duo (Annalena Baerbock and Robert Habeck) representing the pragmatic and centrist faction (*Reformer/Realos*), conforming to true position sharing. While Baerbock and Habeck ran individually for leadership (there was one rival candidate against Baerbock), they positioned themselves as a team afterward and articulated their intention to overcome factional divisions in the party: "Folks, we do not know any party wings, just Greens" (Unfried, 2020). They clearly ascribe to common goals and are complementary in their skills, in addition to fulfilling the gender quota. "For this reason the chairpersons changed rules and perspectives, generating new strength, because they do not neutralize but exponentiate themselves" (Unfried, 2020). One consequence has been an unprecedented overall high in the polls, even overtaking the Social Democrats as the second strongest party in the party system). When a party congress reelected them in November 2019, they achieved impressive results (Baerbock 97.1%, Habeck 90.4%), especially for the Green Party. For the first time, the polls about the importance of Green politicians clearly place the two chairpersons in front of other prominent Greens (see Fig. 4.2). The only Green prime minister of Baden-Württemberg Winfried Kretschmann, the leaders of the parliamentary group Katrin Göring-Eckart and Anton Hofreiter, and Jürgen Trittin all score significantly lower values. Their leadership arrangement is complicated by the overall success of the party. Because of their popularity it was obvious that Baerbock and Habeck would lead the party in the campaign for the federal election 2021 and that there had to be no additional direct vote about this position this time (other than in 2013 and 2017). But the party's enduring strength makes it thinkable that the Greens are able to capture the office of chancellor, leading a government coalition as the strongest party. Therefore, there was pressure to explicitly name one person as a distinct chancellor candidate (as this office cannot be shared). In a seemingly smooth and trouble-free process, Baerbock and Habeck decided that the former should take over this position, and accordingly the executive committee nominated Baerbock as a chancellor candidate in April 2021. Of course, this affects the mandated equality between the two party leadership positions, spelling potential trouble for a coherent and coordinated campaign.

As in the phases before, electoral losses spurred organizational reform, or at least allowed for a shift in the organizational culture. While the strategy of extending coalition options was not decreed from the top, the leadership made incrementally better use of steering the party and gained more expertise in running electoral campaigns. Repeated tenures and a higher chance of being reelected by the party congress stabilized the position of the leaders. With the pairs of Cem Özdemir and Claudia Roth, and currently Annalena Baerbock and Robert Habeck, there was a productive complementarity and effective division of tasks. We can classify the phase since leaving the federal government as planful alignment (with brief episodes of spontaneous misalignment). The tasks or functions of those providing leadership were given prior, planful thought. "Agreements have been worked out among the sources of leadership about which leadership practices or functions are best carried out by which source" (Leithwood et al., 2009).

4.4 The Performance of Plural Leadership: Why It Works (When It Works); Why It Fails (When It Fails)

For the Greens, collective leadership lies at the core of party identity. It is based on a theoretical idea and strongly connected to an alternative style of politics. But as one part of a whole set of new instruments it proved to be dysfunctional at first. Therefore, prominent and charismatic politicians stayed away from this office. Instead, it fell to the factions to take over the role of structuring and leading the party. At the same time, the intentional vacuum at the top handed power to the parliamentary group, and subsequently to the party in government. For a long time factions and groups were decisive in the development and evolution of the party. Party leadership retained a weak role until early 2000, when a productive and effective duo, Kuhn and Künast, took over. With support from the leading figure Joschka Fischer, and a shared goal to see the party organization as a stabilizing element for the party in government, they exhibited clear complementarity and a model of power sharing (see Table 4.4). Both chairs acted as organizers and strategists, in the sense of Rucht's typology (Rucht, 2012), and found a way to divide tasks without friction and competition. That ministers from the Green Party commanded high authority and needed to be included in some model of power sharing could be seen in the ascent of Künast: In the year she switched from party chair to minister position, the number of newspaper articles mentioning her significantly increased from 500 to 1500 (see Fig. 4.3). Parallel to government participation on federal level there were instances of planful alignment and evidence of a transformation into a more influential party leadership.

Table 4.4 Characteristics of the leadership structure in the phases of the Greens/Alliance 90/The Greens

	Foundation stage	*Reform stage*	*Federal government stage*	*Fall and reconstruction*
Type of Leadership	Multimember	Dual	Dual	Dual
Distribution of Leadership	Position- and (distributed) power sharing	Position- and (concentrated) power sharing	Position- and power sharing	Position- and power sharing
Formal hierarchy	No	No	No	No
Labour Organization	Co-performance	Co-performance	Task division and parallel performance	Task division and co-performance
Alignment of leadership functions and roles	Anarchic alignment	Spontaneous misalignment	Spontaneous alignment	Planful alignment and spontaneous misalignment

Source Authors' summary of chapter

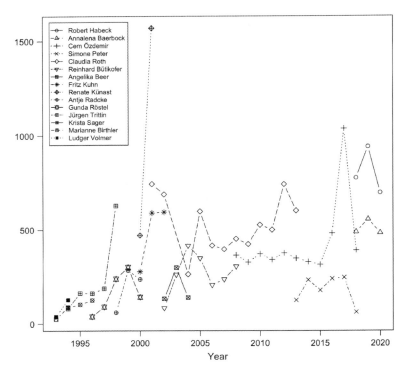

Fig. 4.3 Number of articles mentioning the party chairs of the Greens in three German newspapers, 1993–2020 (*Note* Sum of results for name as search term for each year. *Source* Authors' own compilation based on data collection from online-archives of Süddeutsche Zeitung, Frankfurter Allgemeine Zeitung, die tageszeitung)

The autonomy associated with the position of secretary general allowed Reinhard Bütikofer to gain extensive experience in leading the party. Without being a formal chair, he nevertheless engaged in power sharing, creating enough clout for him to subsequently advance to a chair position. His co-chair Claudia Roth, with her affectionate and sincere style, was the perfect addition as an emotional leader to Bütikofer as an organizer (Richter, 2005). This complementarity held with the successor of Bütikofer, Cem Özdemir, who occupied the position of strategist. He originated in the centrist and pragmatic regional branch in Baden-Württemberg, symbolizing, in a way, the convergence of the party with more conservative positions. The media analysis clearly supports this (see Fig. 4.3). Roth was more visible than Bütikofer and Özdemir in her tenure; there is only a drop for the time where she stepped back from party leadership (2003–2004).

There was a return to a more competitive orientation between the two chairpersons when Simone Peter took over. This, in part, rested on a more pronounced element of factional politics; the leaders switched back to the mode of representing the two major factions, and, accordingly, there was increased tension (Unfried, 2020). "Simone Peter, the new party co-chair, and Anton Hofreiter, the new parliamentary co-leader, both associated with the Left faction, 'emerged' from relative obscurity to become undisputed candidates for these positions" (Rüdig, 2014). This imbalance negatively affected their visibility and overall standing. Özdemir was mentioned in a distinctly higher number of newspaper articles. At the same time, the secretary general, Steffi Lemke, was, at times, at odds with the formal leadership, which created conflicts because of her autonomous position. The influential role of this position complicates the equation of power sharing, as it counterbalances the formal hierarchy between chairpersons and secretary general.

However, this has been paralleled by a challenge to national party leadership since 2008 through the rising prominence of Green politicians in the states. First, this concerned ministers who might become visible in national politics, even more so when they were part of a new coalition model that would attract a lot of attention. In 2011 Winfried Kretschmann became the first Green prime minister in Baden-Württemberg, handing him an outstanding position and heavy influence in the party. In the polls about the importance of Green politicians, Green voters would typically name Kretschmann as an important figure for national politics. Through his position in the second chamber on the national level (*Bundesrat*), his word carried weight for the party as a whole and he advanced into the constructed model of power sharing. This was not without friction because as a prime minister he represented the whole state and electorate, and some of his decisions clashed with Green policy positions (e.g., significance of automobile industry, aggravation of asylum rules).

The power-sharing arrangement with the parliamentary group can be observed through the decision about leading candidates. In the election campaign of 2002, the immensely popular Green foreign minister, Fischer, was the informal top candidate. One campaign slogan ironically portrayed his detachment from the party, hinting that his party membership might not be known to all voters: "Außen Minister, Innen Grün" (minister on the outside, Green on the inside) (Bütikofer, 2003). This question became less relevant later, but with a rise in factional tensions in 2013 and 2017 there were again conflicts about the role and position of the leading candidate which could not be resolved by the chairs or the executive committee. The party leadership turned to the party on the ground to resolve this blockade (Träger, 2015). While this was ultimately the result of a gridlocked situation, it was framed as an appreciation of the founding principles and the legacy of grassroots movements. Conducting a direct member vote could be advertised as realizing the true Green Party identity. In 2013 the party on the ground picked the leadership of the parliamentary group, denying the party chair, Roth, this position. In 2017, the team was more balanced, as members picked the party chair Özdemir and the group leader Göring-Eckart. The high degree of complementarity since Baerbock and Habeck took over the party leadership is confirmed again by the seemingly smooth and trouble-free nomination of Baerbock as the single leading candidate for the federal election in 2021. This is even more surprising as the stakes in 2021 are higher than ever before: The constant polling of the Green party above 20% makes Baerbock not only a leading but also a chancellor candidate, as the chancellor in Germany usually comes from the strongest party in a coalition. However, this also complicates the successful arrangement Baerbock and Habeck set up because it undermines the formal equality between the chairpersons stipulated by the party statute.

Typically, there was informal coordination before leadership elections, but this was confined to intra-factional deliberation in attempting to present a single candidate, or at least narrow the choices. With the initially low importance of this office, there was less pressure to capture the party leadership. Candidates never explicitly ran as a team, but typically their candidacy rested on an informal pre-arrangement. If incumbent chairs both ran for reelection, this resembled a form of team candidacy. However, if there were challengers they only challenged individual candidates and their specific chair position, there were no joint challenges presented by a completely different team.

The streamlined and coherent leadership of Habeck and Baerbock, who both have their roots in the same faction (Heyer & Neukirch, 2020), is an exceptional case of unity and complementarity. The duo reformed the organizational structures, as they use one shared office (previously each leader would have her or his own staff). Habeck combines the roles of emotional leader and president of the party. With his background as a writer and author he excels in political communication, and with his background as deputy prime minister and minister in the state government in Schleswig–Holstein, he demonstrates a distinct expertise for the position. This also explains his significantly higher popularity. But co-leader Baerbock is close to equal; her popularity is significantly higher than most of the leaders before her. Their tenure connotes the first time when Green voters placed the party chairs above other influential Green politicians. Even more so, it fell into their tenure to organize the process of drafting a new basic program, which allowed them to put their mark on the platform of the party. Both were clear and undisputed top candidates for the *Bundestag* elections in 2021. This rendered an additional intra-party vote obsolete, demonstrating their clear authority also vis-à-vis the party in public office. While the decision to nominate Baerbock as a single leading candidate was consensual, her elevated role as chancellor candidate introduced an imbalance into the successful leadership arrangement. This complicates the organization and execution of the election campaign, that already receives more scrutiny than usual because of the particularly strong position of the Green party.

The German Greens are without any doubt an interesting case because collective leadership is deeply rooted in their party identity, and dual leadership has been practiced for a long time in a routinized fashion (see Table 4.4). However, the complementarity rests extensively on the individual team and the structural conditions exerted by the factionalism within the party as well as the government status.

REFERENCES

Ahrens, P., Chmilewski, K., Lang, S., & Sauer, B. (2020). *Gender equality in politics: Implementing party quotas in Germany and Austria*. Springer International Publishing.

Beller, D., & Belloni, F. (1978). *Party and faction: Modes of political competition*. ABC-Clio.

Beste, R. (2011, May 26). Der heimliche Vorsitzende. *Der Spiegel* 24, p. 35.

Boll, B., & Poguntke, T. (1992). Germany: The 1990 all-German election campaign. In S. Bowler & D. M. Farrell (Eds.), *Electoral strategies and political marketing* (pp. 121–143). Palgrave Macmillan.

Bukow, S. (2013). *Die professionalisierte Mitgliederpartei: politische Parteien zwischen institutionellen Erwartungen und organisationaler Wirklichkeit*. Springer VS.

Bukow, S. (2016). The Green Party in Germany. In E. Van Haute (Ed.), *Green Parties in Europe* (pp. 112–139). Routledge.

Bündnis 90/Die Grünen. (2019). *Die Zeiten ändern sich. Wir ändern sie mit*. Bündnis 90/Die Grünen. https://cms.gruene.de/uploads/documents/GRUENE_Chronik_1979-2019.pdf

Burchell, J. (2001). Evolving or conforming? Assessing organisational reform within European green parties. *West European Politics, 24*(3), 113–134.

Bütikofer, R. (2003). Architektur des grünen Wahlsiegs. *Forschungsjournal Soziale Bewegungen, 16*(1), 46–51.

Cross, W. P., & Blais, A. (2012). *Politics at the centre: The selection and removal of party leaders in the Anglo parliamentary democracies*. Oxford University Press.

Detterbeck, K., & Rohlfing, I. (2014). Party leader selection in Germany. In J.-B. Pilet & W. P. Cross (Eds.), *The selection of party leaders in contemporary parliamentary democracies: A comparative study* (pp. 77–92). Routledge.

Doherty, B. (1992). The fundi-realo controversy: An analysis of four European green parties. *Environmental Politics, 1*(1), 95–120.

Egle, C., Ostheim, T., & Zohlnhöfer, R. (Eds.). (2003). *Das rot-grüne Projekt*. VS Verlag für Sozialwissenschaften.

Faas, T., & Klingelhöfer, T. (2019). The more things change, the more they stay the same? The German federal election of 2017 and its consequences. *West European Politics, 42*(4), 914–926.

Forkmann, D., & Schlieben, M. (Eds.). (2005). *Die Parteivorsitzenden in der Bundesrepublik Deutschland 1949–2005*. VS Verlag für Sozialwissenschaften.

Frankland, E. G. (2006). The Green Party's transformation: The "new politics" party grows up. In P. H. Merkl (Ed.), *The Federal Republic of Germany at fifty: At the end of a century of Turmoil* (pp. 147–159). Springer.

Gathmann, F. (2012, July 16). *Nervöse Grüne verzanken sich in Personalfragen*. Spiegel Online. Hamburg. https://www.spiegel.de/politik/deutschland/nervositaet-bei-den-gruenen-streit-zwischen-roth-und-lemke-a-844600.html

Gross, M., & Niendorf, T. (2017). Determinanten der Bildung nicht-etablierter Koalitionen in den deutschen Bundesländern, 1990–2016. *Zeitschrift Für Vergleichende Politikwissenschaft, 11*(3), 365–390.

Heinisch, R., & Mazzoleni, O. (2016). 8 comparing populist organizations. In R. Heinisch & O. Mazzoleni (Eds.), *Understanding populist party organisation* (pp. 221–246). Palgrave Macmillan.

Heyer, J., & Neukirch, R. (2020, January 16). Germany's Greens hit adulthood. *Spiegel Online*. Hamburg. https://www.spiegel.de/international/germany/germany-s-greens-hit-adulthood-a-bec98872-300e-4782-b850-9ff04d43b25a

Hockenos, P. (2008). *Joschka Fischer and the making of the Berlin Republic: An alternative history of postwar Germany.* Oxford University Press.

Hölscher, W., Kraatz, P., & Kommission für Geschichte des Parlamentarismus und der Politischen Parteien (Eds.). (2015). *Die Grünen im Bundestag: Sitzungsprotokolle und Anlagen 1987–1990.* Droste Verlag.

Hopper, R. D. (1950). The revolutionary process: A frame of reference for the study of revolutionary movements. *Social Forces, 3*(28), 270–279.

Inglehart, R. (1971). The silent revolution in Europe: Intergenerational change in post-industrial societies. *American Political Science Review, 65*(4), 991–1017.

Jahn, D., & Korolczuk, S. (2012). German exceptionalism: The end of nuclear energy in Germany! *Environmental Politics, 21*(1), 159–164.

Johnsen, B. (1988). *Von der Fundamentalopposition zur Regierungsbeteiligung: Die Entwicklung der Grünen in Hessen 1982–1985.* SP-Verlag.

Jun, U., & Jakobs, S. (2021). The selection of party leaders in Germany. In N. Aylott & N. Bolin (Eds.), *Managing leader selection in European political parties* (pp. 73–94). Palgrave Macmillan.

Jungjohann, A. (2018). *Grün regieren. Eine Analyse der Regierungspraxis von Bündnis 90/Die Grünen* (No. 44). Heinrich-Böll-Stiftung. https://www.boell.de/sites/default/files/gruen-regieren_3.aufl_web.pdf?dimension1=division_demo

Kitschelt, H. (1989). *The logics of party formation: Ecological politics in Belgium and West Germany.* Cornell University Press.

Kitschelt, H. (2006). Movement parties. In *Handbook of party politics* (pp. 278–290). Sage.

Klein, M., & Falter, J. W. (2003). *Der lange Weg der Grünen: eine Partei zwischen Protest und Regierung.* C.H. Beck.

Korte, K.-R., Michels, D., Schoofs, J., Switek, N., & Weissenbach, K. (2018). *Parteiendemokratie in Bewegung: Organisations- und Entscheidungsmuster der deutschen Parteien im Vergleich.* Nomos.

Lees, C. (2000). *The Red-Green coalition in Germany: Politics, personalities and power.* Manchester University Press.

Leithwood, K., Mascall, B., Strauss, T., Sacks, R., Memon, N., & Yashkina, A. (2009). Distributing leadership to make schools smarter: Taking the ego out of the system. In *Distributed leadership according to the evidence* (pp. 223–252). Routledge.

Mende, S. (2011). *"Nicht rechts, nicht links, sondern vorn": eine Geschichte der Gründungsgrünen.* Oldenbourg.

Merten, H. (2013). Rechtliche Grundlagen der Parteiendemokratie. In F. Decker & V. Neu (Eds.), *Handbuch der deutschen Parteien* (pp. 77–110). Springer Fachmedien Wiesbaden.

Neuner-Duttenhofer, C. (2004). *Bündnis 90/Die Grünen im Bundestagswahlkampf 2002*. LIT.

Niclauß, K. (2002). *Das Parteiensystem der Bundesrepublik Deutschland: eine Einführung* (2. Ed.). Schöningh.

Nishida, M. (2005). *Strömungen in den Grünen (1980–2003): eine Analyse über informell-organisierte Gruppen innerhalb der Grünen*. Lit.

Olivo, C. (2001). *Creating a democratic civil society in eastern Germany: The case of the citizen movements and Alliance 90*. Palgrave.

Panebianco, A. (1988). *Political parties: Organization and power*. Cambridge University Press.

Patton, D. F. (2013). The left party at six: The PDS–WASG merger in comparative perspective. *German Politics, 22*(3), 219–234.

Pilet, J.-B., & Cross, W. P. (Eds.). (2014). *The selection of political party leaders in contemporary parliamentary democracies: A comparative study*. Routledge: Taylor & Francis Group.

Poguntke, T. (1993). *Alternative politics: The German Green Party*. Edinburgh University Press.

Probst, L. (2009). Wie strategiefähig sind Bündnis 90/Die Grünen im Superwahljahr 2009. In J. Raschke & M. Machnig (Eds.), *Parteien zur Wahl 2009. Ihre Ziele. Ihre Stärken. Ihre Schwächen* (pp. 258–264). Hoffmann und Campe.

Probst, L. (2013). Bündnis 90/Die Grünen (GRÜNE). In O. Niedermayer (Ed.), *Handbuch Parteienforschung* (pp. 509–540). Springer Fachmedien.

Probst, L. (2018). Bündnis 90/Die Grünen. In F. Decker & V. Neu (Eds.), *Handbuch der deutschen Parteien* (pp. 203–2018). Springer VS.

Probst, L. (2020). Bündnis 90/Die Grünen: Grüne Erfolgswelle nach enttäuschendem Wahlergebnis. In U. Jun & O. Niedermayer (Eds.), *Die Parteien nach der Bundestagswahl 2017* (pp. 187–219). Springer Fachmedien.

Radcke, A. (2001). *Das Ideal und die Macht: Das Dilemma der Grünen*. Henschel.

Raschke, J. (1993). *Die Grünen: wie sie wurden, was sie sind*. Bund-Verlag.

Raschke, J., & Hurrelmann, A. (2001). *Die Zukunft der Grünen: "so kann man nicht regieren"*. Campus.

Richter, S. (2005). Führung ohne Macht? Die Sprecher und Vorsitzenden der Grünen. In D. Forkmann & M. Schlieben (Eds.), *Die Parteivorsitzenden in der Bundesrepublik Deutschland 1949–2005* (pp. 169–214). VS Verlag für Sozialwissenschaften.

Rucht, D. (2008). Anti-Atomkraftbewegung. In R. Roth & D. Rucht (Eds.), *Die Sozialen Bewegungen in Deutschland seit 1945* (pp. 245–266). Campus.

Rucht, D. (2012). Leadership in social and political movements: A comparative exploration. In L. Helms (Ed.), *Comparative political leadership* (pp. 99–118). Palgrave Macmillan.

Rüdig, W. (2014). The Greens in the German federal elections of 2013. *Environmental Politics, 23*(1), 159–165.

Rupps, M. (2004). *Troika wider Willen: wie Brandt, Wehner und Schmidt die Republik regierten.* Propyläen.

Siegert, J. (1986). *Wenn das Spielbein dem Standbein ein Bein stellt–: Zum Verhältnis von Grüner Partei und Bewegung.* Weber, Zucht & Company.

Switek, N. (2012). Bündnis 90/Die Grünen: Zur Entscheidungsmacht grüner Bundesparteitage. *Zeitschrift für Politikwissenschaft* (Sonderband 2012), 121–154.

Switek, N. (2015). *Bündnis 90/Die Grünen. Koalitionsentscheidungen in den Ländern.* Nomos.

Switek, N. (2019). Bündnis 90/Die Grünen. In U. Andersen, J. Bogumil, S. Marschall, & W. Woyke (Eds.), *Handwörterbuch des politischen Systems der Bundesrepublik Deutschland* (pp. 1–7). Springer Fachmedien Wiesbaden.

Thaa, W., Salomon, D., & Gräber, G. (1994). *Grüne an der Macht: Widerstände und Chancen grün-alternativer Regierungsbeteiligungen.* Bund-Verlag.

Tiefenbach, P. (1998). *Die Grünen: Verstaatlichung einer Partei.* PapyRossa.

Träger, H. (2015). Innerparteiliche Willensbildungs- und Entscheidungsprozesse zur Bundestagswahl 2013: Eine Urwahl, zwei Mitgliederentscheide und neue Verfahren der Wahlprogrammerarbeitung. In K.-R. Korte (Ed.), *Die Bundestagswahl 2013* (pp. 269–289). Springer Fachmedien Wiesbaden.

Unfried, P. (2020, December 8). Können die Grünen Leadership? *taz FUTURZWEI.* Berlin. https://taz.de/Zum-Bundesparteitag-2020/!172 022/

van Hüllen, R. (1990). *Ideologie und Machtkampf bei den Grünen: Untersuchung zur programmatischen und innerorganisatorischen Entwicklung einer deutschen "Bewegungspartei".* Bouvier.

Volmer, L. (2009). *Die Grünen: von der Protestbewegung zur etablierten Partei: eine Bilanz.* Bertelsmann.

Walter, F. (2000). Vom Betriebsrat der Nation zum Kanzlerwahlverein? Die SPD. In G. Pickel, D. Walz, & W. Brunner (Eds.), *Deutschland nach den Wahlen* (pp. 227–252). VS Verlag für Sozialwissenschaften.

Wiesendahl, E. (2006). *Mitgliederparteien am Ende? eine Kritik der Niedergangsdiskussion.* VS Verlag für Sozialwissenschaften.

CHAPTER 5

Alternative for Germany: From Multimember to Dual Leadership

5.1 Introduction

The Alternative for Germany is the most recent addition to the German party system. It was founded in 2013 with the core demand that Germany leave the single currency Euro, or at least conduct an extensive reform of the currency system. This was a reaction to policies of the Christian-Democratic-led federal government toward stabilizing the common currency in the Euro-crisis (Franzmann, 2016). The name of the party is a reference to a quote from chancellor Angela Merkel concerning the financial turbulence in Greece, that there is no alternative to rescuing the Euro. With a mix of Euro-skeptic positions and economic orthodoxy, the activism of the original party founders appealed to a range of smaller organizations that shared a rejection of European integration (Bebnowksi, 2015: 30–32). Despite the prominence of anti-Euro positions, the party was more than a single-issue party. The criticism of the European Union was embedded in a strongly market-liberal platform (Franzmann, 2016). In addition, the party offered conservative and traditional positions in the field of family, gender and migration policies (Bebnowksi, 2015: 25). The decision to set up a collective leadership rested on a recognition of these precursor organizations in combination with the absence of a strong or charismatic leader. Accordingly, Zons and Halsterbach characterize the AfD as a "leaderless party," stating that there is no "[...] concentrated leadership vested in a single undisputed individual" (Zons & Halstenbach, 2019: 7). Contrary to the path of the Green Party, this was not a conscious choice based on an ideological foundation but rather a concession to the groups and organizations that were engaged in building the new party. This implies a deviation from a classical understanding of collective leadership as a way to create a cooperative and balancing exercise of power. This leadership model adds to potential problems of toxic leadership that can often be found in radical-right and far-right parties (Mudde, 2019). Even without this concentrated leadership, Bernd Lucke, as one of the original founders, subsequently became the face of the party. With his background as a professor of economics at the University of Hamburg, he cultivated an expert or technocratic image. Observers noted his ability to summarize complex questions with vocabulary from macro-economic theory and offer clear-cut answers to policy problems (Middelhoff et al., 2017). Intentional or not, with its positions against European integration the party simultaneously sent a subliminal nationalist message that attracted conservative, right-leaning and even right-extremist members and activists. Lucke himself somewhat ambivalently stated: "We also have to talk, free from bias, about unconventional topics" (Lobenstein, 2013: 9). Because of Germany's history and the fascist rule of the Nazi-party, the question of where a party places itself at the right or far-right of the party spectrum is a delicate issue. For the longest time, it was an articulated strategy of the Christian Democratic Party to cover the whole range from center-right to the acceptable end of this dimension, to keep new parties from springing up.[1] Not only do far-right positions provoke public backlash, the federal office for the protection of the constitution has the mandate to examine groups, movements and parties that might place themselves to close to disqualified neo-fascist or neo-Nazi positions. Arzheimer (2019) argues that the successful establishment of the new party rested on a two-step process. With their original soft Euro-skeptic positions, the party voiced legitimate concerns and attracted respected political actors and defectors from other

---

[1] Even Angela Merkel, who noticeably modernized the CDU and moved the party to the left, stated on a party congress of the CDU youth organization, that there should not be a party to the right of the Union (see https://www.sueddeutsche.de/politik/bundestag-merkel-rechts-von-der-union-darf-es-keine-partei-geben-dpa.urn-newsml-dpa-com-20090101-171007-99-356942).

parties. Only when the party had set up its organization, was mostly established, and had secured representation in state parliaments, did it embark on an incremental rightwards shift, accelerated by the refugee crisis in 2015. Here, it moved distinctly to the far-right, ingesting nationalist, nativist, and xenophobic elements into the platform (Arzheimer, 2019). This shifting baseline added fuel to the heavy intra-party conflicts, which, among other factors, led to the exit of the original founders Lucke in 2015 and Frauke Petry in 2017. The various factions divided themselves along a dominant cleavage between national-conservative market-liberal and radical-right (which also resembled a West and East divide). The West German branches tended to be more traditionally conservative with a strategic appeal to the right, while the East German branches, often organized in the far-right *Flügel* are described as ideological far-right with an overlap to right-extremist worldviews (Weisskircher, 2020).[2] This division influenced leadership selection and structured interactions in the young party. Agreements between group leaders managed to provide some volatile stability, but only on an interim basis. Since its foundation, the rightist-faction has continuously pushed to shift the whole organization further to the right (Lau, 2019). This strategy has been supported by the strong electoral results in the Eastern German states.

At the same time, the AfD's populist platform incorporated calls for more direct democracy as a counterbalance to perceived negative consequences of representative democracy, which drove the party to conduct early party congresses as full member assemblies. We assume that differences in rules and processes for the selection of party leaders also influenced the characteristics of collective party leadership.

The AfD secured representation in the federal parliament in 2017; the parliamentary group and its leadership constituted a new intra-party power-center. The conflict between the two factions further escalated in 2020: On the one hand, there were diverging opinions about how to address the Coronavirus pandemic and the multiple groups that organized protests against lockdown measures. On the other hand, the co-chair Jörg Meuthen surprisingly pushed for the expulsion of a member of the executive-committee (Andreas Kalbitz), when evidence of his engagement

---

[2] In April 2020 the Federal Office for the Protection of the Constitution (*Bundesamt für Verfassungsschutz*) decided to observe the AfD faction *Der Flügel* as it was proven to be extremist. The group decided to dissolve itself.

with far-right groups surfaced (Middelhoff, 2020). This further increased the 'with-us-or-against-us'-sentiment in the party.

Even though the AfD is a rather young party, its tumultuous history can be split into distinct phases, which also coincide with leadership turnover (see Table 5.1). The first phase was the foundation phase, where the party was formally founded and secured its first representations on state level (2013–2015); the exit of the de facto leader Lucke marks the beginning of a second stage, where the party continued its trajectory of entering further state parliaments, while shifting the platform distinctly to the right (2015–2017); the third and last phase began with the success of entering the national parliament in 2017, which prompted another leadership change. This phase was characterized by an intensified struggle between a far-right group in the party and less radical forces (2017–2020).

Contrasting the phases with Hopper's (1950) framework, the first and second phase correspond to the popular phase, where the AfD attracted a high degree of attention. The third stage after entering the national parliament aligns with the formal stage, where the party reformed itself to comply with the requirements of parliamentary realities in the German political system. With heavy intra-party conflicts and a pariah status, meaningful government participation seems far away, and a split and a dissolution of the party is still a feasible option.

While there is already quite some research on this new party (Arzheimer 2019; Bebnowski, 2015; Berbuir et al., 2015; Decker, 2016; Franzmann, 2016; Goerres et al., 2018; Lees, 2018), there are fewer studies focusing specifically on the leadership dimensions, the phases of multi-member and dual leadership (Zons & Halsterbach, 2019), and their ramifications for the development of the party as a whole.

5.2 Three Phases in the History of the AfD: Type and Genesis of Plural Leadership

5.2.1 *Founding Phase (2013–2015)*

Bernd Lucke, a professor of economics at the University of Hamburg, became the leading protagonist in the founding phase. He had been an outspoken critic of the Euro for quite some time, and he was one of the three chairs of the new party (Jun & Jakobs, 2020). His authority

Table 5.1 Most significant events in the organizational evolution of the Alternative for Germany (2013–2020)

Date	Event
Foundation stage	
March 2010	Chancellor Angela Merkel calls financial support for Greece to stabilize the Euro 'without alternative'
2012	'Bündnis Bürgerwille' forms as a result to Germany ratifying the European Stability Mechanism (ESM)
6 February 2013	Activists convene in Hesse to formally register a new party, choosing the name Alternative for Germany
14 April 2013	Founding party congress in Berlin; Adam, Lucke and Petry are elected as chairs
May 2013	The AfD has regional branches in all 16 states
22 September 2013	The party misses the threshold in the federal election and in the state election in Hesse
May 2014	The AfD enters the European parliament (7.1%)
August–September 2014	The AfD enters state parliaments in Brandenburg, Saxony and Thuringia
January 2015	A party congress in Bremen accepts Lucke's proposed statute change, that would reduce leadership to a single chairperson
May 2015	The executive committee starts proceedings to expel the Thuringian AfD politician Höcke from the party, referring to his right-extremist positions
May 2015	Lucke organizes the intraparty group Weckruf 2015, to retain control over the party
July 2015	At a party congress in Essen, Lucke and Petry compete for the position of chair; Lucke's loss leads to his exit; Meuthen is elected as co-chair

(continued)

Table 5.1 (continued)

Date	Event
November 2015	A party congress in Hannover rolls back part of the statute reform, reinstating a multi-member leadership (two or three chairpersons)
From Euro-skeptic to (far-)right-populist	
2015	After a drop in public opinion polls, the refugee crisis energizes the party
March 2016	The AfD enters the state parliaments in Baden-Württemberg and Rhineland-Palatia; it receives its best result so far in Saxony-Anhalt (24.3%)
May 2016	A party congress in Stuttgart adopts the first basic program
April 2017	A party congress in Cologne nominates Gauland and Weidel as leading candidates
September 2017	The AfD receives 12.6% at the federal election and entered the Bundestag
September 2017	Party chair Petry declares her exit from party and parliamentary group
Shift to the east stage	
December 2017	A party congress in Hannover reelects Meuthen and elects the leader of the parliamentary group Gauland as second chairperson
May 2018	The expulsion proceedings against Höcke are suspended
Fall 2018	The AfD enters the state parliaments in Bavaria and Hesse; the party is now represented in all 16 state parliaments
2019	A party congress elects Meuthen and Chrupalla as chairs
February 2020	With the votes of the AfD the FDP politician Kemmerich becomes prime minister in Thuringia, sparking massive outrage that compels Kemmerich to resign

(continued)

rested primarily on his scientific expertise rather than charisma or leadership skills. This is one reason the new party was less focused on him as a person, and more open to installing collective leadership. The AfD party statutes defined an executive committee made up of a minimal number of eight members, including a minimum of two party leaders called speakers

Table 5.1 (continued)

Date	Event
April 2020	The federal office for the protection of the constitution declares that it would monitor the faction *Der Flügel* because of its extremist tendencies
April 2020	*Der Flügel* announces its dissolution
May 2020	Meuthen pushes Kalbitz, member of the executive committee and representative of the dissolved *Flügel*, with a narrow vote, out of the party
November 2020	Despite the pandemic the AfD holds an in-person party congress in Kalkar; Meuthen uses his speech to directly attack the right wing of the party; the congress adopts a program on social policy

Source Authors' own summary based on Decker (2020)

(Zons & Halsterbach, 2019: 46). It was up to the party conference to decide on the exact number of the speakers and to elect the members of the executive committee. At the first party conference, the party opted for a multimember leadership made up of three chairpersons, electing party speakers Konrad Adam and Frauke Petry alongside Bernd Lucke.

Under increasing media attention, Lucke assumed the position of most visible representative of the party and de facto leader. He steadily gained more authority over the party on the ground. Consequently, even if the three chairpersons were formally equal, this produced a clear hierarchy among the three leaders which Lucke embraced. However, this hierarchy was less stable than it seemed. This became evident when Lucke started to push for a formal statute change that would have helped to formalize his accentuated position. Initially, he sought to reduce leadership to one person (himself) but sensing skepticism in the party, reverted to a reduction to a dual leadership structure. At the national party congress debating party reform in 2015, Lucke was challenged by one of his co-chairs, Frauke Petry. There was no way to resolve this conflict before the congress, and the two competed for the same chair position. Lucke lost the vote. He had overestimated his support and influence in the party, assuming the party base would trust the founder and most visible face of the party. The delegates' preference for Petry over Lucke signaled that he was in a minority position in the party he had helped to start. Lucke, and a group of party members closely attached to him, exited the party shortly after. Overall, the young party lost about a fifth of its members because of the leadership change (mainly from West German regional branches; Böhmer & Weissenbach, 2019: 253).

The statute based on Lucke's initiative was short-lived and reformed again at the next party congress (Zons & Halsterbach, 2019: 47). The interim version represented Lucke's idea of leadership, reducing the chairpersons to two, while also installing a hierarchy as the first chairperson had the power to select the party secretary. After a transitional phase, the leadership was supposed to shrink to one leader. However, the next statute reform reversed these provisions and again allowed for either two or three party leaders. It also removed the subtle hierarchy introduced by the power of the first chairperson to pick a party secretary. The executive committee was expanded to 12 members (in addition to the chairpersons). As an element of professionalization, the default for party congresses was set to delegates, but member assemblies remained an option.

There are several reasons why there was a build-up in tension within the multi-member leadership, culminating in the head-on collision at the party congress. First and foremost, there was the personal ambition of Lucke to be in more formal control of the party for which he was the figurehead. His co-leader Frauke Petry pushed against this reform: The reform would have curbed her influence, but she could also build on the criticism that Lucke was steering the party in a capricious way, monopolizing decision making (Brost & Ulrich, 2013). His authoritarian and uncompromising leadership style had alienated even some of his supporters. After Petry had won and stepped out of Lucke's shadow, she became more ambitious in vying for the role of prime leader of the party (Amann, 2015b: 34). Beyond the personal rivalry, Lucke and Petry stood for different factions of the party: "Whereas Lucke represented the economically liberal and culturally conservative wing of the party, Petry represented the nationalist, or *völkisch*, part of AfD" (Jun & Jakobs, 2020). Petry had her base in the East German state of Saxony, a stronghold of the party, that achieved three direct mandates in the federal election of 2017. The East German branches tended to be further to the right than the rest of the party (Weisskircher, 2020). It is unclear how far Petry's embrace of the right wing was strategic, as she attempted to table a motion for a moderation at the party congress in Cologne in 2017, but the Eastern delegates nevertheless saw her as one of their own against Lucke with his obvious roots in Western Germany.

5.2.2 From Euro-Skeptic to (Far-)right-Populist (2015–2017)

At a party congress in Cologne in 2017, Petry tabled a motion about orienting the party more to the center-right than the far-right, evidently aiming to make coalitions with the CDU more feasible. The party rejected her proposal, executing a similar playbook as with Lucke, signaling to her that as a party chair she could not simply rely on majorities in the party. To add insult to injury, the congress also denied her a role as a leading candidate for the upcoming election campaign. Instead, Alexander Gauland and Alice Weidel were selected for this position. This foreshadowed her exit, which she conveniently declared right after she had entered the federal parliament on the AfD ticket.

In 2013, the AfD had narrowly missed the 5% electoral threshold, but stable performances in state elections and the successful European elections in 2014 (see Fig. 5.1) strongly suggested a result above five percent for 2017. Unsurprisingly, the AfD managed to clear the five percent threshold necessary for the *Bundestag* in 2017 and even became the largest opposition party (12.6%). With Petry's exit right after the election, the party had to rearrange its leadership once again. While it is typically a shock for a newly founded party to lose its founder, the refugee crisis in 2015, and the strategy of the AfD to fully embrace a position critical of the course of the government compensated both losses of early-stage figureheads and helped to stabilize the party despite the tumultuous organizational politics (Hansen & Olsen, 2019). This is reflected in the membership numbers of the party, which dipped briefly in 2015 but recovered afterward (see Table 5.2). From 2013 to 2019, the membership doubled. Collective leadership allowed for some form of continuity, despite high fluctuation and tumultuous party congresses, as through these several changes, one chairperson stayed in office alongside a new chairperson coming in.

Source Authors' own compilation. Data for party central office and party in public office own data collection; for party on the ground from Niedermayer (2020).

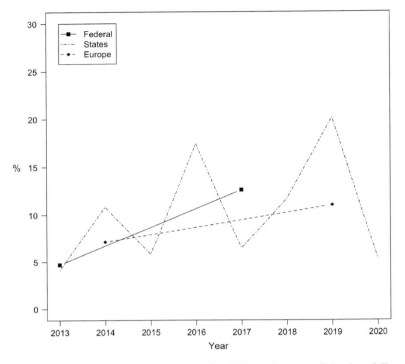

Fig. 5.1 The electoral performance of the AfD at the state, federal and European level, 2013–2020 (%) (*Source* Authors' own compilation with data from https://en.wikipedia.org/wiki/Alternative_for_Germany_election_results)

5.2.3 Power Balance Shifts to the East (2017–2020)

At the party congress in Hanover in 2017, when the party had to elect a new leadership, the undiminished level of intra-party conflict, post-Lucke and Petry, was on full display. Though Meuthen's confirmation was more or less certain, he only received a low percentage of votes (72%). For his co-leader position, two candidates clashed: Doris Sayn-Wittgenstein as a representative of the more radical and far-right wing (from a West German state though) and Georg Padzerski seen as a more center-right and conservative candidate (from the Berlin regional branch). As both repeatedly failed to secure an absolute majority, Alexander Gauland stepped up and was elected as a compromise candidate. As he was already

Table 5.2 The organizational evolution of the AfD

	Founding stage	From Euro-skeptic to (far-)right-populist	Power balance shift to the east
Period	2013–2015	2015–2017	2017–2020
Party Lifespan Threshold	Declaration and Authorization	Authorization	Representation
Party Central Office	Konrad Adam Bernd Lucke Frauke Petry	Jörg Meuthen Frauke Petry	2017–2019 Jörg Meuthen Alexander Gauland Since 2019 Jörg Meuthen Tino Chrupalla
Party in Public Office	2013: 0	2015: 0 MdB, 48 MdL, 7 MdEP	2017: 94 MdB, 186 MdL, 7 MdEP 2020: 89 MdB, 247 MdL, 11 MdEP
Party on the Ground	2013: 17.687	2015: 16.385	2017: 27.621 2019: 34.751

Note MdB—member of the federal parliament; MdL—member of a subnational parliament; MdEP—member of the European parliament

leader of the parliamentary group, this conjoined the two faces of the party, while also giving more influence to his co-chair Jörg Meuthen through Gauland's double burden. In addition to the formal position sharing, this constituted a power-sharing set-up, but Gauland concentrated his efforts on his work in parliament. Even with the potential to advance into a de facto leader position, Meuthen struggled to stabilize and extend his authority and influence. His step into the chair position in 2015 came as a surprise to many as he had stayed virtually invisible next to the dominant Petry before. In addition, there was the increasing impact of a more pronounced right-nationalist shift driven by Eastern German regional branches (which Gauland tacitly approved). Moreover, Meuthen was not uncontroversial in his own regional branch Baden-Württemberg. This was on public display when he proved incapable of preventing a split of the parliamentary group (which later rejoined), and when he was denied the role of delegate to the national party congress by his local chapter in July 2019.

The principle of collective leadership is a prevailing element in the party (see Table 5.3). It started out with a multi member leadership; Lucke's

Table 5.3 Type of leadership in the AfD 2013 to 2020

Period	Type	Leaders
2013–2015	Multimember leadership	Bernd Lucke Konrad Adam Frauke Petry
2015–2017	Dual leadership	Jörg Meuthen Frauke Petry
2017–2019		Jörg Meuthen Alexander Gauland
Since 2019		Jörg Meuthen Tino Chrupalla

Source Authors' own compilation

push for a single leader was ultimately unsuccessful, and the party statutes still allow for two or three leaders (Jun & Jakobs, 2020). In contrast to the German Greens, where the origin in social movements and grassroots ideology substantiated the path of collective leadership, the main motivation of the AfD to implement this model rested on respecting the precursor organizations. Collective leadership emerged to preserve unity and manage internal party divisions. For instance, this enables a strategy wherein two or more leaders can be jointly appointed to represent different wings or groups within the party.

In addition to its Euro-skeptic roots, the party integrated populist rhetoric into its platform (Rosenfelder, 2017; Schwanholz et al., 2020). While there are competing definitions of populism, almost all agree on its anti-establishment core, pitching the pure and virtuous people against the corrupt elite (Mudde & Kaltwasser, 2017; Müller, 2016). As the populist challengers position themselves to speak for the people and represent the real will of the people, they typically include demands for an expansion of direct democracy, as means to challenge the alleged hold of established parties on the political system and as a corrective to the self-interested political class. In this sense, like the Greens, the development of this leadership model was an explicit ideological choice, albeit on a very different foundation. The goal of preserving the influence of the party base was not founded in a grassroots ideology, but rather derived from a negative depiction of a political class that can only be kept in check with instruments of direct democracy. The statutes indirectly capture the objective of implementing consensus in the party's executive committee (Jun & Jakobs, 2020). Furthermore, the AfD highlights membership primaries to decide questions of policies as well as personnel (except for those where the parties act requires a party congress) (Jun & Jakobs, 2020). There is an option of membership consultation, e.g., for the nomination of top-candidates in federal elections.

5.3 The Complementarity Between Different Leaders in the 4 Phases

If we apply our theoretical framework to the AfD, we find virtually no complementarity and consequently low durability and low effectiveness. "Leadership turnover and competitiveness in the AfD demonstrate that the party has not yet had a strong leader who enjoyed unified support over a longer period" (Zons & Halsterbach, 2019: 49). Under these circumstances, the linear establishment in all states and on the federal level is surprising and happened despite the conflicts and tensions between the individual leaders making up the collective leadership. Before the COVID-19 pandemic hit Germany in the spring of 2020, the party was steadily polling around two-digits in public opinion polls. However, the increased infighting showed potential rupture lines and the possibility of a split became more likely.

5.3.1 Informal Leader Overestimates Power (2013–2015)

The original set-up of the new party respected the different backgrounds of the founders. "A closer inspection of the party's origins reveals its ability to draw on an already existing network of social and political structures […]. The party therefore did not have to start from scratch after its official establishment in April 2013" (Decker, 2016: 2). The newcomer superseded predominantly Euro-kceptic and economically liberal groups (e.g., *Bündnis Bürgerwille, Hayek Gesellschaft, Initiative Neue Soziale Marktwirtschaft*), but also the fundamentalist-Christian campaign network *Zivile Koalition* set up by Beatrix von Storch (Bebnowski, 2015). Therefore, the platform constituted a fusion of economically liberal and socially conservative-nationalist positions. This heterogeneity is unusual in comparison to other populist party structures, which often formed around a strong leader figure (Donovan, 2020; Heinisch & Mazzolini, 2016). Even if Lucke subsequently moved into the position of de facto leader, he did not resemble the classical populist chief. "As a slightly wonkish analytical leader he moreover lacked personal charisma" (Decker, 2016: 8).

But this unique complexity and development as a leaderless party masks the central role Bernd Lucke, and activists loyal to him, nevertheless played: "The party was formed top-down by Lucke and his allies […]" (Frankland, 2020: 37). Their influence rested on their previous experience in political parties or alliances as well as their expertise in economic policy. They were socialized in parties and had networks with other political actors: "[…] Lucke, Gauland, and Adam had all a CDU background. They attracted other former Christian Democrats with an expertise on economic issues" (Dilling, 2018: 98). Experienced defectors from established parties made up a significant group in the party at the beginning.

However, Lucke's position weakened as the party started to attract new members more broadly: "[…] activists from pre-existing minor parties, right-wing groups, such as the alt-right identitarian movement, streamed into the AfD, and soon were challenging the center's direction" (Frankland, 2020: 37). In the beginning, this development was understood as an asset rather than a weakness: Lucke and his followers courted market-liberal voters, Adam, Petry and Gauland reached out to social-conservative voters (Dilling, 2018: 98). The two largest factions shared the tasks of mobilizing and attracting their respective sympathizers in the electorate and the party on the ground. At least in the early days of the party there existed a form of task division between the chairs.

In addition to the market-liberal and national-conservative dualism, the party also featured populist elements (Bebnowksi, 2015; Rosenfelder, 2017). In its platform and rhetoric, it pursued a populist focus, emphasizing the common people and their common sense (Bebnowski, 2015: 14). This was fertile soil for mistrust of elites and experts. This worldview was instrumental in attacking perceived adversaries in the political system at large, but subtly undermined the authority of AfD intraparty elites as well. Even if it stemmed from a different ideological (or non-ideological but ideational) foundation, this cultivated a similar mistrust of party leadership as we have seen with the Greens. This helps to explain why the AfD in its short history has mainly experienced unstable and conflictual leadership. The executive committee and multimember (later dual) leadership were made up of representatives of groups that had different strategies for the party in mind (radical and pragmatic, conservative and extreme-right), that were nearly impossible to reconcile. The underlying division into East and West poured additional gas onto the fire.

In any case, a rising demand for Euro-skeptic and anti-immigration positions in the electorate created an externally induced stability. (Hambauer & Mays, 2018). The AfD's rapid ascent to relevant political-player in the German party system was possible because of a vacuum regarding Euro-skepticism which was not addressed by any other party. With the fading permissive consensus for European integration in the electorate, this became a viable platform. In combination with the high saliency of European integration during the time of the Euro crisis, fueled by the debate about austerity measures and debt relief for Greece, the party profited from being able to capture a truly contrarian position with respect to the established parties. The crisis of the single currency served as a window of opportunity, but another crucial factor was the long-term dissatisfaction with the CDU, due to its neglect of conservatism under Merkel (Franzmann, 2016: 458).

As a professor of economics, Lucke was the right person at the right time to inject macro-economic expertise and dissenting ideas into the debate. "Lucke, 50, sounds refreshingly non-professorial; he articulates his views in simple and clear terms" (Neukirch, 2013). He quickly ascended into the role of sole representative of the party; he was invited to talk-shows, but not his co-chairs. If AfD voters and sympathizers were asked about the importance of politicians, Lucke was the only relevant actor they named from the AfD (see Fig. 5.2). The formally equal co-leaders Adam and Petry were relegated into the second row. This held true not just for public appearances but also for intra-party communication. Lucke wrote long and elaborate e-mails without consulting with his co-leaders. He single-handedly published position papers on the role of Islam, codes of conducts for party members, and questionnaires for membership applicants. Criticism grew, that there was no opportunity for his co-leaders, the executive committee, or even the party on the ground to participate in the formation of will. The chair of the Lower Saxony branch, Gerhard Nadolny, who left the AfD shortly after its founding in 2013, called Lucke "einen autoritären AfD-Führer" (an authoritarian AfD-leader; Lobenstein, 2013). "Part of the problem could undoubtedly be found in the person of Lucke who was neither willing nor capable of bridging ideological divides to keep the party united. The AfD's founder was not just completely committed to the party's moderate economically

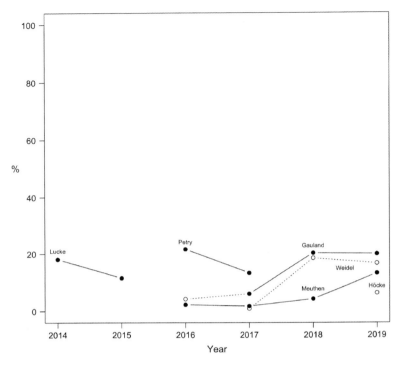

Fig. 5.2 Popularity of leading AfD politicians with AfD voters/sympathizers (%) (*Note* Question: Who are currently the most important politicians in Germany? Mentions of AfD politicians by respondents who intended to vote for the AfD, if there was a federal election next Sunday. *Source* Authors' own compilation with data from Jung, Matthias; Schroth, Yvonne; Wolf, Andrea: Politbarometer 1993–2019. GESIS Data Archive, Cologne. https://www.gesis.org/en/elections-home/politbarometer)

liberal wing; he also practiced an authoritarian leadership style that placed virtually no value on incorporating other positions and was therefore criticized as high-handed" (Decker, 2016: 8). The briefly effective division of tasks evolved into a parallel performance, where the chairs performed the same functions and routines but with minimal coordination (Spillane, 2006: 40). This resulted not only in ineffectiveness and redundancy but crossed over into the realm of toxic leadership, where the chairpersons engaged in destructive behavior and actively butted heads, pursuing their own goals that they believed were right for the party as a whole.

While different backgrounds can sometimes be conducive to complementarity in leadership, for the AfD this was not the case: Lucke cultivated the role as an academic expert in economic policy. He had a background of engagement in multiple political contexts and experiences as a political entrepreneur. Frauke Petry had recently filed for bankruptcy for her company and was a newcomer to the political sphere. The AfD was her first attempt to engage in politics. The third co-chair Konrad Adam was a pensioner with a long history in the conservative milieu of Germany, as a journalist and intellectual. He had nothing to prove and like Gauland was mainly driven by the perception that Merkel had significantly changed their former home, the CDU, in leading it away from true conservatism.

In addition to tensions created by his work style and personal background, Lucke differed from his co-chairs in party strategy. It seemed that he attempted to keep the party on a primarily Euro-skeptic course as a legitimate and accepted right-wing alternative to the CDU/CSU. Nevertheless, he was aware of the close overlap of Euro-skepticism with nationalist, right-extremist positions that used anti-EU platforms to disguise nativism and xenophobia. His rhetoric at times veered in this territory, strategically expanding the base in this direction. "If you read his e-mails, it becomes clear how he courted extreme voters from the beginning, and also tried to win over the provocateur Thilo Sarrazin" (Amann, 2015a).[3] This was at odds with Lucke's formal call for rules to exclude extremist party members from the AfD. His co-chairs, Adam and Petry on the other hand, were less critical regarding the right fringe and saw nationalist voters and members as natural allies. Petry later started a discussion about the term '*völkisch*', which is vocabulary strongly associated with Germany's fascist past and the Nazi-party (Chase, 2016).

Lucke understood the AfD as his creation. He disapproved of coordinating with his co-chairs, or the executive committee, and accordingly pursued a clear strategy to become more autonomous in his position.

---

[3] Sarrazin was a member of the Social Democratic Party and a board member of the German central bank. He published a controversial and best-selling book in 2009 (Deutschland schafft sich ab; Germany Abolishes Itself) which was widely seen as xenophobic and specifically anti-Islam. A first attempt to terminate his party membership in 2010 failed, but after similar public comments and further publication, a party arbitration committee excluded him from the party in 2019.

Hesitant to propose an abrupt shift to solo leadership, he devised a two-step process. In the first step, the co-chair elected first (presumably him) would have the power to appoint the party secretary. This meant a new formal hierarchy, in contrast to the previously equal multimember leadership. In a second step, collective leadership would be abolished, installing one single leader. When Lucke sensed the growing resistance in the party, he recognized that it was going to be difficult to execute this organizational change in a group based heavily on anti-establishment sentiment. He tried to rally his supporters in preparation for the decisive party congress in the city of Essen. He organized a semi-formal group inside the party (*Weckruf 2015*, wakeup call 2015) to solidify and gather his base behind his organizational reform, and to signal to the rest of the party the influence he commanded. There was another practical reason for this strategy: because of the anti-establishment stance, coupled with direct-democratic demands, the first congresses were open to all members, and all attendees had voting rights (other German parties typically use a delegate system). The leadership could not rely on "natural majorities" (Böhmer & Weissenbach, 2019: 257). This made it harder for the leadership to gauge the support they could rely on in assemblies. Lucke's strategy in formalizing his support in an intra-party group backfired though, as this further substantiated his opponents' allegations that he was driving a wedge into the party (Zons & Halstenbach, 2019: 52). The interactions in the run-up to the party congress and at the congress itself are unambiguous indicators of a high degree of toxicity between the chairpersons and between the factions they represented. There was destructive behavior that inflicted harm on the followers and the party organization (Heppell, 2011).

These leadership struggles culminated at the party congress in Essen in 2015. The delegates voted for Petry as party chair, rather than for Lucke, expressing their dislike for his organizational plans through this personnel decision. Petry's win signaled to Lucke that, despite his merits as founder, he was in a minority position in the party. Shortly afterward, he decided to leave the party (about a fifth of all party members followed him). This reduced the share of members with economically liberal preferences, but other founding members, like Alexander Gauland, remained in place and continued to provide veteran guidance (Frankland, 2020).

Collective leadership allows a new party to divide the organizational burdens of creating a new organization. Lucke, however, monopolized multiple roles at once: He acted as an organizer, a strategist and president. He ceded no ground to his co-chairs and left no room for them to contribute. At the same time, he was missing the charismatic qualities of an emotional leader who could channel the extensive enthusiasm typically widespread among members of a new challenger in the party system. This unfortunate combination accelerated conflicts with his co-chairs. While Petry pursued a strategy of openly voicing opposition, Adam kept his criticism muted. In March 2015, he took over a new role as head of the AfD party foundation. While he voluntarily abstained from competing for a chair position at the party congress in Essen, even his attempt to be elected to the executive committee failed. This is reflected in the survey of AfD voters and sympathizers, in which he never made the list of influential AfD politicians (see Fig. 5.2). Adam declared his exit from the party in September 2020.

The statutes defined collective leadership with equal rights, where two or three chairpersons would share positions. However, de facto Lucke concentrated power around him, which was supported by his prominence and popularity. This corresponds to anarchic misalignment, where the statutes do not offer clear guidance, and the specific constellations of leadership undermine collaboration. Lucke's power did not last though, and his credibility as party founder was spent faster than he had expected.

The party followed a path similar to that of other newcomer or challenger parties, which rely heavily on the enthusiasm and motivation of the original activists. These organizations resemble communities, creating a strong sense of meaning and belonging for their members. Their goal is to push a particular, overlooked issue onto the public agenda, and their reward is seeing the movement, and cause, getting recognition. For the first two years, the AfD functioned as an amateur movement, and only around the time of the first federal election exhibited signs of professionalization.

5.3.2 New Leadership, Same Trajectory (2015–2017)

The refusal of the delegates to accept Lucke as party chair was a decisive triumph for Petry, and Lucke's departure instantly moved her into the limelight. While the party statutes delineated a path to single leadership, this was quickly reversed and the option of a two- or three-person leadership readopted (thus far the party had settled on dual leadership). Apparently, their experience with Lucke's authoritarian style wasn't enough to teach the party's top leadership their lesson. Quite the contrary: Petry followed in his footsteps. This was accentuated by the asymmetrical power balance with her co-leader, Meuthen, who, as a newcomer, naturally had less visibility and authority. On the one hand, Petry had led the party for two years (albeit in Lucke's shadow); on the other hand, Meuthen's advance to the top was a concession to the moderate forces in the AfD. Petry did not consider him an equal chairperson and regularly delegated tasks to him in meetings of the executive committee: "Jörg, could you get this done by Tuesday?" (quoted in Amann, 2016a). Meuthen accepted this hierarchy, engaged himself in writing proposals and attempted to manage and steer the fragmented party. There were multiple instances when the imbalance was unwittingly reinforced, for example, when Petry was mistakenly introduced as national and Meuthen as regional leader, or when a greeting message from the Austrian FPÖ only mentioned Petry (Amann, 2016b). This was also reflected in the answers of the AfD voters and sympathizers, when, in 2016 and 2017, roughly 20% named Petry as an important AfD politician, while Meuthen merely reached a few percentage points. Petry was clearly more popular with the party on the ground.

Petry positioned herself as the president of the party, mainly representing the party in the public. She left the role of organizer to Meuthen, but at the same time closely guarded her influence. For instance, she declined to work with the official AfD press spokesperson in the party central office but instead relied on external advisors and spin-doctors she hired herself (Amann, 2016c). The dual leadership was lacking in basic team spirit that could have laid the groundwork for successful complementarity. The leadership change had not reduced the toxic spirit between the chairpersons or in the executive committee at large. "Petry, whose selection had initially been met with high hopes by her party, has for quite some time now been the subject of criticism for a leadership style defined by going it alone, as well as making comments that are not run by other party officials and frequently not thought-through" (Decker, 2016: 12). One factor which nevertheless boosted her leadership capital was her womanhood (Campus, 2013). The combination of a female leader and right-wing party captured media attention—similar to the phenomenon of Marine Le Pen and the Front National. There is an inherent tension between traditional-authoritarian positions of right-wing parties and the leadership of an independent and modern woman: "An evolution is represented by [Le Pen's] appearance as a modern woman who dresses in casual but elegant clothes, is divorced, and supports secular policies such as abortion rights" (Campus, 2013: 109). In the case of the AfD, this was reflected in the number of newspaper articles about Petry (see Fig. 5.3). In her first tenure, from 2013 to 2015, Lucke was mentioned most often. However, right after he left the AfD, Petry surpassed him and in 2016 garnered more than 1000 mentions, about 300 more than Lucke at his highest point in 2015.

The change in leadership did not result in a discernible change in the level of factionalization within the party: "The split, however, did not put an end to the infights within the AfD, which underlines that it has

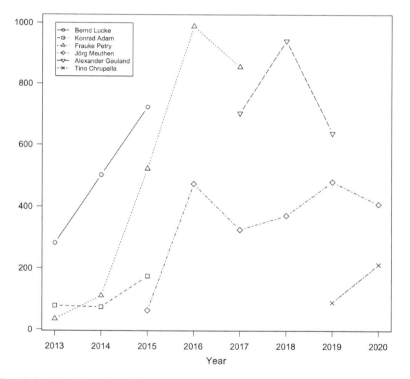

Fig. 5.3 Number of articles mentioning the party chairs of the AfD in three German newspapers, 2013–2020 (*Note* Sum of results for name as search term for each year. *Source* Authors' own data collection from online-archives of Süddeutsche Zeitung, Frankfurter Allgemeine Zeitung, die tageszeitung)

so far lacked essential mechanisms to resolve internal conflicts. Conflicts emerged between a group behind Petry, promoting more national-conservative positions, and proponents of a far-right course, including Alexander Gauland and Björn Höcke" (Dilling, 2018: 99). Petry had used the right-wing to defeat Lucke, but she herself was not affiliated with this group. For the party congress in Cologne in 2017 she tabled a motion that read like a moderation of the party, ultimately allowing for coalitions with the CDU/CSU, and therefore further distancing herself from this group. "She argued that in the medium term, the AfD should follow the example of the Austrian FPÖ and the Norwegian Progress Party and become available as a coalition partner for the centre right. In a bid to soften the image of the party while consolidating her own power base, like Lucke before her she tried but failed to expel Björn Höcke, party leader in Thuringia and, more importantly, the leader of a semi-official faction called 'Der Flügel' (the 'Wing' or 'Tendency') that is particularly strong in eastern Germany" (Arzheimer, 2019: 93).

While the role and influence of Björn Höcke in the party was and is obscure, he received nationwide attention with his provocative, revisionist and anti-Semitic speech in Dresden in 2017. He was seen as the informal leader of the radical-right *Flügel*. He has, so far, never held an office on the national level, but through a combination of far-right credentials and his formal party and group leadership in Thuringia he seems to be part of a power-sharing model. Next to the party chair, Meuthen, and the two leaders of the parliamentary group, Gauland and Weidel, Höcke is the only other AfD politician that is recognized by AfD voters (with a rather low percentage though; see Fig. 5.3). He enjoys the tacit support of Gauland, who was instrumental in burying the expulsion proceedings against him.

"Höcke has many influential supporters in the party. Moreover, many others were simply wary of Petry's ambitions, and so a rift began to grow between her supporters and her detractors. At the 2017 conference, the party refused to even discuss Petry's plan for the long-term strategic development of the AfD and denied her the role of the 'Spitzenkandidat'. Instead, Alexander Gauland and Alice Weidel led the AfD's national campaign. So far, Weidel had been counted as an ally of Petry and as a leading moderate, but given the top spot, she quickly adopted the inciting rhetoric the party base seems to demand" (Arzheimer, 2019: 93).

While initially, intra-party groups were heterogeneous, eventually, the radical right *Flügel*, which had the most supporters in the East German branches, became dominant. Until its dissolution in 2020, it pushed the party platform to the right and sought to place party members sympathetic to their cause in high-ranking offices.

From 2015 to 2017, there was slightly more complementarity. Frauke Petry positioned herself as president and strategist, and left the organizing work to her co-chair, Meuthen. This resembled a form of task division but was not based on mutual agreement or collaboration, leading to instances of parallel performance as well (Spillane, 2006: 40). Power remained imbalanced, as visibility, prominence, and power rested solely with Petry. She created an informal hierarchy by delegating tasks to Meuthen. Petry, at times, ignored party structures and tried to build a network centered on herself, which raised resistance in the executive committee.

5.3.3 Radical-Right Exerts Pressure on Leadership (2017–2020)

When Petry resigned and left the party altogether, a new dual leadership had to be elected. As with the change two years before, dual leadership allowed for some continuity amidst the turmoil. Yet, the invisible Meuthen received only 72% of the delegates' votes at the party congress in November 2017, indicating his unsteady position. There was more drama regarding his co-chair position, where the voting demonstrated a rift in the party. The executive committee favored Georg Padzerski (a moderate national conservative). At the party conference itself, Doris von Sayn-Wittgenstein announced her candidacy without any prior notice. Sayn-Wittgenstein claimed that she was part of the *Flügel*, but as a new and unknown member, her blank slate made it hard to assess her credibility and capabilities. As part of his strategy to elevate or at least integrate the right fringe of the party, the leader of the parliamentary group, Gauland, lauded her performance: in his eyes she was able to "appeal to the heart of the party, and it did not matter where she stands or where she comes from" (quoted in ZEIT Online, 2017). While the *Flügel*, as the strongest intra-party faction, aimed to be represented in the national leadership, the duo Meuthen and Sayn-Wittgenstein would produce a purely West German leadership. Padzerski from the AfD regional branch Berlin, could—at least partly—represent the East German component of the party; in this case both chairs would be part of the less radical faction though. This incompatibility led to a gridlock. Ultimately, neither Pazderski nor Sayn-Wittgenstein were able to obtain the necessary majority. Consequently, Gauland saw himself as the only candidate who could bridge the widening gap between the different party wings; despite his age—already 76 years old—he was elected co-chair. Sayn-Wittgenstein later was excluded from the party but refused to give up her position as regional party leader in Schleswig-Holstein (Jun & Jakobs, 2020). With Gauland holding two offices at the same time, the party entered a phase of power sharing. Despite the intra-party strife, this allowed for some form of task division that rested mainly on the different arenas the chairs prioritized.

Gauland focused his work on the parliamentary group. His holding two leadership positions at the same time made him more visible than his co-chair Meuthen (see Fig. 5.3). This also translated into a higher popularity with the AfD party on the ground (see Fig. 5.2). If we contrast this with his parliamentary co-leader, Weidel, she was also viewed as significantly more influential than Meuthen. Eventually, as a result of his long tenure, Meuthen's standing grew. In 2019, the gap between Gauland and Weidel on the one side, and Meuthen on the other had shrunk. The power-sharing agreement was skewed toward the group leadership in the national parliament, but Meuthen's position improved over time.

Gauland's role resembled that of a president; he presided over group and party, repeatedly stating his goal to integrate the party, including the right-extremist *Flügel*. He typically defended provocative rhetoric, even if other executive committee members called for an expulsion. He did not engage in day-to-day politics but rather addressed larger questions. In the party organization, this left more room for Meuthen. In this case, the leadership mechanism resembled a parallel performance in which similar (organizational) tasks are performed in different contexts (i.e., party central office and party in public office).

In 2019 Gauland stepped back from party leadership. "Gauland's retirement as co-chair of the federal party in December 2019 (he remains co-chair of the Bundestagsfraktion) has not created a succession crisis. The other party co-chair Jörg Meuthen, an economist who is moderate by AfD standards, was reelected, and the newly elected party co-chair Tino Chrupalla had prevailed over more extreme challengers" (Frankland, 2020: 47). This duo exhibited a mechanism similar to the previous collective leadership teams. As, yet again, one new leader joined an incumbent chairperson, the established chair naturally commanded more experience and authority. This was encouraged by the method of leadership election adopted by AfD, that dual leadership is not elected in tandem but individually. In combination with the high degree of factionalization this does not foster or incentivize complementarity between co-leaders. There is minimal coordination and merely parallel performance in the division of labor.

Meuthen's strategy did not leave room for complementarity and balance with his co-chair. Instead, he used his superiority to engage against the right-wing. In a surprising move he called for an exclusion of Andreas Kalbitz, member of the executive committee, from the party. This was a clear escalation of intra-party factional struggles and this demonstrated his willingness to push for extreme measures, even if they further eroded the common ground. This was based on evidence that Kalbitz did not disclose a former membership in a right-extremist organization, which was a reason to void his membership and his position in leadership (Muthen argued that this merited a committee vote instead of a formal procedure in front of a party arbitration court). The vote was close and his co-chair Chrupalla voted against it. This showed the clear line of conflict between the two, based on factional representation. The now-honorary party chair, Gauland, has also criticized this measure. The camps in the executive committee are locked in a power struggle to gain dominance over the party and there is no base for collaborative or inclusive leadership.

Factionalism plays a decisive role in intra-party politics. The influence and power of actors in the party are derived from factional support. Björn Höcke never held a formal position of leadership, but by representing extreme right positions he informally exerted power. He continually tested out his limits and repeatedly provoked national attention: "His demeanor and speech at a gathering of *Der Flügel*, called Kyffhäuser-Meeting, in 2019 provoked an intra-party call, signed by top officials at the federal and subnational level, condemning his appearance" (Zons & Halsterbach, 2019: 55).

5.4 The Performance of Plural Leadership: Why It Works (When It Works); Why It Fails (When It Fails)

The AfD is part of a wave of new parties that European party systems have experienced in the last fifteen years. While the party is new, it was not built completely from scratch. Our analysis showed relevant precursor organizations that can provide one explanation for the development of collective leadership, which is rather atypical for right-wing or right-populist parties. What lessons can we draw from our detailed analysis of collective leadership in the AfD?

The implementation of collective leadership was driven by a desire to respect several precursor organizations, as well as to honor the elements of direct democracy integral to a populist platform. This was a less stable foundation than that of the Green Party and the actual chairpersons had no real strategic interest in creating a productive collective leadership. After a brief period of effectively dividing labor in a productive way to reach shared goals, based on the different backgrounds of the three original chairpersons, Lucke quickly advanced into the de facto role of decisive leader. His leadership style suffocated any real possibility for a complementarity of roles or tasks. Amann described the AfD during his tenure as a "One-Man-Show" (Amann, 2014). He monopolized relations- and task-oriented functions. This worked for a short foundational phase with his credibility as a founder but created tension as the party established itself: "While Lucke performed well as the party's messenger in the identification phase, his power-seeking revealed his flaws as an organizer in the next phase of the party institutionalization" (Zons & Halsterbach, 2019). The leaders did not coordinate tasks but engaged in a disconnected parallel performance.

Despite this negative experience, the party viewed the model as basically sound. The party's action was less strategically organizational, and more a repudiation of Lucke's personal authoritarian leadership style. The far-right faction spent less energy attempting to place representatives in chair positions, but rather chose to support allies or sympathizers. They viewed informal power sharing as a legitimate method, and less susceptible to intelligence service observation or public backlash than holding a formal position.

So far, processes of leadership pre-selection and the nomination of leadership candidates in the AfD have been characterized by crude and intense competition. The party leadership was and is a collection of competitive players (Cannella et al., 2008: 126). The initial heterogeneity of groups, which evolved into a cleavage between a strong radical right and a less structured group, which is mainly kept together by their opposition to the former, is mirrored in the leadership and prohibits an effective complementarity. In the AfD, the representation of factions or faction sympathizers in the collective leadership fuels conflicts because it releases leaders of the need to build a compromise. While this fuels toxic leadership on the one hand, on the other hand, it paradoxically functions as a safeguard: when Lucke and Petry overstepped certain boundaries, even their leadership capital as founders of the party could not compensate for the increasing criticism coming from their own followers and base.

Except for the first leadership election, there was never a pre-agreed team that collaborated in a leadership election. Individuals as representatives for intraparty groups would try to reach a majority in contested and close elections. In case of decisive leadership elections, compromise candidates were sought on short notice to fill a vacancy (i.e., Meuthen because Lucke stepped back, Gauland because of gridlock between Padzerski and Sayn-Wittgenstein).

In comparison with other right-wing parties, the AfD is an outlier and an in-depth analysis substantiates this mismatch. As an organization built on a right-populist platform, and considering the preferences of its membership, collective leadership has been an unusual choice. It briefly helped the new party to gain traction, but subsequently provoked conflicts rather than ameliorating them. This held even more true as the question of leadership itself became part of the intra-party struggle, ultimately leading to the exit of founder Lucke. A second phase hinted at a new productive set-up: There was a brief phase of planful alignment while Meuthen and Gauland led the party. There was tacit agreement about the division of tasks and functions (see Table 5.4). Gauland only acted as a placeholder in the party organization and was primarily interested in the parliamentary group. However, because of the cleavage in the party, Meuthen could not profit from this complementarity but rather engaged in trying to limit the influence of the radical right, in part to secure his position, in part to avoid an observation by the *Bundesverfassungsschutz* (Federal Agency for the Protection of the Constitution).

The anti-establishment base of the party coupled with the high degree of factionalization has impeded any chance for productive collective leadership based on a planful alignment so far. "Instead, the party has rather tolerated than embraced its leaders" (Zons & Halstenbach, 2019: 50).

Table 5.4 Characteristics of the leadership structure in the phase of the AfD

	Founding stage	From euro-skeptic to (far-)right-populist	Power balance shift to the east
Type of leadership Distribution of leadership	Multimember Position Sharing	Multimember Position Sharing and Power Sharing	Multimember Position Sharing and Power Sharing
Formal hierarchy	No	Briefly	No
Labor Organization	Task division and parallel performance	Task division and parallel performance	Parallel performance
Alignment of leadership functions and roles	Spontaneous misalignment	Spontaneous misalignment	Spontaneous alignment and spontaneous misalignment

Source Authors' summary from the chapter

References

Amann, M. (2014, March 17). Luckes Ermächtigungsgesetz. *Der Spiegel*, p. 30.
Amann, M. (2015a, January 17). Das Tabu brechen. *Der Spiegel*, p. 16.
Amann, M. (2015b, July 4). Ich. Ich. Ich! *Der Spiegel*, p. 34.
Amann, M. (2016a, July 9). Die Meuterei. *Der Spiegel*, p. 26.
Amann, M. (2016b, November 19). Zeit für Gespräche. *Der Spiegel*, p. 38.
Amann, M. (2016c, December 17). Herz der Macht. *Der Spiegel*, p. 48.
Arzheimer, K. (2019). Don't mention the war! How populist right-wing radicalism became (almost) normal in Germany. *Journal of Common Market Studies, 57*(S1), 90–102.
Bebnowski, D. (2015). *Die Alternative für Deutschland*. Springer Fachmedien Wiesbaden.
Berbuir, N., Lewandowsky, M., & Siri, J. (2015). The AfD and its sympathisers: Finally a right-wing populist movement in Germany? *German Politics, 24*(2), 154–178.
Böhmer, A., & Weissenbach, K. (2019). Gekommen, um zu bleiben? Zum Zusammenhang des Institutionalisierungsprozesses der AfD und ihrer Erfolgschancen nach der Bundestagswahl 2017. In K.-R. Korte & J. Schoofs (Eds.), *Die Bundestagswahl 2017* (pp. 245–265). Springer Fachmedien Wiesbaden.
Brost, M., & Ulrich, B. (2013, May 21). Die Spaltung. *Die ZEIT*, p. 3.
Campus, D. (2013). *Women political leaders and the media*. Palgrave Macmillan.

Cannella, A. A., Park, J.-H., & Lee, H.-U. (2008). Top management team functional background diversity and firm performance: Examining The roles of team member co-location and environmental uncertainty. *Academy of Management Journal, 51*(4), 768–784.

Chase, J. (2016, September 11). AfD co-chair Petry wants to rehabilitate controversial term. *DW*. https://www.dw.com/en/afd-co-chair-petry-wants-to-rehabilitate-controversial-term/a-19543222

Decker, F. (2016). The "alternative for Germany": Factors behind its emergence and profile of a new right-wing populist party. *German Politics and Society, 34*(2), 1–16.

Decker, F. (2020, October 26). Etappen der Parteigeschichte der AfD. *Bundeszentrale für Politische Bildung*. https://www.bpb.de/politik/grundfragen/parteien-in-deutschland/afd/273130/geschichte

Dilling, M. (2018). Two of the same kind? *German Politics and Society, 36*(1), 84–104.

Donovan, T. (2020). Right populist parties and support for strong leaders. *Party Politic*. https://doi.org/10.1177/1354068820920853

Frankland, E. G. (2020). The alternative for Germany from breakthrough toward consolidation? *German Politics and Society, 38*(1), 30–54.

Franzmann, S. T. (2016). Calling the ghost of populism: The AfD's strategic and tactical agendas until the EP election 2014. *German Politics, 25*(4), 457–479.

Goerres, A., Spies, D. C., & Kumlin, S. (2018). The electoral supporter base of the alternative for Germany. *Swiss Political Science Review, 24*(3), 246–269.

Hambauer, V., & Mays, A. (2018). Wer wählt die AfD? – Ein Vergleich der Sozialstruktur, politischen Einstellungen und Einstellungen zu Flüchtlingen zwischen AfD-WählerInnen und der WählerInnen der anderen Parteien. *Zeitschrift Für Vergleichende Politikwissenschaft, 12*(1), 133–154.

Hansen, M. A., & Olsen, J. (2019). Flesh of the same flesh: A study of voters for the Alternative for Germany (AfD) in the 2017 Federal Election. *German Politics, 28*(1), 1–19.

Heinisch, R., & Mazzoleni, O. (2016). 8 comparing populist organizations. In R. Heinisch & O. Mazzoleni (Eds.), *Understanding populist party organisation* (pp. 221–246). Palgrave Macmillan.

Heppell, T. (2011). Toxic leadership: Applying the Lipman-Blumen model to political leadership. *Representation, 47*(3), 241–249.

Hopper, R. D. (1950). The revolutionary process: A frame of reference for the study of revolutionary movements. *Social Forces, 3*(28), 270–279.

Jun, U., & Jakobs, S. (2020). The selection of party leaders in Germany. In N. Aylott & N. Bolin (Eds.), *Managing leader selection in European political parties* (pp. 73–94). Palgrave Macmillan.

Lau, M. (2019, July 11). Wo geht es hier nach rechts? *Die ZEIT*, p. 7.

Lees, C. (2018). The 'alternative for Germany': The rise of right-wing populism at the heart of Europe. *Politics, 38*(3), 295–310.
Lobenstein, C. (2013, December 12). Wie rechts ist die Alternative für Deutschland? *Die ZEIT*, p. 9.
Middelhoff, P. (2020, May 20). Lauter Verräter. *Die ZEIT*, p. 1.
Middelhoff, P., Simon, J., & Wahba, A. (2017, July 20). Die Stunde der Gründer. *Die ZEIT*, pp. 15–25.
Mudde, C. (2019). *The far right today*. Wiley.
Mudde, C., & Kaltwasser, C. (2017). *Populism: A very short introduction*. Oxford University Press.
Müller, J.-W. (2016). *What is populism?* University of Pennsylvania Press.
Neukirch, R. (2013, April 8). Haste mal ne Mark? *Der Spiegel*, p. 34.
Rosenfelder, J. (2017). Die Programmatik der AfD: Inwiefern hat sie sich von einer primär euroskeptischen zu einer rechtspopulistischen Partei entwickelt? *Zeitschrift Für Parlamentsfragen, 48*(1), 123–140.
Schwanholz, J., Lewandowsky, M., Leonhardt, C., & Blätte, A. (2020). The upsurge of right-wing populism in Germany. In I. Khmelko, R. Stapenhurst, & M. L. Mezey (Eds.), *Legislative decline in the 21st Century* (pp. 184–197). Routledge.
Spillane, J. P. (2006). *Distributed leadership*. Jossey-Bass.
Weisskircher, M. (2020). The strength of far-right AfD in Eastern Germany: The East-West divide and the multiple causes behind 'populism.' *The Political Quarterly, 91*(3), 614–622.
ZEIT Online. (2017, December 3). *Alice Weidel als Beisitzerin in AfD-Vorstand gewählt*. https://www.zeit.de/politik/deutschland/2017-12/alternative-fuer-deutschland
Zons, G., & Halstenbach, A. (2019). The AfD as a 'leaderless' right-wing populist party: How the leadership-structure dilemma left an imprint on the party's leadership. *Polish Political Science Review, 7*(1), 41–60.

CHAPTER 6

Five Star Movement: From Dual to Multimember Leadership

6.1 THE MOVIMENTO 5 STELLE: A NEW 'HYBRID' PARTY IN THE ITALIAN POLITICAL LABORATORY

Officially established in October 2009, the *Movimento 5 Stelle* (M5S, Five Star Movement) attained its first national electoral success in the 2013 parliamentary elections. It was not a 'normal' or predicable breakthrough. In 2013, in fact, for the very first time that the M5S participated in a national election, it became the most-voted party in Italy. Almost nine million Italians voted for a party that, only few years earlier, was described as a collection—and collector—of local lists, sponsored by meet-up groups at the municipal level and supported by the flamboyant leadership of a well-known comedian (Beppe Grillo) who, at that time, was famous for his personal blog, his harsh criticism of the Italian ruling class and his interests in environmental issues and some kind of utopian electronic democracy.

Looking at the M5S from this point of view, it could be interpreted simply as a late, or delayed, product of that 'silent revolution' (Inglehart, 1977) that, during the 1980s, set the stage for the emergence of ecologist or new left libertarian political parties. As we shall see throughout this chapter, indeed, the M5S shares some principles and organizational practices with the Green parties that have developed in Europe at the sunset of the twentieth century, such as emphasis on the ideal of grassroot democracy; (formal) rejection of any hierarchical structure within the organization; distrust of professional, office-seeking politicians and a programmatic platform based on self-expressive or post-materialist values.

Nevertheless, the M5S is much more than that, not only because it was established almost 20 years later than the other ecologist and libertarian parties. To begin with, the Italian party founded by Beppe Grillo and Gianroberto Casaleggio in 2009 is, partially, the intended result of the 'digital revolution' that arrived in Italy during the early 2000s.[1] The blog created by Grillo in 2005, with the 'advice and consent' of Casaleggio,[2] and then the decision to support the formation of local meet-up groups, would have been unthinkable without the infrastructure provided by new information and communication technology (Bailo, 2020; Calise & Musella, 2019). In this sense, the M5S is a product of its time.

In addition, as many scholars have correctly pointed out, this party is also one of the best exemplars of that groups of actors who emerged in reaction, or as a response, to the Great Recession that severely hit European economies between 2009 and 2013 (della Porta et al., 2017; Corbetta, 2013; Vassallo & Valbruzzi, 2018; Karremans et al., 2019). According to della Porta et al. (2017), along with Podemos in Spain or Syriza in Greece, the M5S perfectly fits the category of "movement parties against austerity" (16), emerging from the axes of "the crisis of late neoliberalism in Europe" (29). To a certain extent, the party founded by Grillo and Casaleggio is a by-product of the digital revolution while the Great Recession 'exploded' in the early twenty-first century throughout Europe (Gerbaudo, 2019).[3]

---

[1] In this context, by 'digital revolution' we mean, in particular, "the explosion of Internet services and applications spearheaded by social networking services" (Bailo, 2020: 33).

[2] In this sense, it is difficult to say who comes first, whether Grillo involved Casaleggio in his enterprise, or if it was the other way around. According to some scholars or political pundits, Grillo is just an "asset" for the web communication company owned by Casaleggio or, as Iacoboni (2018: 34) put it, the "patient zero" of Casaleggio Associates. In other viewpoints, the role of the comedian is considered of paramount importance since the "movement has been built, developed and directed by Beppe Grillo" (Biorcio & Natale, 2013: 77). Rather than trying to solve this 'chicken or the egg dilemma', in this chapter we shall treat both Grillo and Casaleggio as the co-leaders and co-founders of the M5S.

[3] For the same reasons, the M5S has been aptly described, regarding its technological infrastructure, as an "internet-fuelled party", given its "reliance on the Web as a tool for

Although the M5S shares some features with the new wave of anti-austerity actors, its political trajectory is absolutely *sui generis*. That is also the reason why it cannot be locked into rigid categories and most of the time eludes too stringent definitions. To illustrate further this point, it is useful to start by saying that a political party can be mainly defined and analyzed along four dimensions: (1) genesis (party formation); (2) party ideology; (3) party organization; (4) its role within the party system.[4] As we will discuss below, shortly, the M5S shows peculiar features in all four of these dimensions.

With regard to the process of party formation, there should be no doubt, following the analytical distinction suggested by Maurice Duverger (1964) between parties of internal and external origin, that the M5S was created *outside* (and to some extent, also against) parliament. Its organizational roots were not from some pre-existing parliamentary groups but from societal groups that represent the backbone of the future party.

Yet, the question becomes more complex once we move from the seminal Duvergerian distinction to the one put forward by Panebianco (1988). According to his so-called genetic model (50), a party's organizational development is strictly linked to its pattern of formation, which can occur through a process of: (a) territorial *penetration*; (b) territorial *diffusion*; (c) a combination of these two. If territorial penetration entails a crucial role for the 'centre' in coordinating, stimulating and organizing the 'peripheral' branches of the party, territorial diffusion implies a "spontaneous germination" (50) of local association that only later is coordinated and federated at the 'centre'. Following this useful distinction, the case of the M5S presents some ambiguities. On the one hand, it cannot be denied that "there was a starting input from the – partially

---

organization, decision-making, communication, and identity-building (Mosca et al., 2015: 127; see also Mosca and Vaccari, 2013; Lanfrey, 2011). In a similar vein, Bennett et al. (2018: 12) include the M5S in the category of "connective parties", that is, "*organizations in which technology platforms and affordances are indistinguishable from, and replace, key components of brick and mortar organization and intra-party functions*".

[4] Another dimension that can be taken into consideration for the analysis of the political parties concerns their "primary emphases or orientations" (Wolinetz, 2002: 151). Accordingly, parties can be described as vote-seeking, policy-seeking and office-seeking. Since this dimension overlaps, to some extent, with both the ideological and organizational dimensions, we exclude it from the following analysis. In any case, in this perspective as well, the 'hybrid' nature of the M5S is seen, given its partial transformation from a purely policy-seeking party to a more office-seeking party with a strong vote-seeking attitude.

virtual – center represented by Grillo's blog and that it continues to be an essential reference point for all the members of the Movement" (Passarelli et al., 2013: 128). In this sense, the *penetration* process seems to prevail. On the other hand, given its movement-based, loosely organized format, the M5S appears to be "closer to the second (formation by diffusion)" process (128), according to which the degree of autonomy between rank and file activists at the local level and the party founders/centralizers is maximum.[5] In any event, the pathway leading to the creation of the M5S can be better described as a hybrid process in which territorial penetration and diffusion combine and stimulate one another. Perhaps, the first movers were Grillo and Casaleggio but then the local meet-up groups acted in a context of high autonomy from the center.

A similar argument applies if we adopt the recent distinction suggested by Bolleyer (2013), according to which new parties can be described as "rooted" or "entrepreneurial" by observing the existence of "societal groups which predate the party formation" (Bolleyer, 2013: 17). In the case of the M5S, officially established in 2009, there were municipal associations loosely aligned with the new, ill-defined (at that moment) political project launched by Grillo and Casaleggio. In this sense, the M5S had pre-existing societal roots but these roots had been planted and cultivated by the two political entrepreneurs in the previous years. It is also true that the Movement in many circumstances tried to 'jump in' other pre-existent protest movements, (such as "*No Gronda* in Genova, *No Dal Molin* in Vicenza, *No Muos* and *No Ponte* (Sicily), *No Tap* in Puglia and *No Ilva* (Taranto), as well as groups campaigning against the construction of new waste incinerators") (Biancalana, 2020: 156), but in all these cases it simply acted as a hub or as an amplifier of these local associations, a sort of "movement of the movements" (Casaleggio & Grillo, 2011: 71).[6] In any case, although the 'entrepreneurial' activity of both Grillo and Casaleggio can hardly be underestimated, the hybrid nature of the M5S has

---

[5] A different perspective is provided by Vittori (2019: 45), according to whom in the formation of the M5S we "observe an expansion by penetration, that is, from the centre to the periphery [...], it was the centre, Beppe Grillo's blog and the Casaleggio Associates to support the structuration at the subnational level".

[6] On the role of Beppe Grillo's blog as the "central hub" or the "central node" in the network of protest movements widespread in Italy in the early 2000s, see De Rosa (2013: 130–131).

found further confirmation (Biancalana & Piccio, 2017; Bordignon & Ceccarini, 2015; Diamanti, 2014).

As said, a political party can also be defined in relation to its ideology, which concerns, specifically, "the characterization of a belief system that goes right to the heart of a party's identity" (Mair & Mudde, 1998: 220). Hence, what is the ideological identity of the M5S? Many scholars have dealt with this issue intensively, and most of the time they have come to the conclusion that the M5S is a "post-ideological" actor,[7] with a "polyvalent" (Pirro, 2018) or "eclectic" (Mosca & Tronconi, 2019) identity. Precisely for this reason, the party founded by Grillo and Casaleggio has been frequently related to the all-embracing concept of populism, albeit in combination with other factors (Bobba & McDonnell, 2015; Biorcio, 2015; Tarchi, 2018; Zulianello, 2020). For instance, Corbetta (2013) emphasizes the digital nature of the party in saying that the essence of the M5S lies in its "web-populism", whereas other scholars attach greater weight to the set of ideas that are considered typical of the "technopopulist parties" (Deseriis, 2017; see also Caruso, 2015; Bickerton & Invernizzi, 2018; Mosca, 2020). At any rate, in line with that stream of literature that studies populism as an extremely 'thin ideology' (Mudde, 2004), with a strong chameleon-like posture, M5S's identity reveals once again its hybrid nature, with a set of core values that is absolutely elusive, changing and ill-defined.

If we now come to party organization as a criterion for analyzing political parties, the ambiguity surrounding the M5S increases enormously. Although the industry of 'party models' is alive and well, there is no consensus among party scholars on the model that fits the "strange animal" (Corbetta, 2013: 197) known as Five Star Movement. For some, the M5S is just the latest episode in the trajectory of Italian "personal parties" (Calise, 2000). A trajectory that links Silvio Berlusconi's *Forza Italia* (McDonnell, 2013) to, more recently, Grillo's party (Bordignon, 2013; Corbetta & Gualmini, 2013). However, the M5S does not meet all the criteria that define a personal party, "not only because the founder-leaders are two (Grillo and Casaleggio), but also because their role within the organization does not reflect that of other emblematic cases of this kind of party" (Tronconi, 2018: 176). As we will discuss in the next

---

[7] The post-ideological posture of the M5S is also stressed by Casaleggio and Grillo (2011: 13), in line with their suggestion/prediction that the "new world will be post-ideological".

section, the role of Grillo has been—and to some extent still is—relevant, but also other actors have (had) a crucial role within the M5S.

Likewise, also the description of the M5S as a "business firm party" does not fit with the organizational model designed by Grillo and Casaleggio. Following Paolucci and Hopkin (1999), a business firm party originates from the private initiative of a political entrepreneur and functions as a commercial company, with a constant overlapping between private and party interests. Even though the role of Gianroberto Casaleggio and his company (*Casaleggio Associati*, Casaleggio Associates) has been crucial for the launch and the organizational persistence of the party, his control of the M5S as well as the degree of autonomy enjoyed by the local groups affiliated to the Movement cannot be equated by any means to those of a real business firm.

At the same time, other scholars have emphasized the loose connection that exists between the 'party in the central office' of the M5S and its ramifications 'on the ground', at the local level. The relative autonomy between these two 'faces' of the party was seen as an indicator of the stratarchical nature of the organizational model, typical of that type of party that Carty (2004) has dubbed as a "franchise party". According to this model, the 'centre' of the party owns the party brand and determines both the product line and the marketing strategy. In turn, the local branches of the franchise-like organization enjoy a great deal of liberty in selling and targeting the 'product' to their own local market. In sum, brand standardization from above goes hand in hand with local marketization from below. This type of party model seems to effectively describe the *statu nascenti* of the M5S, during its incubation phase between 2005 and 2008. But then, after that "latency phase" of the Movement (della Porta et al., 2017: 57), the stratarchical and franchise-like organization model gave way to more hierarchical or centralized patterns of decision-making (Vittori, 2020).

Another type of party model that has been frequently associated with the M5S is the 'party movement'. According to the original definition put forward by Kitschelt (2006: 180), "movement parties are coalitions of political activists who emanate from social movements and try to apply the organizational and strategic practices of social movements in the arena of party competition". This definition originates mainly from the analysis of the European Green parties, with a strong emphasis on their assembly-based organization, the exaltation of the principles of grassroot democracy and the rejection of any internal hierarchies. To a certain degree, this description fits with the history of the M5S, in particular, in the early stage of its organizational development. During the years of the 'collective effervescence' of the Movement, approximately before entry into parliament in 2013, the party did resemble the 'movement type' as defined by Kitschelt. In the following years, though, other factors took over, starting with a growing centralization of power in the hands of a fistful of leaders. This is why Vittori (2020: 14) prefers to describe the M5S as a "plebiscitarian movement party", which is capable of combining "a bottom-up design structure with top-down control of decision-making processes" (14); or, as indicated by Ceccarini and Bordignon (2018), as a "*hybrid movement party*" in which personalization, centralization and direct participation create a strange organizational mix (Passarelli et al., 2017).

Finally, a party can be also defined by looking at the role it plays in the party system or, more precisely, by the pattern of interactions that it creates with other parties (Sartori, 1976). When considering the case of the M5S, the whole arsenal of 'anti-' types of parties has been mobilized. For instance, the Movement has been defined as an "anti-establishment" party (Vittori, 2018; Corbetta & Vignati, 2014), rejecting the possibility to make a deal with traditional or establishment parties. In a similar vein, for the M5S the label of "anti-party party" (Bordignon & Ceccarini, 2015) has been retrieved, which aims to emphasize its antipolitical nature, language and attitude. In addition, and taking into account its uncompromising opposition to the legitimacy of the Italian party system, the party founded by the duo Grillo and Casaleggio has been traced back to the category of anti-system parties (Zulianello, 2018; Ceccanti & Curreri, 2015; Pasquino & Valbruzzi, 2013) or, in a slightly different form, to the more nuanced notion of "challenger parties" (Hobolt & Tilley, 2016; De Vries & Hobolt, 2020). However, all these 'anti-' labels describe a phase in the lifespan of the M5S that predates its decision to accept the 'cost of governing' and forming coalitions with other mainstream parties. In 2018, with the formation of a cabinet led by Giuseppe Conte, the M5S formed a coalition, as a major partner, with the League until August 2019, and then (until February 2021) with the Democratic Party. In one blow, the protest movement that originally emerged as a reaction against the *casta* (the 'caste', the pejorative term for the political class) became part and parcel of that party system that at one time it wanted to destroy, losing its anti-establishment credentials and its deeply-rooted anti-system charge (Corbetta, 2018).

In summary, the M5S is a peculiar party with an elusive organizational model (Tronconi, 2018; Vignati, 2015b). The adjective that best grasps its nature is 'hybrid'—a notion that describes both its ideological stance, its organization, its formation and also its role in the party system, which is constantly oscillating between power and opposition. However, there is an aspect that has up to now been generally neglected by party scholars working on the M5S, that is, the nature and, in particular, the structure of its leadership. Certainly, the role of Beppe Grillo as the charismatic, plebiscitarian or personal leader of the party has been commonly recognized in the literature.[8] Similarly, the relevance of Gianroberto Casaleggio for the functioning of the M5S, albeit with some delay and difficulty, has not been overlooked (Di Maggio & Perrone, 2019).

Nevertheless, a thorough analysis of the nature of the collective leadership at work in the M5S and of its relationship with the performance of the party over time is still missing. Therefore, in the following sections we will focus on the specific pattern of leadership in the Five Star Movement, following the analytical framework elaborated in the first part of this volume.

6.2 The Leadership Structure in the M5S

No other parties in West European political systems have reached electoral success with the proportion and the rapidity of the M5S. Many factors, both institutional and behavioral, have been considered to explain the rise of the M5S. As we have seen in the previous section, the Great Recession created perfect conditions for the emergence of a new protest, anti-establishment party. Furthermore, the rule by a technocratic government (2011–2013),[9] supported by all the mainstream parties from left to right, represented a perfect target for the criticism of an outsider actor with strong anti-elitist rhetoric. The austerity measures suggested by the EU institutions and implemented by the Italian government fuelled the protest even more against the establishment and its representative,

---

[8] Here we do not to discuss whether, and on what basis, the leadership of Beppe Grillo can be defined as 'charismatic'. For a detailed discussion of this aspect, see: Chiapponi (2017) and Tarchi (2018).

[9] On the formation of the technocratic cabinets in Europe, before and after the Great Recession, and their consequences, see: Bertsou and Caramani (2020), McDonnell and Valbruzzi (2014), Pasquino and Valbruzzi (2012).

at both national and supranational levels. All these factors, to which is added a long-lasting anti-party sentiment in the Italian society at large (Bardi, 1996; Ignazi, 2020), provided a window of opportunity for the emergence of a social movement with the specific characteristics of the M5S.

Nevertheless, the opportunity produced by the economic, social and political crises was not mechanically linked to the formation of a new party actor. To exploit such an opportunity, strategic leadership with a political project was needed. And this is where, in the case of the M5S, the agency came in. Like other social movements that emerged from a period of social unrest, the history of the Five Star Movement can be divided into four different phases or stages and, as we will demonstrate, each of these has been characterized by a specific leadership structure in which the role of the founding duo Grillo-Casaleggio evolved over the years until giving way to a group of multiple leaders. However, before turning to the question of how the M5S shared executive power at the top, it is necessary to see how a movement-party can organizationally evolve over time, from its incubation to full-blown institutionalization (Ceri & Veltri, 2017; Navarria, 2019: 167–216).

6.2.1 *The four stages of a movement-party*

The first phase is the 'preliminary stage' and this serves to describe, on the one hand, the social and political context in which the movement appears and, on the other, the original characteristics of the new social actor. In other words, the preliminary stage reveals how the leadership of the social movement has prepared the ground for its subsequent formation. The second phase in the life cycle of a social movement is the 'popular stage', namely, that phase in which the protest becomes popular and sufficiently widespread in the society. As Hopper (1950) put it, it is "a time of *popularization* of unrest and discontent; a time when the dissatisfaction of the people results in the development of collective excitement" (Hopper, 1950: 273). After this period of collective excitement, it is time for the 'formal stage' in the development of a social movement in which "the roots of the movement must strike deeper than sensationalism, sentimentalism, fashion, and fad" (Hopper, 1950: 275). This is the phase in which the movement formally begins its routinization and institutionalization, setting the internal 'rules of the game' and, albeit vaguely, the boundaries of the organization. Finally, the fourth phase in the movement's life cycle is the 'institutional stage', when the routinization process is completed. A process by "which collective behaviour which begins outside formal offices and without formal rules, engaged in unconventional groups of people, in unexpected situations, or in ways contrary to use and wont, develop formal offices, organized groups, defined situations, and a new body of sanctioned use and wont" (Hopper, 1950: 278). If we apply this four-stage developmental schema to the evolution of the M5S, the transition from M5S-as-a-movement to M5S-as-a-party is clear, even though—as we will discuss below—its full institutionalization is not yet complete.

By looking at the history of the M5S through the lens of the four stages of organizational development, there are at least three aspects that we should bear in mind. First, there is nothing deterministic in the process described above (from the preliminary to the institutional stage). A social movement can remain stuck at one stage, without making any progress or taking a step forward. Or, alternatively, it can move back and forth, and even prematurely disappear.

Second, the four stages in the organizational evolution of a social movement roughly match the 'thresholds' that a political party must overcome during its lifespan in order to reach the final institutional stage. According to Pedersen (1982), the first threshold is the threshold of declaration, "the point in time when a political group declares its intention to participate in elections and thus becomes a party" (6). This phase corresponds to the preliminary stage in the life cycle of a social movement in which the leaders of the group declare their existence and their intention to get involved in the political process. The second step is the threshold of authorization, which implies that the party in the making fulfills all the requirements necessary for participation in the electoral process. In the case of the M5S, this phase matches with the popular stage in which the 'movement party' becomes strong and popular enough to fill electoral lists and nominate candidates (at the local or regional level). Then, the third challenge is the threshold of representation, "to barrier which all parties have to cross in order to obtain seats in the legislature" (Pedersen, 1982: 7). For the M5S, this barrier was crossed in 2013, that is, during the first parliamentary elections in which it participated. Lastly, there is the threshold of executive power, that is to say, the moment when "parliamentary strength could be translated into direct influence on executive decision-making" (Rokkan, 1970: 79). The M5S crossed this threshold in 2018, when it decided to form a coalition government with the League.

The third and final aspect to stress is that each stage in the organizational development of a social movement (as well as of a party) would ideally require different types of leaders. In fact, "we would expect that there are different types of leaders who are more or less suited to play their roles in different contexts and with regard to different challenges" (Rucht, 2012: 109). For instance, the agitator or the prophet type of leader is more suitable for the preliminary or popular stages, whereas the administrator or the statesman is more in line with the necessity of the organization during the formal or institutional stages. To a large extent, the success or the sustenance of an organization in the long run depends, among other factors, on the combination of these leadership types over time and in relation to the stage of organizational development.

The evolution of the M5S can, therefore, be usefully explored along the dimensions discussed so far, and within the analytical framework for the study of collective leadership as presented in the first part of the volume. At this point, in particular, we will focus on the development of the organizational model of the M5S and of the nature of its leadership. As reported in Table 6.1, the history of the party founded by Grillo and Casaleggio can be roughly divided into four phases: (a) preliminary stage (2005–2008); (b) popular stage (2009–2012); (c) formal stage (2013–2017); (d) (partial) institutional stage (2018–2021).

6.2.2 *The preliminary stage (2005–2008)*

As we have already anticipated, the preliminary stage prepares the foundation for the emergence of the future 'movement party'. It is a phase in which the social movement works undercover, sometimes with different names, undefined roles, imprecise rules and uncertain boundaries. For the M5S, this phase covers the period from 2005 to 2008, that is, from the decision of Beppe Grillo, technologically supported and powered by Gianroberto Casaleggio's Internet services company, to launch his popular blog and the subsequent creation of a network of online and offline local groups through the tools provided by the Meetup platform. In other words, this is the phase of "latency on the web" (della Porta et al., 2017: 58) for the future Five Star Movement, in which the founder-leaders made extensive use of new digital technologies to set up a movement that, at

Table 6.1 Most significant events in the organizational evolution of the M5S (2005–2021)

Date	Event
Preliminary Stage	
22 January 2004	Founding of the company Casaleggio Associati S.r.l
1 April 2004	First meeting between Beppe Grillo and Gianroberto Casaleggio in Livorno
16 January 2005	Founding of the blog 'www.beppegrillo.it'
16 July 2005	Initial diffusion of Grillo's meet-up groups
25 January 2007	Creation of 'certified' Five Star local lists
8 September 2007	Organization of the first V-Day against the political class
10 February 2008	Publication of the first 'political communiqué' in Grillo's blog
25 April 2008	Organization of the second V-Day against the mainstream media elite
3 December 2008	Presentation of the party symbol for Five Star local lists
8 March 2009	National meeting of Five Star local lists and presentation of the 'Chart of Florence' (the party platform for the local lists)
1 August 2009	Grillo announces participation in the 2010 regional elections
Popular stage	
4 October 2009	Foundation of the M5S in Milan
25–26 September 2010	At the party gathering, 'Five Star Woodstock', Grillo announces participation in the next parliamentary election
28 October 2012	Regional election in Sicily: M5S is the largest party
18 December 2012	Formation of the association, 'Movimento 5 stelle', needed for participation in the 2013 national elections
Formal stage	
28 February 2013	M5S is the most-voted party on the national stage in the 2013 parliamentary election (at the Chamber of Deputies)
1 December 2013	Organization of the third V-Day, mainly on European issues
28 November 2014	Grillo steps aside ('I'm a bit tired') and suggests the formation of a Directorate
24 December 2014	New regulations for the internal organization of the M5S and identification of the 'political leader' (capo politico)
8 April 2016	Foundation of the Rousseau Association (chair: Davide Casaleggio)
12 April 2016	Death of Gianroberto Casaleggio

(continued)

Table 6.1 (continued)

Date	Event
25 April 2016	Beppe Grillo's blog becomes the new 'Blog of the Stars' (Blog delle stelle) and launch of the Rousseau platform
11 November 2016	Grillo announces the end of the Directorate
23 September 2017	Luigi Di Maio selected as the new 'political leader' of the M5S
30 December 2017	Approval of the new party Statute
Institutional stage	
4 March 2018	In the 2018 parliamentary election the M5S is the largest party, in terms of both votes and seats
18 May 2018	Online membership vote approving the formation of a coalition cabinet with the League led by the prime minister Giuseppe Conte
3 September 2019	Online membership vote approving the formation of new cabinet led by Conte with the Democratic Party
15 December 2019	Creation of the 'Team of the Future' (Team del futuro, 204 members) and nomination of 18 national facilitators
22 January 2020	Resignation of Luigi Di Maio as 'political leader' and nomination of Vito Crimi as the new caretaker, political leader
15 November 2020	Party congress ('Stati generali') and approval of a formal multimember leadership
9–11 February 2021	Online membership vote approving the formation of new cabinet led by Draghi and the changes to the party Statute

Source Authors' own compilation.

that time, combined participation, information and mobilization (Bailo, 2020).

Right from the start, the relationship between the comedian Grillo and the web entrepreneur Casaleggio was crucial for understanding the formation of the M5S. They met for the first time in Spring 2004, after a show that Grillo had in a Livorno theater. From that time on, their collaboration was constant and strict, working together on all aspects regarding the organization of the Movement. The partnership between the two co-founders/leaders was based on a real pattern of collaboration with many elements of complementarity. This collaborative leadership is well described by Grillo when he stated, "Gianroberto has the synthesis, I have the analysis. I speak, speak, speak…. It all begins from confrontation and conversation" (Grillo, 2013: 12). With such a spirit of cooperation, they wrote articles/posts together, they defined the strategy for the groups at the local level and they also prepared the framework for the future party organization. Their ideas and strategies were so intertwined that it was difficult to realize who was the author of what. In Casaleggio's (2013: 13) own words, "it is just the two of us who write but no one can understand who is the one or the other".

In this phase, Grillo gradually put aside the attire of the comedian and, instead, wore the mantle of the political entrepreneur, using his blog to convey his message and to promote the political involvement of citizens at the municipal level on very local issues. At that time, national politics remained in the background. Similarly, Gianroberto Casaleggio put aside his attire as manager and owner of a relatively small company, (*Casaleggio Associati*, working in the field of web marketing and online editorial strategy consultancy), and became a strategist interested in public and political affairs. In short, the meeting between Grillo and Casaleggio was a meeting between two distinct political entrepreneurs, with a common interest and very different skills and professional expertise.

During this phase, Grillo used his fame to spread the message both online, through his successful blog, and offline, with the invitation to create local groups of 'civic', nonpartisan activists (the so-called Friends of Beppe Grillo). Besides the development strategy, Casaleggio provided both the material and immaterial infrastructure for the diffusion of the message embodied by Grillo. Nevertheless, as noted by della Porta et al. (2017: 59), during this incubation phase of the M5S "[p]ublic visibility and media coverage of the Movement were extremely limited at this stage, and the new (pre)political creature was mostly known to the limited circuit of supporters and activists". It took almost four years to move the M5S from the shadow of the preliminary stage to the next phase of its popularization.

6.2.3   *The popular stage (2009–2012)*

In moving from the latency on the web to the so-called popular stage, there were two events in the history of the M5S that prepared the ground for its official breakthrough at the national level. The first event was the organization, on 8 September 2007, of a public demonstration—called 'V-Day'[10]—which was held in Bologna and other Italian cities and aimed

---

[10] The reasons behind the choice of this name for the national events organized by the M5S are manifold: (a) V stands for *Vaffanculo* (fuck off), an insult directed especially at

against the political class and in favor of a 'clean parliament' (i.e., cleared of convicted MPs). Although the national mainstream media did not pay enough attention to that event, in terms of citizens' participation it was a success and, more importantly, it helped to move the activity of the Movement from the local domain to the national arena.

A similar event—the second 'V-Day'—was organized one year later in Turin (on 25 April 2008), and this time the target of the criticism was the mainstream media. Traditional journalism and journalists were considered as 'traitors' or false/fake mediators of the will of public opinion. As Casaleggio and Grillo (2011: 35) declared, there are to be "no filters between power and citizens". The intermediation role of journalists between the public and the political realm was rejected on the basis of the principle of disintermediation, that is, citizens are, at the same time, users and producers of information and they do not need any mediating actor. Again, the public demonstration turned out to be a success, mobilizing hundreds of thousands of people, and the Movement acquired even greater national resonance.

After these successes on the national stage, Grillo and Casaleggio decided to make the first entry into the electoral arena. Initially, they proposed or actively incentivized the formation of civic (i.e., nonpartisan) local lists for the municipal elections (Biorcio, 2014; Natale, 2014). After a previous process of screening and evaluation carried by the duo Grillo and Casaleggio with their staff, the 'acceptable' lists received a formal 'certificate' from the Movement and could take part in local elections. Yet, that decision was just the beginning of a more profound change. In fact, one year later, the Movement first approved the so-called *Carta di Firenze* (Charter of Florence), a political manifesto for the civic lists contesting local elections, and then, on 4 October 2009, announced the official establishment of the new political actor, the *Movimento 5 Stelle*.

Although the role of Beppe Grillo is commonly considered crucial in the creation of the M5S, it is important to not underestimate the importance of Casaleggio in this phase. Actually, as Casaleggio himself was keen

---

politicians and journalists; (b) V also recalls a famous graphic novel by Alan Moore and David Lloyd, V for *Vendetta*; (c) V-day also reminds the 'D-day' landing of the Allies in Normandy during World War II; and finally (d) V stands for '5' in Roman numerals and refers to the five stars (water, environment, mobility, development, energy) that should inspire the political commitment of the M5S members.

to stress in a letter written to the oldest and most prestigious Italian newspaper, *Il Corriere della Sera*, "I want to make it clear that I have never been 'behind' Beppe Grillo, but by his side. Basically, I am the cofounder of this movement along with him".[11] In sum, as many scholars have correctly pointed out (Tronconi, 2015a; Iacoboni, 2018; Vignati, 2013; Vittori, 2020), at the top of the M5S there was a "diarchy", a duo or a tandem made up of Grillo and Casaleggio that, in the terms presented in Chapter 2, can be described as a form of dual leadership. Yet, unlike the previous (preliminary) phase, at this stage the dual leadership of the M5S has been partially formalized. In fact, in October 2009 the approval of the so-called party 'non-statute'[12] (a slim document of only seven articles) established that the name and symbol of the Movement are "registered in the name of Beppe Grillo, the only titleholder with rights to their use" (art. 3), thereby making a formal distinction between Grillo, as the owner of the party logo, and Casaleggio, who was not even mentioned in the document.

Moreover, beyond these differences in the (formal) distribution of power within the organization, the division of labor between the party leaders remains unchanged. Grillo continued to perform the role of the expressive or emotional leader, while Casaleggio kept on being the task-oriented strategist of the Movement. The apex of this distinction occurred between 2012 and 2013, that is, respectively, during the electoral campaigns for the 2012 Sicilian regional elections and the 2013 parliamentary elections. Especially during the latter, the expressive role of Grillo, both inside and outside of the Movement, reached a record high. On that occasion, all M5S's electoral campaign was based on the figure

---

[11] The role of Casaleggio has been acknowledged by Grillo himself when, in a post announcing the passing of the co-founder of the Movement, he stated that: "This morning Gianroberto Casaleggio, the co-founder of the Five Star Movement, passed away". More in general, on the role of Casaleggio and his company in the formation/organization of the M5S, see also Becchi (2016), Iacoboni (2019), Biondo and Canestrari (2018, 2019), Morosini (2019).

[12] The M5S rejects the definition and the label of 'party' and prefers to present itself as non-party or a 'non association'. As Art. 4 of the non-statute specifies, the Movement "is not a political party, nor is it intended that it should become one in the future". The idea of having a 'statute non-statute' stems from the need to take a critical distance from all the categories of traditional party politics.

of Beppe Grillo.[13] In addition to being the one and only spokesman of the party, he transformed the electoral campaign of the M5S into his own personal tour (called *Tsunami tour*) "played out in the piazzas, making the most of Grillo's theatrical rhetoric to draw the crowds" (De Rosa, 2013: 134).[14]

Even though Grillo was, in Duverger's (1964) terms, the "titular" leader of the M5S, that is, the 'voice' and the 'face' of the Movement, "the role of Gianroberto Casaleggio is certainly significant in shaping the strategy of the party" (Tronconi, 2015b: 218), for that which concerns both the organization and communication strategy. It is difficult to say if the balance of power weights more in favor of the former or the latter; but what cannot be disputed is that the founding of the M5S originates from "Grillo's alliance with Gianroberto Casaleggio" (Vignati, 2015a: 14), and vice versa.

6.2.4 *The formal stage (2013–2017)*

After the popularization of the movement all across Italy, the next step in the organizational development of the M5S entailed entry into the formal stage, in which the party started to build up a more stable structure and a less imprecise collective identity. The starting point of this new phase came with the 2013 parliamentary elections, in which the party, led by Grillo and Casaleggio, was the most-voted on the national level. With the entry into the national legislature of 163 representatives, the 'face' of the 'party in public office' became, for the first time, a relevant actor within the organization (see Table 6.2).

---

[13] In contrast to other political leaders, Grillo did not seek public visibility on television or in national newspapers. Actually, he adopted a mix-method strategy of 'pre-modern' and 'post-modern' electoral campaign, through which his old-style rallies in the squares of all Italian provinces were amplified by the Internet (mainly, his own blog). Nevertheless, these gatherings became, through a "skilfully executed communications strategy" and "a game of smoke and mirrors" (Bordignon & Ceccarini, 2019: 146), immediately newsworthy and part of national TV debates.

[14] Grillo's 2013 election tour reached all the major Italian cities. The three events with the largest media impact, according to Bobba et al. (2013: 373) "were the rally in Turin (February 16), the one in Milan (February 19) and the final campaign rally held in Rome (February 22).

Table 6.2 The organizational evolution of the M5S

	Preliminary stage	Popular stage	Formal stage	Institutional stage
Period	2005–2008	2009–2012	2013–2017	2018–2021
Party lifespan threshold	Declaration	Authorization	Representation	Executive power
Party in central office	Grillo/Casaleggio Sr	Grillo/Casaleggio Sr	Grillo, Casaleggio (Sr. and Jr.), Directorate (2014–16)	Grillo, Casaleggio Jr., Di Maio, 'collegial leadership'
Party in public office	-	2012: 213 municipal councillors, 4 mayors, 19 regional councillors	2013: 324 municipal councillors, 6 mayors, 42 regional councillors, 163 MPs	2020: 1,655 municipal councillors, 39 mayors, 113 regional councillors, 287 MPs, 14 MEPs
Party on the ground	2005: 35 meetups	2012: 560 meetups; 31,612 registered members	2013: 1,217 meetups; 48,292 registered members	2020: 647 meetups; 186,664 registered members

Source Authors' own compilation on data provided by Tronconi (2015a, 2018), Lanzone & Tronconi (2015), Vittori (2019), Bischof and Kurer (2020)

Up to that time, if we exclude the extremely limited number of mayors and municipal or regional councillors elected at the local level, the structure of the M5S revolved around the relationship between the 'party in the central office', on the one hand, represented by Grillo and Casaleggio, and the 'party on the ground', that is, the group of supporters at the local or digital level, on the other hand. This relationship was unmediated and relatively loose or weak. In the stylized model of the 'digital party' suggested by Gerbaudo (2019), that has been tailored by keeping in mind the case of M5S, there is no mediation between what he calls the "hyperleader", namely, "the plebiscitary-charismatic figure tasked with representing the party in the media and internet spectacle" (21), and the "superbase" composed of activists or sympathizers whose role in the organization is mainly to react, by voting in online referenda, to the decisions of the central office.

This very rudimental organizational structure came to an end with the formation of large parliamentary groups, which were located in between the national/central leaders and the rank-and-file of the party. Inevitably, the organization became more complex as well as the relationships between the relevant groups within the party. The first decision made by the two founder-leaders was to impose, in 2014, "the presence of 'communication groups', both in the two chambers of the national parliament and in the European parliament" (della Porta et al., 2017: 87). These communication groups, whose members were "indicated by the leaders, ratified by the MPs, and funded with the resources of the parliamentary groups" (87), had the task of supporting, coordinating and monitoring the behavior of the 'party in public office'. They were, in other words, the *longa manus* of the dual leadership on the parliamentary groups.

Over time, the strict control of the leaders over the MPs caused tension and conflict within the party, which eventually led to a massive wave of expulsion of dissidents from the ranks of the parliamentary groups. In fact, almost one quarter of Movement's MPs left, or were expelled from, the party in the 2013–2018 parliamentary term. This situation revealed the need to introduce a structure of mediation and representation within the party that would be capable of channelling the interests and preferences of the 'party in public office'. This need became much more pressing after the worsening of Gianroberto Casaleggio's health between 2014 and 2016, and the declaration of Beppe Grillo (2014) to 'take a step aside' from the leadership of the Movement because he felt 'pretty tired'.

If in the past "Grillo and *Casaleggio Associati* were the sole points of reference for all sub-national meet-ups and newly elected councillors" (Vittori, 2020: 9), the weakening and then (in April 2016) the passing of one member of the dual leadership pushed for a complete re-organization of the Movement and a reform of the leadership structure. The first attempt to move in that direction was the formation of the so-called *Direttorio* (Directorate), a board of influential MPs with the task of coordinating the activities of the parliamentary groups and representing their intentions to the inner circle of the party. As noted by Ceccarini and Bordignon (2016: 138), the "formation of the Directorate is undoubtedly the most significant indicator of the strengthening of the

Movement's internal organization", which, for the first time in the history of the M5S, explicitly broke the principle of a "leaderless" movement (Casaleggio, 2013: 11), with no formal hierarchical structure.[15]

In this regard, it is important to add that the formation and composition of the Directorate was established 'from above', directly by Grillo and Casaleggio, and approved 'from below', "in an online vote in the space of just one day" (Ceccarini & Bordignon, 2016: 138) by the registered members of the party. In other words, the co-leaders of the M5S selected the five members of the Directorate (Luigi Di Maio, Alessandro Di Battista, Carla Ruocco, Roberto Fico and Carlo Sibilia) and then the party members expressed their approval. The experience of this new body within the party was short-lived and, after less than two years in which it had been, in fact, inoperative, it was simply dismissed by Grillo in an interview ("the Directorate does not exist anymore"). However, its formation is relevant for our argument because it reveals a phase of transition in the organizational model of the M5S, in particular, from an undisputed dual leadership to a more collective and distributed form of leadership in which other relevant actors are involved and new representative or executive bodies are created.

In fact, at the end of 2017, the M5S approved further organizational changes that had a significant impact on the hierarchical structure of the party.[16] First of all, Beppe Grillo was no longer the formal "political leader" of the Movement, but was indicated as the *Garante* (Guarantor), a new office created *ad personam* for the founder of the party. Also in recent years, Beppe Grillo depicted himself as the guarantor of the party, as a political figure with the task of controlling and monitoring, from above, the behavior of the M5S representatives and their adherence to the basic principles of the party. For the same reason, from time to time Grillo enjoys proclaiming himself as the 'Elevated' (*Elevato*), as a sort of neutral, mystical, semi-divine entity supervising from above his own

---

[15] On the formal aversion to the figure of a leader in the M5S and the tension between "a political movement with a strong 'leaderist' stamp" and its ideology that "professes an equally strong 'leaderless' nature", see Vignati (2015a: 9–12).

[16] In that occasion, the previous 'non-statute' was replaced by a party statute to all effects. More importantly, the "control over the logo, the Rousseau Platform and the blog, rather than to Beppe Grillo alone, now goes to a new '5-Star Movement Association' that replaces the 2012 body and envisages the election of the guarantor, but only from 2021, after Grillo's 'renewed' four-year mandate" (Musso & Maccaferri, 2018: 13).

political 'creature'. But only with the new regulations and the organigram approved in 2017, the role of the Guarantor has been completely clarified and certified (Vignati, 2017).

Second, the role of 'political leader' that in the past was held by Beppe Grillo was transferred to one of the most powerful spokespersons of the party, Luigi Di Maio.[17] As a former member of the Directorate and, more significantly, as deputy-chair of the Chamber of Deputies, Di Maio was the undisputed frontrunner in the online closed primary elections held in order to choose the new political leader and the candidate for the premiership. With the participation of one quarter of the eligible voters (37,442 out of approximately 142,000 certified members), unsurprisingly, the result was that Di Maio won with 83% of the total votes and was announced as the new formal leader of the party.

The only aspect that was still in the dark was the role of the company *Casaleggio Associati*. While Gianroberto Casaleggio was still alive, he acted as the main strategist of the Movement, playing "the role of the shadow leader of the organizational structure" (Tronconi, 2018: 165) or, better yet, the *éminence grise* of the M5S. With his passing in April 2016, the shadow leadership of the Movement was inherited by Casaleggio's son, Davide, who took charge of the family-run business, and of the whole ICT infrastructure behind the M5S (blogs, Web sites, communication groups, social media, etc.) and, most importantly, of the 'Rousseau platform', which was the new decision-making system of 'direct democracy' within the party (Musso & Maccaferri, 2018: 13; Lioy et al., 2019).

Thus, both formally and informally, *Casaleggio Associati* controls some of the most important "zones of uncertainty" (Panebianco, 1988: 33–36) within the party organization.[18] For example, the whole process of

---

[17] Along with these two new political figures (the Guarantor and the political leader), the regulation also requires the formation of three further bodies: the Guarantee Committee (composed of Vito Crimi, Roberta Lombardi and Giovanni Cancelleri), the Board of Arbitrators (composed of the MPs Nunzia Catalfo, Paola Carinelli and Riccardo Fraccaro) and the Treasurer (Luigi Di Maio). Incidentally, if the creation of the Directorate in 2014 could be considered as a false start in the process of party institutionalization and routinization, the new organizational structure set up in late 2017 marked, instead, a significant step in that direction.

[18] By "zones of uncertainties", a concept that Panebianco borrows from Crozier (1964), we refer to a source of organizational power that allows actors to make important decisions in areas of organizational unpredictability. Hence, those who are in control of the zones of uncertainty in the party organization "hold a trump card, a resource that is 'spendable' in the internal power games" (Panebianco, 1988: 33).

leadership election and candidate selection is managed by the Rousseau Association through the Rousseau operating system. The same applies for the 'registration' or 'certification' of the membership. Indeed, only certified members of the Movement can participate in the online primaries or referenda. So, the database of the "superbase", as Gerbaudo (2019) called it, that is, the full list of the registered party members, is under the strict control of the Rousseau Association, whose president is Davide Casaleggio.

In addition, the flow of information and the main channel of communication, beginning with the Blog of the stars (*Blog delle stelle*), are under the technical direction of the Web site managers provided by *Casaleggio Associati*. Finally, the Rousseau Association also has partial control over the funding of the organization. In fact, as clarified in the 'code of conduct' (*codice etico*) signed by the MPs before their election, all M5S representatives at regional, national or supranational levels are "obliged to use the so-called 'Rousseau Platform' as the main tool of communication" and "to provide an economic contribution for the maintenance of the technological platforms that support the activity of the parliamentary groups or the individual representatives and councillors" of the Movement. In short, the most important zones of uncertainty in the M5S (i.e., communication, funding, recruitment, technological expertise, etc.) are in the hands of a private company that has only a very loose link with the formal organizational chart of the M5S. But how does this power configuration affect the leadership structure of the Movement?

As we have seen, the 'formal stage' in the organizational development of the M5S marks the passage from a dual leadership, with a clear division of tasks, roles and functions between Grillo and Casaleggio, to a new multimember leadership in which a formal hierarchy within the party goes in tandem with, on the one hand, an informal structure of power controlled by *Casaleggio Associati* and, on the other hand, the continued existence of a 'real political leader' (i.e., the Guarantor, Beppe Grillo) who "still has the non-negotiable last word on interpretation of the party statute" (Vittori, 2020: 12) and who owns the party logo. As a consequence, during this phase the leadership structure of the M5S is still based on a power-sharing arrangement in which, however, the distribution of tasks, functions and roles between the leaders is not as clear as it was in the previous phases. To begin with, there exists a tension between the *titular* political leader (Luigi Di Maio) and the *real* political leader (the founder-guarantor Grillo). Although they should perform relatively different tasks, the risk of the overlapping of these two 'political' roles is inevitably high, especially when the party faces new challenges, such as entry into the executive arena.

In a way, the cohabitation between Grillo and Di Maio created a situation of potential 'co-performance', in the sense that both leaders had the function to present the manifesto and the values of the Movement to society at large. To varying degrees, they were the 'face' and the 'voice' of the party. Hence, if the original dual leadership of Grillo and Casaleggio Sr. was based on a clear division of tasks, in the case of Grillo and Di Maio that division is much more blurred. So much so that it would be better described as a case of co-performance.

Moreover, the power within the M5S is not strictly confined to the formal boundaries of the party organization. As we have seen, the external influence of a private company on the activities of the party is crucial for understating the distribution of power in the M5S. As a matter of fact, it is not farfetched to say that "[t]wo thirds of the actual leadership – the president of the *Associazione Rousseau* and the Guarantor – is outside the party in public office but can nonetheless constrain, and impose decisions on, the party in public office" (Vittori, 2020: 14). And, regarding the role of *Associazione Rousseau* (proprietor of the homonymous Rousseau platform), the control and influence over the party comes from a company located outside the organizational boundaries of the party. This circumstance creates a situation in which the power within the party is distributed, or more appropriately, diluted among different actors and, in some cases, an overlapping of tasks and functions between these actors can be observed.

We have already discussed the potential tension between the guarantor and the political leader of the party, but another source of potential conflict derives from the distribution of tasks between, again, the political leader (Di Maio) and the manager of the Rousseau platform and association (Casaleggio Jr.), who continues to be in full control of the organizational apparatus. In a way, the multimember leadership at work in this phase of M5S's lifespan can be described as the sum of two dual leaderships. On the one hand, the formal dual leadership operating within the organizational boundaries of the Movement, embodied by Grillo and Di Maio. They performed similar tasks in a relatively collaborative fashion, according to a logic that can be described as 'co-performance'.

On the other hand, there is also the informal dual leadership composed of the political leader and the shadow leader (Casaleggio Jr.), who are both in charge of the party machinery. In this case, the logic of action is closer to what can be defined as a 'parallel performance' in which similar (organizational) tasks are performed in different contexts (inside and outside the party). Therefore, the resulting multimember leadership originates by the intertwining of these double, dual leaderships in which the distribution of tasks and functions is not as clear-cut as it was at the origin of the Movement.

6.2.5 The institutional stage (2018–2021)

The final turning point in the M5S's organizational development came with the crossing of the 'executive threshold' after the success in the 2018 parliamentary elections (Corbetta, 2017; Biorcio & Natale, 2018). Until that point, the Movement confirmed its "isolationist purity" (Bordignon & Ceccarini, 2019: 156), that is, the refusal of any alliances with other parties before or after the election. As one of the most visible and influential representatives of the M5S, Alessandro Di Battista, declared in the run-up to the 2018 elections, "the day on which the M5S decides to coalesce – though it will never happen – with the parties responsible for Italy's destruction is the day I will leave the Five Star Movement" (Di Battista, 2018). Contrary to Di Battista's expectations, that day came twice in a matter of a few months. Initially, with the post-electoral alliance with the League that led to the formation of the first Conte government and lasted from May 2018 to August 2019. Then, with the decision to form a different cabinet that was headed by the same prime minister (Giuseppe Conte), but that was supported by a different coalition partner, the *Partito Democratico* (Democratic Party).[19] In sum, the M5S's isolationist purity suddenly became a broken taboo (Bordignon & Ceccarini, 2019: 156).

Inevitably, the crossing of the 'executive threshold' brought about a new set of organizational challenges for the M5S. First, the 'party in public office' became larger and more diversified, with the addition of a new stratum composed of those representatives that were included in the executive arena. Second, the formation of government required a new coordinating system between the two sides of the party in public offices (parliamentary groups vs. cabinet members) and, in turn, between the

---

[19] In February 2021, after the fall of the second Conte cabinet, the M5S decided to support the new governing coalition headed by Mario Draghi.

representatives of the party in the institutions and in both the central leadership and the membership. The third challenge was presented by the hybrid role played by prime minister Giuseppe Conte, within or on the edge of the party.

Formally, Conte is not a member of the M5S. In the run-up to the 2018 elections, he was indicated as a potential minister in a hypothetical 'Five star government' but he did not participate as a candidate in the electoral contest. As a lawyer and professor of Civil Law at the University of Florence, Conte was a technician who was led to politics. In light of this 'neutral' background, he was appointed prime minister for the coalition made up of the M5S and the right-wing party led by Matteo Salvini (*Lega*, League). Especially during the first months of the new cabinet, Conte was frequently depicted as a sort of 'puppet' in the hands of the political leaders of two parties (Di Maio and Salvini).[20] However, over time Conte has become more autonomous vis-à-vis their supporting parties and, in particular, after his first government fell, he has acquired more personal power. Consequently, also his influence over the M5S has significantly increased, adding even more uncertainty to the leadership structure of the Movement.

Indeed, as indicated in Fig. 6.1, when asked to indicate their preferred leader, in October 2020 almost one-third of the M5S voters named Giuseppe Conte. In this perspective, it is also interesting to observe the trajectory of the founder of the Movement. In 2013, Grillo was undoubtedly the most preferred leader, indicated by almost 80% of M5S voters. Seven years later, only 5% of M5S sympathizers named the founder of the party as their most favorite leader. It is also important to notice that, in line with his character of shadow leader acting behind the scenes, Casaleggio is not even taken into consideration in the surveys on the leadership of the Movement. He was simply taken for granted, as a constant in the changing landscape of the M5S.

All the factors that we have listed above contributed to make the organizational model of the M5S more complex and its distribution of

---

[20] For instance, during a plenary session of the European Parliament the Liberals' leader Guy Verhofstadt described Conte as "the puppet moved by Salvini and Di Maio". A similar description was frequent in the Italian media. However, it is telling how the French newspaper, *Le Figaro*, entitled the news concerning the crisis and then the fall of the first Conte government: "Giuseppe Conte, a puppet turned into a puppeteer" (*"Giuseppe Conte, un pantin devenu marionnettiste*, 28 August 2019).

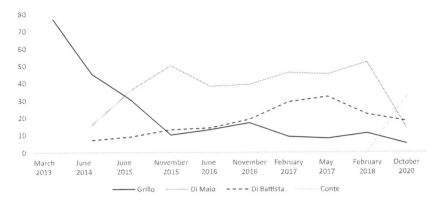

Fig. 6.1 Preferred leaders of the M5S voters/sympathizers (%) (*Source* Authors' own compilation based on data provided by the Demos & Pi survey (Ceccarini and Bordignon 2018: 357) (N = 1,014 cases) up to 2018, and SWG survey (N = 2,000) for the 2020 figure. *Note* In addition to Conte in 2020, we have reported the data for the three most preferred leaders over time)

leadership more uncertain. A situation has been exacerbated after the resignation of Luigi Di Maio as the 'political leader' of the party in January 2020 because of the M5S's poor electoral performance in the 2019 European elections and in the subsequent electoral contests at the regional level (Tronconi & Valbruzzi, 2020).[21] As reported in Fig. 6.2, after the huge electoral successes obtained in the 2013 and 2018 general elections, the electoral support for the M5S followed a steady downward trend, especially in the last two regional elections (in 2019 and 2020) where the Movement received, on average, less than ten percent of the total votes.

In order to cope with these new political, electoral and organizational challenges, the M5S has introduced relevant changes to its internal structure. The first change was introduced in mid-December 2019, with the creation of new roles at both the regional and national level: the so-called facilitators (*facilitatori*). The 90 regional facilitators have the tasks of connecting national and supranational representatives with the

---

[21] After the resignation of Luigi Di Maio, Vito Crimi has been appointed as the acting 'political leader' of the M5S until the approval of the new 'collegial leadership' in early 2021.

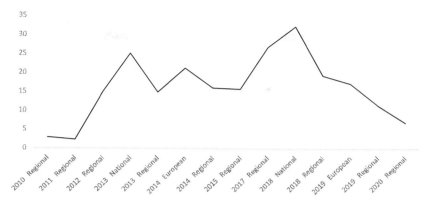

Fig. 6.2 The electoral performance of the M5S at the regional, European and national elections, 2010–2020 (% list vote on the total valid votes cast) (*Source* Authors' own compilation based on data provided by the Italian Ministry of the Interior Web site. *Note* For the regional elections, we have taken into account only the regions in which the M5S participated in the elections)

local activists; coordinating the behavior of the elected members in the different institutional arenas, and providing political training to the party membership. In contrast, the 18 national facilitators are divided into two types: "six are responsible for organizational aspects of the party, while 12 are responsible for the party's policy development. The latter leads the so-called *teams del futuro* (teams of the future), each of which supervises a specific policy field. Each *team del futuro* is composed of eight members" (Vittori, 2020: 12). It is not clear whether these new political bodies represent the 'party in central office' or, simply, the middle-level elite of the M5S. Thus far, they have remained pretty much inoperative and with no direct impact on the functioning of the party.

The second relevant change in the party organization occurred at the end of 2020, when the M5S held what many journalists described as the 'first party congress'. The so-called *Stati Generali* (Estates-General convention), which is the name chosen for the party congress, changed

M5S's Statute and introduced, at least formally, a new leadership structure.[22] At the top of the party, and replacing the role of the 'political leader', there should be now a board of leaders composed of five members (presented by the journalists as a 'collegial leadership'). On paper, this decision marked the passage from the informal multimember leadership that we have observed in the previous 'formal stage', to a new situation characterized by the existence of a formal multimember leadership in which different actors are involved. Formally, there is no hierarchy within this new multimember body and no predefined distribution of tasks. According to new party statute, all five members are collectively responsible for "the function of determining the political direction" of the Movement. Therefore, co-performance appears to be the logic of coordination between the members of the multimember leadership.

Despite the formalization of the new executive body, the organizational model of the M5S still presents various elements of ambiguity. First, the relationship between the multimember leadership and the role of the national 'facilitators' is unclear. In fact, both groups of actors share the responsibility for organizational aspects of party life. Second, the guarantor, Beppe Grillo still has the 'power of the last word' on the most important decisions of the M5S and, for this reason, he shares the task of determining the political direction of the Movement with the newly formed board of leaders. Third, Davide Casaleggio is still in control of the decision-making platform used by the M5S to make relevant decisions within the Movement and of the channels of communication or information used by the representatives.

As a consequence, the multimember structure of M5S's leadership cannot be restricted to the new formal body created in 2020 (the so-called collegial leadership or, more precisely, the Steering Committee), but it must also include other actors who continue to play a crucial role in the party organigram, such as Beppe Grillo and Davide Casaleggio (see Table 6.3). Looking at the type of labor organization, we find a situation of co-performance for the functioning of the new multimember leadership, in that the five member-leaders perform together the same task (i.e., setting political direction for the Movement). At the same time, we observe a 'parallel performance' in relation to the organizational aspects

---

[22] In addition to the changes introduced in the leadership structure, the party congress has also decided to strengthen their organizational roots at the local level, thereby setting aside the 'post-bureaucratic' principle on which it was originally based.

6 FIVE STAR MOVEMENT: FROM DUAL TO MULTIMEMBER LEADERSHIP

Table 6.3 Type of leadership in the M5S from 2005 to the present

	Type	Leaders
2005–2008	Dual leadership	Beppe Grillo, Gianroberto Casaleggio
2009–2012	Dual leadership	Beppe Grillo, Gianroberto Casaleggio
2013–2017	Multimember leadership	Beppe Grillo, Gianroberto Casaleggio, Davide Casaleggio, Luigi Di Maio, members of the Directorate (2014–2016)
2018–2021	Multimember leadership	Beppe Grillo, Davide Casaleggio, Luigi Di Maio, members of the Steering Committee

Source Authors' own compilation

of the party, which are performed separately by Casaleggio and his staff, on the one hand, and the new internal bodies created in the M5S, on the other hand.

In summary, the organizational evolution of the M5S, from the preliminary to the (partially) institutional stage, has been characterized by a changing leadership structure. In the two initial phases and until the formation of the so-called Directorate in 2014, dual leadership with a clear division of tasks between Grillo and Casaleggio has been the norm in the Movement. In the subsequent phases, we have observed the creation of a multimember leadership, either informally (especially between 2013 and 2018) or formally established through the formation of a new Steering Committee in 2020.[23]

Thus far, however, we have not investigated in detail the composition of M5S's leadership structure and, in particular, the way in which the different skills of the leaders have combined with each other in order to have a more or less effective control over the organization. In the next section, we will focus on these aspects.

---

[23] In this new organizational context, the role that Giuseppe Conte will play within the M5S is still uncertain and unclear after his resignation as prime minister in February 2021. It is important to point out that, although formally approved by the party membership, the new Steering Committee of the M5S has not yet (as of June 2021) come into force.

6.3 The configuration of leadership in the different phases

As we have already anticipated, different types of leadership may change over time, during the evolution of the party organization. The leader who is suitable for the preliminary stage may not be equally suitable or effective for the formal or the more institutionalized stages.[24] Therefore, it is important to analyze the type of leaders—and the type of leadership—that has characterized the trajectory of the Five Star Movement from 2005, when the two co-founders of the Movement decided to launch a new social (and then political) project.

Basically, the history of the M5S begins with a "decisive meeting" (Vignati, 2015a: 18), which was between Grillo and Casaleggio. However, it was not just a meeting of two individuals but a perfect match between their skills, wills and attitudes. Indeed, "Grillo, a leader able to seduce crowds with the skill of a born performer, found in Casaleggio a managerial organization" (19). In other words, a famous showman who was banned from public TV because of his satire against the Italian ruling class met an unknown digital communication expert with a passion for the Web and a dream for direct democracy.

If we adopt the typology of leadership profiles illustrated in Chapter 2,[25] during the preliminary stage (2005–2008) we see the perfect combination between two types of leaders performing different tasks. On the one hand, there is Beppe Grillo who acts both as the 'motivator' and the 'president' of the party. He is the "orator who does not seek public office" (Vignati, 2015a: 11) and who seduces the crowds with his very peculiar political satire (Cosenza, 2014); while, at the same time, he acts as a president-in-chief, the embodiment of the movement for the outer world. In this more formal role, Grillo is the titleholder of the party symbol or the one who 'certifies' whether a local list can participate in the electoral contest in representation of the Five Star Movement. Using the metaphor of Ernst Kantorowicz (1957), Beppe Grillo embodies both of

---

[24] In party politics literature, the relationship between leadership profiles and party development has been explored by Harmel (1985), Harmel and Svåsand (1993), Harmel et al. (1995).

[25] This typology of leadership profiles was originally formulated by Rucht (2012: 110–111) for the analysis of social movement leaders.

the 'the King's two bodies'—the institutional and the natural, or ideal, face of the Movement.

On the other hand, Gianroberto Casaleggio is in charge of the organizational aspects of the M5S. Especially during the incubation phase of the Movement, he was both the 'strategist' and the 'organizer' of the future party. Indeed, "Casaleggio's role is not one of mere technical support, as was initially depicted; rather, he is claimed to contribute to defining the political contents" (Vignati, 2015a: 19). In light of this, he can be described as the strategist or the "spin doctor, ideologist" (Bordignon & Ceccarini, 2013: 13) of the M5S, namely, the person who had "a clear idea about what directions to go in and how to ultimately reach the stated goals" (Rucht, 2012: 111). At the same time, he (along with his staff) was responsible for the whole organization of the Movement, especially in its early stage when there was no rule to follow and everything was built from scratch. If the M5S can be described as an 'experiment in social engineering', the "author of the experiment" is Gianroberto Casaleggio (Iacoboni, 2018: 77).

In terms of division of labor between the two founder-leaders, it is clear that there was a neat division of tasks and roles between them, as a function of their different skills and attitudes. Casaleggio, as a secretive and reserved person, preferred to remain behind the scenes, whereas Grillo as a consummate performer enjoyed being in the limelight. As a duo, they were "the perfect Mr. Inside/Mr. Outside team" (Tyrnauer, 2004: 102). As a result, the division of tasks in this combination of dual leadership was perfect: the 'head' and 'hands' sharing a strong commitment to launch a new socio-political enterprise.

In addition, the two co-leaders were also perfectly complementary with each other, both in terms of roles (motivator/president vs. strategist/organizer), tasks (expressive vs. instrumental), cognitive characteristics and expertise. In short, Grillo and Casaleggio were *compatible* in terms of values, *complementary* in terms of roles and *committed* to the same political mission. Theirs was a fortunate combination of characteristics that is not easy to replicate and that fits the definition of a 'united career' perfectly. In fact, their co-leadership went far beyond a temporary professional collaboration and, in line with other cases of united career leaders, it was based on "a tighter coupling of the relationship" (Alvarez & Svejenova, 2005: 175). If a united path assumes the fact that co-leaders "consider each other's trajectory when making career decisions and undertake career moves" (175), then there can be no doubt about the trajectory that unified the duo Grillo-Casaleggio.[26]

Regarding the patterns or configurations of leadership functions, it is relevant to notice that there is a slight difference between the dual leadership in the incubation phase of the Movement (2005–2008) compared to the subsequent period (the popular stage, 2009–2013). In fact, in the incubation phase of the movement we observe a full-fledged 'planful alignment' of leadership functions, which "have been given prior, planful thought by organizational members" (Leithwood et al., 2006: 225). At that time, the organizational members of the M5S, particularly at the top level, were mainly two, Grillo and Casaleggio (with their often intertwined staff). Consequently, the distribution of leadership roles and functions was the result of a planned process, according to which Grillo became the 'megaphone' of a protest/civic movement and Casaleggio provided, in addition to the overall strategy, the necessary organization and communication infrastructure. If Grillo was the 'megaphone', Casaleggio was the man who plugged it in. In this way, leadership functions were deliberately distributed to the individuals who had the necessary resources for performing specific tasks.

A similar configuration also occurred in the subsequent 'popular stage' in the history of the M5S even though the co-leaders in this phase had to adapt their 'plans'—and, accordingly, their functions—to a new and more complex organizational environment. Some tasks were still planned in advance, on the basis of previous, pertinent experience, while in other circumstances Grillo and Casaleggio had to adapt their skills and attitudes to perform functions there were not contemplated in their professional expertise.

In light of the above, leadership roles and functions in this phase assumed a configuration that could be placed somewhere between the 'planful alignment', that is specified above, and the so-called spontaneous alignment. According to the latter configuration, leadership tasks were distributed in a less predefined or deliberate way, where "tacit and intuitive decisions about who should perform which leadership functions result in a fortuitous alignment of functions across leadership sources"

---

[26] The united trajectory of Grillo and Casaleggio has been strengthened also by the fact that both co-leaders did not seek public office and did not participate in national elections. Since the beginning, they remained 'outsider leaders', controlling the party from outside public office.

(Harris et al., 2007: 344). It is precisely during this period that Grillo played the roles of both the 'motivator' and the 'president', with no prior expertise in that field (as 'guarantor' of the basic principles of a political party). Likewise, Casaleggio had to reinvent himself as a party-builder, trying to provide efficient organization to a very loose and magmatic social movement. Therefore, the resulting alignment of leadership roles and functions was not based on a predefined plan but originated from a spontaneous process of trial and error, through which the two leaders came to share the power.

The dual leadership of Grillo and Casaleggio that we have just described lasted until 2014 when, for different reasons, both co-leaders took a 'step to the side' from their leading roles within the organization. That decision led, first, to the formation of the short-lived board of directors (or Directorate) and, then, to the selection of Luigi Di Maio as the formal 'political leader' of the M5S. Meanwhile, in accordance with the typical rules of inheritance, Davide Casaleggio became the president of the newly formed *Associazione Rousseau*, which is in control of the platform used by the Movement as a tool for internal decision-making.

Hence, the year 2014 inaugurated the beginning of a new type of leadership for the M5S (i.e., based on a multimember structure), with a different division of labor and a more complex configuration of leadership roles, profiles and functions. The degree of complementarity that we have seen above between Grillo and Casaleggio was no longer present and the division of labor presented various elements of confusion and ambiguity. For instance, Grillo continued to be the 'motivator' and the 'president' of the party, although over time the latter role was carried out in collaboration with the newly elected party leader, Luigi Di Maio, the new "television 'face' of the M5S" (Ceccarini & Bordignon, 2018: 361) for the outside world. At the same time, new (potential) 'motivators' emerged from the ranks of the 'party in public office', for instance, to name perhaps the most relevant, Alessandro Di Battista, a member of the Directorate and MP from 2013 to 2018.

The competition for the role of new 'motivator' in the M5S can be analyzed by looking at the number of interviews given by Grillo in comparison with other M5S leaders (see Fig. 6.3), or the number of newspaper articles mentioning the main party leaders over time (Fig. 6.4). As the figures make clear, until 2013 Grillo was the one and only 'voice' of the M5S, both in the newspapers and in television (Nizzoli, 2012;

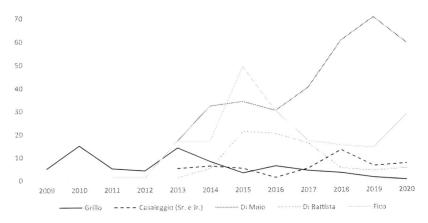

Fig. 6.3 Number of interviews given by the main leaders of the M5S in Italian newspapers, 2009–2020 (*Source* Authors' own compilation based on all articles included in the press review of the Chamber of Deputies)

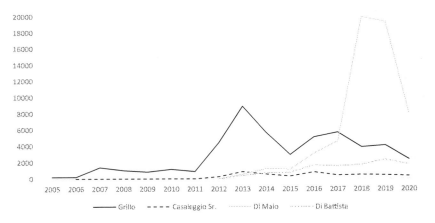

Fig. 6.4 Number of articles mentioning the main leaders of the M5S in Italian newspapers, 2005–2020 (*Source* Authors' own compilation based on the articles included in the press review of the Chamber of Deputies)

Barbieri, 2014; Bianchi et al., 2014; Bentivegna, 2014).[27] Then, with the advent of the formal stage in the history of the Movement, Grillo's monologue has been replaced by a cacophony of 'voices' of the new emerging leaders who are involved (in particular, Di Maio, Fico and Di Battista). In the final analysis, Grillo remained the guarantor and guardian of the Movement, acting as the formal 'president' of the party even though the role of 'motivator' was passed on to other actors who were in competition with each other. More specifically, this competition was strong especially during the three-year period from 2014 to 2016 among three emerging leaders: Alessandro Di Battista, Luigi Di Maio and Roberto Fico. As shown in Fig. 6.3, all three leaders surpassed Grillo in terms of number of interviews given to national newspapers. They were about to become the new spokespersons of the M5S and, at that time, it was still unclear who would become the political leader of the party. This period of uncertainty, that for a while was filled with the formation of the Directorate, came to an end only in summer 2017, when M5S members crowned Di Maio as the political leader of the Movement, while the "other aster of the 5-Star firmament, Di Battista, chose instead not to run in the [2018] legislative elections" (Ceccarini & Bordignon, 2018: 360), thus leaving a 'reserve' for future leadership.

Instead, concerning the organizational leadership of the Movement, many of the tasks performed by Gianroberto Casaleggio were passed in inheritance to his son, who became the new 'organizer' of the M5S, and who was responsible for the communication groups within the movement, the coordination between the elected members, the process of political recruitment and the supervision of the data concerning party membership. Davide Casaleggio was, in other words, the organizational manager of the M5S, the gatekeeper monitoring who is in and who is out of the Movement.

However, with the passing of one of the two co-leaders, one position remained open in the Movement: the 'strategist'. As we have previously explained, Gianroberto Casaleggio was the 'mind' behind the creation

---

[27] It is important to stress that Grillo's centrality in the communication strategy of the M5S also originated from the critical attitude of the party toward the traditional media. Therefore, going on television as talk-show guests was completely forbidden for both candidates and elected members of the Movement. This internal policy lasted until approximately 2015–2016 and, after that period, many high-profile M5S representatives became "veritable stars of talk shows" (Bordignon & Ceccarini, 2019: 148).

of the M5S and he had a plan for its organizational development. After his death in 2016, the function of setting a political direction for the Movement has been shared between different actors (Grillo, Di Maio, Casaleggio Jr., the Directorate), however, in not a very collaborative way because there was no longer a common vision of the future of the party organization. In some cases, especially for what concerned domestic politics, the strategic decisions were made by the political leader (Di Maio) in accordance with other high-profile MPs, the members of the Directorate and Casaleggio. Grillo was only involved in the most relevant or delicate decisions. In other circumstances, such as international relations and alliances with other parties at the EU-level (Iacoboni, 2018: 72), Davide Casaleggio has been the principal strategist. For instance, in 2014, when the M5S decided to join the group of the radical right in the European Parliament (EFDD: Europe for Freedom and Direct Democracy), the "agreement was reached personally between Davide Casaleggio and the leader of the EFDD's main party (UKIP), Nigel Farage, thus excluding M5S's MPs and MEPs from the decision-making process. M5S leaders did not meet with any other representatives of parliamentary groups" (Vittori, 2020: 10). A similar episode occurred two-and-a-half years later when Davide Casaleggio, in tandem with Grillo, tried to change the group affiliation in the European Parliament and to make a (failed) alliance with the Liberals led by Guy Verhofstadt.

Unlike the previous two phases in the evolution of the M5S, in the third 'formal stage' (2013–2017) leadership roles and tasks were, in many cases, overlapping. The "organizational leadership" of Casaleggio (Vittori, 2020: 10) was shared, to some extent, with the political leader Di Maio and (while it lasted) the members of the Directorate. As we have seen in the previous section, a clear task division between the two co-leaders with complementary skills and attitudes gave way to a less effective 'co-performance' structure in which a fistful of leaders exercise the same or a very similar function. This holds true for both the relations-oriented functions, mainly performed by Di Maio, Grillo and some other high-profile MPs, and the task-oriented function in which Casaleggio's organizational leadership is shared with other relevant actors.

As a consequence, the third phase of the M5S has been characterized by a configuration of leadership roles and functions that resembles what Leithwood et al. (2006) have defined as 'spontaneous misalignment'. In this case, despite the efforts made to build a more effective organizational structure, the roles and profiles within the organization were distributed in an unplanned manner. This situation within the M5S eventually led to a misalignment of leadership activities, where the same tasks were performed simultaneously by different leaders or different functions were exercised by a single actor.

Finally, the fourth and last phase in the organizational evolution of the M5S, which began in 2018, underwent significant changes. Beppe Grillo continued to play a modest role in the activities of the party. In many cases, especially when the stakes are very high, Grillo used his role and legitimacy as a kind of last-resort decision-maker, trying to solve the potential conflicts within the party. For instance, during the political crisis that in August 2019 brought about the fall of the first Conte government, the summer house of Beppe Grillo in the province of Livorno became headquarters for meetings between the most prominent leaders in the M5S (Davide Casaleggio, Alessandro Di Battista, Luigi Di Maio and Roberto Fico). A similar intervention occurred at the end of 2020, when Grillo (2020), with a post on his personal blog, clearly expresses his opposition to the activation of the European Stability Mechanism (ESM) credit line intended for health spending (Grillo, 2020).[28]

In some ways, the decision to replace the monocratic office of the political leader with a multimember body (the new Steering Committee) responded, on the one hand, to the need to reduce conflict concerning the control of the party's helm. On the other hand, the multimember arrangement tried to accommodate the preferences of the different party factions that emerged during the last years within the Movement. Although at this stage of the organizational development it is still difficult to distinguish between types of party sub-units in the M5S, we can certainly say that there are at least two *tendencies*, although they are loosely organized. On the one hand, in Panebianco's (1988: 25–27) terms, there are the "careerists" who have an office-oriented and pragmatic attitude, and on the other hand, there are the "believers" who have a more policy-oriented and ideological behavior. The 'collegial leadership' has been designed with the more or less explicit aim of accommodating the conflicting preferences of these two party factions/tendencies and has no intention to calibrate its composition on the basis of the different abilities of the leaders.

---

[28] An even more important role was played by Grillo in early 2021, after the termination of the second government led by Giuseppe Conte and the decision to support the new cabinet headed by Mario Draghi.

Indeed, the composition of the multimember body does not reflect a planful attribution or distribution of roles, tasks and functions. All five members are called upon to perform the same task, that is, setting the political direction of the M5S. In addition, this 'co-performance' arrangement does not take into consideration the possible complementarity, in terms of skills or expertise, between the members of the Steering Committee and, unlike in the past, within it there is neither a common vision nor a strong commitment on the future of the party organization.

With regard to the organizational aspects within the M5S, Davide Casaleggio is still playing a leading 'parallel' role in that field. Although his organizational leadership has been increasingly put into question by some M5S members, he remains in full control of the 'operating system' of the Movement. As the 'organizer-in-chief' of the party, he is in the position to exert a great deal of influence over the most important activities of the organization, from political recruitment to funding. Nevertheless, at the party congress held in November 2020, most of the delegates approved the proposal to transform the strict partnership between the M5S and the *Associazione Rousseau* (controlled and chaired by Davide Casaleggio) into a sort of business relationship, according to which the Association becomes nothing more than an external service provider for the party. It is too early to evaluate the consequences and the effectiveness of these changes, but what is already clear is that this decision has opened up a new line of conflicts within the M5S regarding the control over the party apparatus.

Overall, the new configuration of leadership roles and functions that we have just illustrated and that is currently at work in the M5S can be described as a case of 'anarchic misalignment' (see Table 6.4), characterized by "active rejection, on the part of some or many organizational leaders, of influence from others about what they should be doing in their own sphere of influence" (Leithwood et al., 2006: 227). As we have just seen, this 'active rejection' does not concern only the 'organizing' role of Casaleggio, which is overtly questioned especially by the members of the 'party in public office', but also other prominent figures of the party whose leading roles are increasingly disputed.

As a result, all current leadership roles and functions in the M5S are performed highly independently from each other, with a low degree of coordination among the different units and in competition on matters such as organizational goals and access to key resources. This situation has fuelled a sentiment of mistrust among the leaders and has put at

Table 6.4 Characteristics of the leadership structure in the four phases of the M5S

	Preliminary 2005–2008	Popular 2009–2012	Formal 2013–2017	Institutional 2018–2021
Type of leadership	Dual	Dual	Multimember	Multimember
Distribution of leadership	Power sharing	Power sharing	Power sharing	Power sharing
Formal hierarchy	No	No	Yes	Yes
Labor organization	Task division	Task division	Task division, co-performance	Co-performance, parallel performance
Alignment of leadership functions and roles	Planful alignment	Planful/spontaneous alignment	Spontaneous misalignment	Anarchic misalignment

Source Authors' own compilation

risk both the electoral performance and the organizational persistence of the party. If, after more than ten years from its creation, the M5S is still going through an uncertain process of institutionalization (Tronconi, 2015a; Vittori, 2020), a part of the explanation lies in its indeterminate and unstable leadership structure.

6.4 In conclusion: lessons from M5S plural leadership

The category of 'newborns', that is, parties completely formed from scratch, has been on the rise in the last fifteen years or so. Certainly, the Five Star Movement is one of the most successful exemplars in this category. Stemming from a spin-off from a blog created by two web gurus, Grillo and Casaleggio, it has become the largest party in Italy and a major partner in two consecutive governments. All this has happened in less than a decade.

As we have seen throughout this chapter, the role and nature of the leadership structure have exerted, among other factors, a major influence on the political trajectory of the Five Star Movement, from its foundation to its still tentative institutionalization. In particular, there are four lessons that can be drawn from the plural leadership adopted—and adapted over time—by the M5S.

The first lesson, which is in line with the analytical framework outlined in the first part of the book, is that plural leadership in political parties can also be based on a power-sharing arrangement rather than a more traditional (especially in the political realm) position-sharing distribution of tasks and roles. What is more, the case of the M5S shows that this particular distribution of power within the organization can be as effective as other modes of power distribution or concentration. This is especially true in the preliminary or the formative phases of a political party in which the flexibility and adaptability offered by a power-sharing solution can be more aligned with the needs of a party in the making. The history of the M5S is a case in point because its initial 'post-bureaucratic organization' and its peculiar leadership structure turned out to be crucial factors for understanding the subsequent evolution of the party.

The second lesson concerns the nature of the dual leadership that brought the M5S to a point of success. As we have stressed in the two previous sections, the duo made up of Grillo and Casaleggio is not just a fortuitous combination of individuals with different skills, expertise and attitudes. Quite the contrary, their meeting and, in particular, the perfect match between their different roles were strategically prepared in advance. It came from a planned alignment of their skills and orientations. The result was a 'united career' phenomenon, where the trajectories of the two co-leaders were so intertwined that they could not be easily disentangled. To a certain extent, the duo became a single, unified leadership, in which the face of the one was the flip side of the other. Obviously, both the flexibility and the effectiveness offered by a well-designed 'united career' are closely linked to the survival of the original dual leadership. Once that kind of relationship falls apart and it is put into question or loses its grip on the party organization, then the asset might become a liability for the party. Again, this is what happened in the M5S when the (united) dual leadership of Grillo and Casaleggio began to show the first signs of deflating between 2014 and 2016, with the passing of the latter and the 'stepping to the side' of the former. From that moment on, the initial dual leadership has developed, somewhat confusingly, into a multi-member leadership, which is, as we know, a whole new ballgame for a party organization.

The third lesson that can be drawn from the case study of the M5S relates precisely to the new multimember leadership that replaced the

Grillo-Casaleggio duo. In an organizational context that is still characterized by the existence of a power-sharing arrangement, the transition toward multimember leadership is full of obstacles and risks. In fact, if the distribution of roles, tasks and functions is to work, according to the logic of power sharing, when there are two complementary leaders who collaborate, having a common vision, the situation becomes far more complicated when there are multiple leaders in competition with one another, who have different strategies for the development of the party. In a way, the power-sharing arrangement for plural leadership is much more demanding than position sharing in terms of role complementarity and for the overall distribution of tasks and functions. Indeed, it requires a planned distribution of roles between various actors as well as a common framework for action. Instead, the M5S decided to build up a multimember leadership, still based on a power-sharing arrangement, but with no prior and clear distribution of labor among its circle of leaders. This brought about, first, a spontaneous and, then, an anarchic misalignment of leadership roles and functions, which led the M5S to the verge of an internal organizational crisis.

Finally, the fourth lesson derives from the interplay between leadership structure and the different stages in the organizational evolution of a political party. To put it differently, the challenges of party formation are different from the challenges of party institutionalization, and both may require different configurations of the leadership structure. As the case of the M5S makes clear, the formation of the M5S has benefitted greatly from the type of dual leadership embodied by its founding tandem Grillo-Casaleggio, that operated in a flexible and creative way thanks to the characteristics supplied by the power-sharing arrangement.

In contrast, the stage as well as the challenge of party institutionalization needs a completely different set of skills and profiles. As Bolleyer (2013: 52) put it, "the process of institutionalization is characterized by the need to balance and reconcile effective leadership and extraparliamentary structure formation". This is, in essence, the *"leadership-structure dilemma"* (Bolleyer, 2013: 52). That is, in other words, the inherent need in each new party's development, to find a balance between the leadership interests and those of the overall organization. As we have seen in this chapter, a carefully planned rearrangement of the leadership structure, in which different interests are combined into a multimember executive body, may be an option, if not a solution, to solving such an organizational dilemma. Up to now, the prospects offered by the recent evolution of the M5S do not look that promising but the jury is still out.

References

Alvarez, J. L., & Svejenova, S. (2005). *Sharing executive power: Roles and relationships at the top*. Cambridge University Press.

Bailo, F. (2020). *Online communities and crowds in the rise of the Five Star Movement*. Palgrave Macmillan.

Barbieri, G. (2014). Lo Tsunami Tour. *Comunicazione Politica*, 6(1), 171–185.

Bardi, L. (1996). Anti-party sentiment and party system change in Italy. *European Journal of Political Research*, 29(3), 345–363.

Becchi, P. (2016). *Cinquestelle & Associati. Il MoVimento dopo Grillo*. Kaos edizioni.

Bennett, W. L., Segerberg, A., & Knüpfer, C. B. (2018). The democratic interface: technology, political organization, and diverging patterns of electoral representation. *Information, Communication & Society*, 21(11), 1655–1680.

Bentivegna, S. (2014). Beppe Grillo's dramatic incursion into the Twittersphere: talking politics in 140 characters. *Contemporary Italian Politics*, 6(1), 73–88.

Bertsou, E., & Caramani, D. (Eds.). (2020). *The technocratic challenge to democracy*. Routledge.

Biancalana, C. (2020). From social movements to institutionalization: the Five-star Movement and the high-speed train line in Val di Susa. *Contemporary Italian Politics*, 12(2), 155–168.

Biancalana, C., & Piccio, R.D. (2017). L'organizzazione del Movimento 5 stelle: continuità o cambiamento? *Quaderni di Scienza Politica*, 24(3), 435–462.

Bianchi, V., Chianale, C., & Pulvirenti, A. (2014). La campagna elettorale 2013 in Tv. *Comunicazione Politica*, 6(1), 47–60.

Bickerton, C. J., & Invernizzi Accetti, C. (2018). 'Techno-populism' as a new party family: the case of the Five Star Movement and Podemos. *Contemporary Italian Politics*, 10(2), 132–150.

Biondo, N., & Canestrari, M. (2018). *Supernova. I segreti, le bugie e i tradimenti del Movimento 5 Stelle: storia vera di una nuova casta che si pretendeva anticasta*. Ponte alle Grazie.

Biondo, N., & Canestrari, M. (2019). *Il sistema Casaleggio. Partito, soldi, relazioni: ecco il piano per manomettere la democrazia*. Ponte alle Grazie.

Biorcio, R. (2014). The reasons for the success and transformations of the 5 Star Movement. *Contemporary Italian Politics*, 6(1), 37–53.

Biorcio, R. (2015). *Il populismo nella politica italiana. Da Bossi a Berlusconi, da Grillo a Renzi*. Mimesis.

Biorcio, R., & Natale, P. (2013). *Politica a 5 stelle. Idee storia e strategie del movimento di Grillo*. Feltrinelli.

Biorcio, R., & Natale, P. (2018). *Il Movimento 5 Stelle: dalla protesta al governo.* Mimesis.

Bischof, D., & Kurer, T. (2020). Does partisan grassroots mobilization matter in the digital age? https://doi.org/10.31235/osf.io/q3awj.

Bobba, G., & McDonnell, D. (2015). Italy: A strong and enduring market for populism. In H. Kriesi & T. S. Pappas (Eds.), *Populism in the shadow of the great recession* (pp. 159–174). ECPR Press.

Bobba, G., Legnante, G., Roncarolo, F., & Seddone, A. (2013). Candidates in a negative light. The 2013 Italian election campaign in the media. *Italian Political Science Review, 43*(3), 353–379.

Bolleyer, N. (2013). *New parties in old party systems: Persistence and decline in seventeen democracies.* Oxford University Press.

Bordignon, F. (2013). *Il partito del capo. Da Berlusconi a Renzi.* Apogeo-Maggioli.

Bordignon, F., & Ceccarini, L. (2013). Five stars and a cricket. Beppe Grillo shakes Italian politics. *South European Society and Politics, 18*(4), 427–449.

Bordignon, F. & Ceccarini, L. (2015). The five-star movement: A hybrid actor in the net of state institutions. *Journal of Modern Italian Studies, 20*(4), 454–473.

Bordignon, F., & Ceccarini, L. (2019). Five stars, five years, five (broken) taboos. In L. Ceccarini & J. L. Newell (Eds.), *The Italian general election of 2018: Italy in uncharted territory* (pp. 139–163). Palgrave Macmillan.

Calise, M. (2000). *Il partito personale.* Laterza.

Calise, M., & Musella, F. (2019). *Il Principe digitale.* Laterza.

Carty, K. R. (2004). Parties as franchise systems: the stratarchical organizational imperative. *Party Politics, 10*(1), 5–24.

Caruso, L. (2015). Il Movimento 5 Stelle e la fine della politica. *Rassegna Italiana Di Sociologia, 56*(2), 315–340.

Casaleggio, G., & Grillo, B. (2011). *Siamo in guerra. Per una nuova politica.* Chiarelettere.

Casaleggio, G. (2013). Censure e pregiudizi. Dalla Grecia antica alla rete. In D. Fo, G. Casaleggio, & Grillo, B., *Il Grillo canta sempre al tramonto. Dialogo sull'Italia e il Movimento 5 Stelle* (pp. 5–26). Chiarelettere.

Ceccanti, S., & Curreri, S. (2015). I partiti antisistema nell'esperienza italiana: il MoVimento 5 Stelle come partito personale autoescluso. *Diritto Pubblico Comparato Ed Europeo, 1*(3), 799–832.

Ceccarini, L., & Bordignon, F. (2016). The five stars continue to shine: The consolidation of Grillo's 'movement party' in Italy. *Contemporary Italian Politics, 8*(2), 131–159.

Ceccarini, L., & Bordignon, F. (2018). Towards the 5 Star party. *Contemporary Italian Politics, 10*(4), 346–362.

Ceri, P., & Veltri, F. (2017). *Il movimento nella rete. Storia e struttura del Movimento 5 Stelle*. Rosenberg & Sellier.

Chiapponi, F. (2017). *Democrazia, populismo, leadership: il Movimento 5 Stelle*. Epoké.

Corbetta, P. (2013). Conclusioni. Un web-populismo dal destino incerto. In P. Corbetta, & E. Gualmini (Eds.), *Il partito di Grillo* (pp. 197–214). Il Mulino.

Corbetta, P. (Ed.). (2017). *M5s. Come cambia il partito di Grillo*. Il Mulino.

Corbetta, P. (2018). M5s: i nodi che verrano al pettine. In M. Valbruzzi, & R. Vignati, *Il vicolo cieco. Le elezioni del 4 marzo 2018* (pp. 243–249). Il Mulino.

Corbetta, P., & Gualmini, E. (Eds.). (2013). *Il partito di Grillo*. Il Mulino.

Corbetta, P., & Vignati, R. (2014). Direct Democracy and scapegoats: the Five Star Movement and Europe. *The International Spectator, 49*(1), 53–64.

Cosenza, G. (2014). Grillo's communication style: from swear words to body language. *Contemporary Italian Politics, 6*(1), 89–101.

Crozier, M. (1964). *Bureaucratic phenomenon: An examination of bureauracy in modern organizations and its cultural setting in France*. The University of Chicago Press.

Della Porta, D., Fernández, J., Kouki, H., & Mosca, L. (2017). *Movement parties against austerity*. Polity Press.

De Rosa, R. (2013). The Five Stars Movement in the Italian political scenario. A case for cybercratic entralism? *eJournal of eDemocracy and Open Government, 5*(2), 128–140.

De Vries, C. E., & Hobolt, S. B. (2020). *Political entrepreneurs: The rise of challenger parties in Europe*. Princeton University Press.

Deseriis, M. (2017). Technopopulism: The emergence of a discursive formation. *TripleC: Communication, Capitalism & Critique, 15*(2), 441–458.

Diamanti, I. (2014). The 5 Star Movement: a political laboratory. *Contemporary Italian Politics, 6*(1), 4–15.

Di Battista, A. (2018). Di Battista: "Mai alleanze con chi ha distrutto il Paese o lascio il M5S". https://www.youtube.com/watch?v=Z5kyeXqzEfQ&feature=emb_title. Accessed 20 Jan 2021.

Di Maggio, M., & Perrone, M. (2019). The political culture of the Movimento Cinque Stelle, from foundation to the reins of government. *Journal of Modern Italian Studies, 24*(3), 468–482.

Duverger, M. (1964). *Political parties: Their organization and activity in the modern state*. Methuen.

Gerbaudo, P. (2019). *The digital party: Political organisation and online democracy*. Pluto Press.

Grillo, B. (2013). Censure e pregiudizi. Dalla Grecia antica alla rete. In D. Fo, G. Casaleggio, & Grillo, B., *Il Grillo canta sempre al tramonto. Dialogo sull'Italia e il Movimento 5 Stelle* (pp. 5–26). Chiarelettere.

Grillo, B. (2014). Consultazione Online - Comunicato Politico Numero Cinquantacinque. www.beppegrillo.it.
Grillo, B. (2020). La Mes è finita. https://www.beppegrillo.it/la-mes-e-finita/.
Harmel, R. (1985). On the study of new parties. *International Political Science Review, 6*(4), 403–418.
Harmel, R., & Svåsand, L. (1993). Party leadership and party institutionalisation: Three phases of development. *West European Politics, 16*(2), 67–88.
Harmel, R., Heo, U., Tan, A., & Janda, K. (1995). Performance, leadership, factions and party change: An empirical analysis. *West European Politics, 18*(1), 1–33.
Harris, A., Leithwood, K., Day, C., Sammons, P., & Hopkins, D. (2007). Distributed leadership and organizational change: Reviewing the evidence. *Journal of Educational Change, 8*(4), 337–347.
Hobolt, S. B., & Tilley, J. (2016). Fleeing the centre: the rise of challenger parties in the aftermath of the euro crisis. *West European Politics, 39*(5), 971–991.
Hopkin, J., & Paolucci, C. (1999). The business firm model of party organisation: cases from Spain and Italy. *European Journal of Political Research, 35*(3), 307–339.
Hopper, R. D. (1950). The revolutionary process: a frame of reference for the study of revolutionary movements. *Social Forces, 28*(3), 270–279.
Iacoboni, J. (2018). *L'esperimento. Inchiesta sul Movimento 5 Stelle*. Laterza.
Iacoboni, J. (2019). *L'esecuzione. 5 Stelle da movimento a governo*. Laterza.
Ignazi, P. (2020). The failure of mainstream parties and the impact of new challenger parties in France, Italy and Spain. *Italian Political Science Review*. https://doi.org/10.1017/ipo.2020.26.
Inglehart, R. F. (1977). *The silent revolution. Changing values and political styles among Western republics*. Princeton University Press.
Kantorowicz, E. (1957). *The King's two Bodies: A study in medieval political theology*. Princeton University Press.
Karremans, J., Malet, G., & Morisi, D. (2019). Italy – The end of bipolarism: restructuration in an unstable party system. In S. Hutter & H. Kriesi (Eds.), *European party politics in time of crisis* (pp. 118–138). Cambridge University Press.
Kitschelt, H. (2006). Movement parties. In R. S. Katz & W. Crotty (Eds.), *Handbook of party politics* (pp. 278–290). Sage Publications.
Lanfrey, D. (2011). Il Movimento dei Grillini tra meetup, meta-organizzazione e democrazia del monitoraggio. In C. Vaccari, & L. Mosca (Eds.) *Nuovi media, nuova politica? Partecipazione e mobilitazione online da MoveOn al Movimento 5 stelle* (pp. 143–166). Franco Angeli.
Lanzone, M. E., & Tronconi, F. (2015). Between blog, social networks and territory: activists and grassroots organization. In F. Tronconi (Ed.), *Beppe Grillo's*

Five Star Movement: Organisation, communication and ideology (pp. 53–73). Ashgate.

Leithwood, K., Mascall, B., Strauss, T., Sacks, R., Memon, N., & Yashkina, A. (2006). Distributing leadership to make schools smarter. In K. Leithwood, B. Mascall, & T. Strauss (Eds.), *Distributed leadership according to the evidence* (pp. 223–251). Routledge.

Lioy, A., Esteve Del Valle, M., & Gottlieb, J. (2019). Platform politics: Party organisation in the digital age. *Information Polity, 24*(1), 41–58.

Mair, P., & Mudde, C. (1998). The party family and its study. *Annual Review of Political Science, 1*(1), 211–229.

McDonnell, D. (2013). Silvio Berlusconi's personal parties: from Forza Italia to the Popolo della Libertà. *Political Studies, 61*(S1), 217–233.

McDonnell, D., & Valbruzzi, M. (2014). Defining and classifying technocrat-led and technocratic governments. *European Journal of Political Research, 53*(4), 654–671.

Morosini, M. (2019). *Snaturati. Dalla social-ecologia al populismo*. Castelvecchi.

Mosca, L. (2020). Democratic vision and online participatory spaces in the Italian Movimento 5 Stelle. *Acta Politica, 55*(1). https://doi.org/10.1057/s41269-018-0096-y.

Mosca, L., & Vaccari, C. (2013). Il Movimento e la rete. In P. Corbetta & E. Gualmini (Eds.), *Il partito di Grillo* (pp. 169–196). Il Mulino.

Mosca, L., Vaccari, C., & Valeriani, A. (2015). An internet-fuelled party? The Movimento 5 Stelle and the web. In F. Tronconi (Ed.), *Beppe Grillo's Five Star Movement: Organisation, communication and ideology* (pp. 127–151). Ashgate.

Mosca, L., & Tronconi, F. (2019). Beyond left and right: the eclectic populism of the Five Star Movement. *West European Politics, 42*(6), 1258–1283.

Mudde, C. (2004). The Populist Zeitgeist. *Government and Opposition, 39*(4), 541–563.

Musso, M., & Maccaferri, M. (2018). At the origins of the political discourse of the 5- Star Movement (M5S): Internet, direct democracy and the "future of the past." *Internet Histories, 2*(1–2), 98–120.

Natale, P. (2014). The birth, early history and explosive growth of the Five Star Movement. *Contemporary Italian Politics, 6*(1), 16–36.

Navarria, G. (2019). *The networked citizen: Power, politics, and resistance in the Internet age*. Palgrave.

Nizzoli, A. (2012). Il Grillo silente. La comunicazione del Movimento 5 Stelle nelle amministrative 2012. *Comunicazione politica, 4*(3), 525–532.

Panebianco, A. (1988). *Political parties: Organization and power*. Cambridge University Press.

Passarelli, G., Tronconi, F., & Tuorto, D. (2013). Dentro il Movimento: organizzazione, attivisti e programmi. In P. Corbetta & E. Gualmini (Eds.), *Il partito di Grillo* (pp. 123–167). Il Mulino.
Passarelli, G., Tronconi, F., & Tuorto, D. (2017). "Chi dice organizzazione dice oligarchia": cambiamento e contraddizioni della forma organizzativa del Movimento. In P. Corbetta (Ed.), *M5s. Come cambia il partito di Grillo* (pp. 163–194). Il Mulino.
Pasquino, G., & Valbruzzi, M. (2012). Non-partisan governments Italian-style: decision-making and accountability. *Journal of Modern Italian Studies, 17*(3), 612–629.
Pasquino, G., & Valbruzzi, M. (2013). Post-electoral politics in Italy: institutional problems and political perspectives. *Journal of Modern Italian Studies, 18*(4), 466–484.
Pedersen, M. N. (1982). Towards a new typology of party lifespans and minor parties. *Scandinavian Political Studies, 5*(1), 1–16.
Pirro, A. L. P. (2018). The polyvalent populism of the 5 Star Movement. *Journal of Contemporary European Studies, 26*(4), 443–458.
Rokkan, S. (1970). *Citizens, elections, parties.* Universitetsforlaget.
Rucht, D. (2012). Leadership in social and political movements: a comparative exploration. In L. Helms (Ed.), *Comparative political leadership* (pp. 99–118). Palgrave Macmillan.
Sartori, G. (1976). *Parties and party systems. A framework for analysis.* Cambridge University Press.
Tarchi, M. (2018). *L'Italia populista. Dal qualunquismo a Beppe Grillo.* Bologna: Il Mulino.
Tyrnauer, M. (2004). So Very Valentino. *Vanity Fair*, August.
Tronconi, F. (Ed.). (2015a). *Beppe Grillo's Five Star Movement: Organisation, communication and ideology.* Ashgate.
Tronconi, F. (2015b). Conclusion: the organisational and ideological roots of the electoral success. In F. Tronconi (Ed.), *Beppe Grillo's Five Star Movement: Organisation, communication and ideology* (pp. 213–229). Ashgate.
Tronconi, F. (2018). The Italian Five Star Movement during the crisis: towards normalisation? *South European Society and Politics, 23*(1), 163–180.
Tronconi, F., & Valbruzzi, M. (2020). Populism put to the polarisation test: The 2019–20 election cycle in Italy. *South European Society and Politics.* https://doi.org/10.1080/13608746.2020.1821465.
Vassallo, S., & Valbruzzi, M. (2018). I partiti della Grande Recessione contro i partiti della Grande Depressione. Un nuovo *cleavage* o un'altra bolla? *Stato e mercato, 38*(1), 87–116.
Vignati, R. (2013). Beppe Grillo: dalla Tv ai palasport, dal blog al Movimento. In P. Corbetta & E. Gualmini (Eds.), *Il partito di Grillo* (pp. 29–63). Il Mulino.

Vignati, R. (2015a). Beppe Grillo and the Movimento 5 Stelle: a brief history of a 'leaderist' movement with a leaderless ideology. In F. Tronconi (Ed.), *Beppe Grillo's Five Star Movement: Organisation, communication and ideology* (pp. 9–28). Ashgate.

Vignati, R. (2015b). The organization of the Movimento 5 Stelle: A contradictory party model. In F. Tronconi (Ed.), *Beppe Grillo's Five Star Movement: Organisation, communication and ideology* (pp. 29–52). Ashgate.

Vignati, R. (2017). Dai comuni al Parlamento: il Movimento entra nelle istituzioni. In P. Corbetta (Ed.), *M5s. Come cambia il partito di Grillo* (pp. 23–62). Il Mulino.

Vittori, D. (2018). Party change in anti-establishment parties in government: the case of Five Stars Movement and SYRIZA. *Italian Political Science, 13*(2), 78–91.

Vittori, D. (2019). *Il valore di uno. Il Movimento 5 Stelle e l'esperimento della democrazia diretta.* Luiss University Press.

Vittori, D. (2020). Which organization for which party? An organizational analysis of the five-star movement. *Contemporary Italian Politics.* https://doi.org/10.1080/23248823.2020.1838868.

Wolinetz, S. W. (2002). Beyond the catch-all party: approaches to the study of parties and party organization in contemporary democracies. In R. Gunther, J. R. Montero, & J. J. Linz (Eds.), *Political parties: Old concepts and new challenges* (pp. 136–165). Oxford University Press.

Zulianello, M. (2018). Anti-System parties revisited: concept formation and guidelines for empirical research. *Government and Opposition, 53*(4), 653–681.

Zulianello, M. (2020). Varieties of populist parties and party systems in Europe: from state-of-the-art to the application of a novel classification scheme to 66 parties in 33 countries. *Government and Opposition, 55*(2), 327–347.

CHAPTER 7

Conclusion

7.1 The Theoretical Framework Put to the Proof

This book presents the exploration of a phenomenon that has not, as yet, been thoroughly studied and that should be examined further, which is, namely, the presence of two or more leaders at the apex of political party organizations. Therefore, our first step was to build a theoretical framework in order to provide a guide to the empirical research. In Chapters 2 and 3, a conceptualization of collective leadership and advanced heuristic hypotheses about its functioning and sustenance have been proposed. Then, in Chapters 4, 5 and 6, a detailed analysis of three cases has been offered, which we consider to be relevant and particularly paradigmatic of the many faces that collective leadership may assume.

In this concluding chapter a summary of the main findings is presented. First, we illustrate what we have learned from the three case studies, the Alliance 90/The Greens, Alternative for Germany (AfD) and the Five Star Movement (M5S), with the objective of checking the usefulness and the explicatory potential of our theoretical framework. Then, we proceed to offer reflections about the mechanisms underlying plural leadership in the hope that they could serve as fruitful guidelines for further analyses. In particular, through a presentation of similarities and differences among the three cases, we attempt to advance some possible generalizations, and also to highlight the relevance of specific country characteristics. Finally, the chapter concludes by proposing directions for future research.

First, among the several observations derived from the analysis of the three political parties we analyzed, it is worth stressing the adaptability of the organizational structure of collective leadership. We selected our cases in part because they seem to be characterized by plural leadership as a constant feature; therefore, they were preferred to others in which collective leadership appeared to be a more exceptional and temporary experience. However, if adherence to the general model proved to be stable over time, actually, all three parties experienced changes in the configuration of the number of leaders. A structural simplification characterized the history of the German Greens, which went from multimember to dual leaderships, paralleled by a slow and continuous process of increased acceptance of formal leadership in a grassroots party. The AfD has recently been led by couples, after an initial triad was in power (even though, in principle, there has not been any restriction as the statute contains the provision for leadership to be shared among two or three chairs). On the contrary, the M5S was founded by a duo, which then shifted toward forms of multimember leadership whose specific configuration seems to respond to contingent factors. This suggests that collective leadership is not a rigid structure, but it is likely to evolve through a process of adjustments and revisions. Therefore, it can be prefigured as a flexible instrument that is adaptable to different institutional settings and multiple circumstances.

Let us proceed now by discussing in detail the conceptualization presented in Chapter 1 in light of the main findings. One of the key dimensions we have adopted for classifying instances of collective leadership has been the distinction between position sharing and power sharing. The three cases were selected because they seem to present a certain variety in this respect, since the German Greens and the AfD appear to be examples of formal collective leadership, while the M5S has always relied on informal arrangements in which people holding different positions have shared power and influence. In this regard, the empirical analysis has shown that the two types are not always actually alternative arrangements.

In some cases, the scenario certainly appears to be streamlined. In the AfD, for instance, initially formal party chairs shared the most prominent position in the party and only over time did group leadership and factions gradually become included in a power-sharing agreement. The M5S has been confirmed to be a case of typical power sharing. But things are not always so crystal-clear, since, for example, the German Greens have for the most part experienced phases in which position sharing between formal chairs or spokespersons was sidelined by the involvement of other individuals with different roles, who participated in a *de facto* multimember leadership. In particular, this was evident during the years when Joschka Fischer was a minister in the federal government. He never held a formal leadership position in the party in central office; nevertheless, he was the most prominent and popular figure among green politicians. More generally, it should be observed that, in the early years especially, the Greens' formal leaders were actually party spokespersons (as was their official title). They were not in charge of classical leadership functions, which were instead distributed among a larger group of people. In most of the phases of party history, the ruling team included party representatives in public offices, such as ministers, heads of parliamentary groups and other prominent people in the executive body, such as the party secretaries. The current leadership duo seems to be the sole exception in which the two party chairs command clear authority and constitute the undisputed and unchallenged heads of the party.

In other words, it could be concluded that the existence of position sharing gives certain shape and structure to the relationship between two or more leadership partners who have the same role and rank. However, the two categories that we have defined—position sharing and power sharing—should not, necessarily, be regarded as being mutually exclusive. Only the analysis of how the several functions of leadership are distributed can tell us how many people are active parts of the ruling team and, therefore, whether there are other leaders, beyond the formal ones, that should be included in the group who exerts real influence at the top. In principle, a formal individual leader may also share power with other people, so forms of power sharing may in fact exist without any formal position sharing.

This reflection suggests that, in order to truly understand how a collective arrangement works and who really performs essential leadership functions, the most important factor to be considered is the second dimension which we have identified, that is, the division of labor and, consequently, the complementarity among leaders.

The analysis of the three cases allowed us to highlight some aspects regarding the division of labor and complementarity in different configurations of plural leadership. Considering the German Greens, there has been an evolution from an initial diffusion of power among a group of people (including some who were officially appointed, mainly those in charge of speaking for the party, as well as others performing further tasks), to an arrangement in which the appointed party chairs have gradually become more authoritative leaders. The division of labor, and its effectiveness, has depended on the individual characteristics of leaders and on specific contextual features. The current leadership duo, composed of Annalena Baerbock and Robert Habeck, is a good example of a well-integrated team that is based on a division of tasks, but also capable of supporting and complementing each other. Their decision to merge the offices of the two party chairs into a single office is a distinct indication of their cooperative attitude, which is facilitated by their affiliation to the same party wing. With their efficient division of tasks and their attempt to present a truly equal team, it is hard to assign clear-cut roles according to Rucht's (2012) category. However, by taking into account their slightly different popularity with the base, Habeck could be considered as the president and Baerbock as the organizer. In their handling of the new, basic program, they shared the role of strategist and defined a path forward as a pragmatic, environmentalist-left wing party that is more or less abandoning any remaining radical impulses. It remains to be seen how Annalena Baerbock's additional role as chancellor candidate destabilizes this model that was built on formal equality of the two chairpersons.

The scenario appears quite different in the AfD where the dominant aspect of all leadership duos and teams seems to be the high degree of competition among leaders. Soon after the party foundation, the leadership style of Bernd Lucke proved to be incompatible with a collective leadership arrangement. His departure, however, has not made room for the formation of genuine cooperative duos. The relationship of his successors, Frauke Petry and Jörg Meuthen, was far from affable. In principle, there could have been an improved complementarity with Petry as the 'face' of the party and with Meuthen more concerned with the organization. However, Petry's attitude for pushing herself to the fore, and her attempts to gather followers that were loyal to her, prevented the establishment of a harmonious arrangement. Among the highs and lows, the AfD leadership has remained predominantly conflictual and dominated by factionalism, with a distribution of tasks and power that is not planned but, rather, to use Leithwood et al. (2006)'s terminology, that is conducive to "spontaneous alignments" or "misalignments" of leadership functions depending on the circumstances.

Finally, the M5S is a particularly interesting case study due to the fact that the founding and popular stages of the party have been characterized by a perfectly designed division of labor. The co-leaders/co-founders possessed complementary skills and attitudes. They shared a common project and were strongly committed to the future of the party. They were two sides of the same coin. Grillo was the public face of the party (president and motivator), while Casaleggio was the 'private' leader, working behind the scenes as the organizer, but also acting as the strategist who provided direction and vision. It can, therefore, be argued that the initial success of the M5S was due, among other factors, to a successful alignment of leadership roles and functions, especially while the two co-founders remained 'in the game'. In contrast, the difficulties that eventually emerged in the subsequent phases of the party can be, at least partially, interpreted as failed attempts to replace the original harmonious arrangement between Grillo and Casaleggio.

In Chapter 3 we advanced a number of heuristic hypotheses about the genesis and the sustenance of collective leadership. Such hypotheses stemmed both from the research on collective leadership in other fields and from various examples of interactions within dyads or teams at the top of political organizations and institutions. Now we will discuss whether they have or have not been confirmed through the analyses of the three cases. As for the reasons leading a party to the adoption of collective leadership, it can be said that the detailed illustration of the history of the German Greens has confirmed what we have observed regarding the political family of Greens and their ideological adherence to a democratic governance in which hierarchies are kept to a minimum. In other words, in the case of the German Greens, collective leadership may be regarded as a matter of vocation, although over the passage of time they moved toward an increasing verticalization, with the current party chairs now having more central authority than the party spokespersons in the early phases. In contrast, the case of AfD is highly representative of position sharing that has little to do with ideal choices but that emerges from a very pragmatic need to handle factionalism and preserve the unity of the party. Finally, the path of the M5S seems to follow the typical evolution of those movements for which collective leadership is a genetic trait, which is also maintained during the phase of institutionalization. At the same time, however, if one looks at the M5S in the context of the crisis of Italian mainstream parties, it may be suggested that the preference for a form of collective leadership, which in M5S's case is entangled with the refusal of politics as a profession and the myth of direct democracy, has also represented a powerful signal of renewal. Moreover, in the last stage of the party's organizational evolution, the search for an arrangement based on a new type of multimember leadership that could also be sanctioned in formal way through the establishment of a collegial executive body, instead of the former political chief, may also be considered to be a response to emerging party factionalism.

In Chapter 3, among the heuristic hypotheses, we also included the suggestion that differences in the institutional or formal mechanisms exert a remarkable impact on the shaping of collective leadership. In this regard, our three cases offer several stimulating insights. First, the analysis of Greens and AfD has confirmed that collective leadership may imply different selection methods of party leaders. For a long time the Greens were committed to a high turnover, but this aspect was considered less important with the passage of time, coinciding with the increasing centrality of party leaders. Without formal provisions, a routine was established in order to avoid complete leadership turnovers, (despite the anti-elitist sentiments within the "party on the ground"), to allow for at least some form of continuity. Nevertheless, the composition changed annually or biannually from 2005 when longer tenures of four or more years became the norm (Claudia Roth chaired the party for nine years from 2004 to 2013, and Cem Özdemir for 10 years). While there was typically some pre-electoral coordination to generate a balanced ticket (e.g., gender, factions, regions), ultimately the candidates competed individually. This was the same in the AfD, where, after the original founding meeting, the first three-person leadership was undisputed. The end of their first term resulted in the election loss and subsequent departure of Lucke. Petry exited the party abruptly after the federal elections in 2017. Meuthen managed to secure his election as party chair multiple times, each time with a different person by his side. In principle, this fuels a competition that cannot be easily transformed into friendly and productive cooperation once in office (the several narrow votes of the AfD executive committee on crucial issues demonstrate this). As for leadership tenure, the Greens abolished rotation requirements in their reform phase, and the AfD never defined any restrictions in this respect.

Second, albeit in different ways, all three cases directed attention to the role of electoral leaders, since their relationship with party leaders could become a crucial point in collective leadership arrangements. In presidential and semi-presidential systems, the direct election of the head of state requires a formal procedure of nomination of the presidential candidate, which is not necessarily the party leader. In France, for instance, the coincidence of the two roles is frequent. However, it is not to be taken for granted, especially for parties adopting the primary system. For instance, Ségolenè Royal in 2007, François Hollande in 2012 and François Fillon in 2017 were all nominated although they were not the party leaders. In parliamentary systems, since the prime minister is not directly elected by the people, the identification of the lead electoral candidate is usually not formally defined. The party leader is often the most prominent candidate and, during the electoral campaign, he or she is in charge of leading the campaign. It may occur that the party leader presents himself or herself as the prospective prime minister in case of a victory even if it is well known that post-electoral agreements may produce coalition governments that are not led by the leader of the largest party.

Interestingly enough, the scenario has never been that simple in our three cases, also due to country-specific practices. In Germany the top electoral candidates (*Kanzlerkandidaten*) are not necessarily the party leaders (Helms, 2020). The German Greens presented a distinct, single, leading candidate for the first time with Joschka Fischer by taking into account his enormous popularity that superimposed the intraparty norms against strong individual leaders. The Greens came to understand the value of promoting prominent, popular green politicians for election campaigns. At the same time, this was a strategy to reduce the complexity of the two dual leaderships of party and group to at least two accentuated candidates. This elevates two candidates from the power-sharing arrangement in order to more clearly signal a coherent party strategy than offer a multitude of competing voices. The decision in 2013 and 2017 to appoint these candidates through a direct intra-party vote also meant a way to overcome factional gridlock. Currently, the Green leadership of Annalena Baerbock and Robert Habeck entertains an elevated position, based on their actual division of labor, their apparent complementarity and their popularity within the party. This meant that the party chair positions were automatically understood as leading candidates for the 2021 election. The situation in 2021 is in so far different, as the enduring strength of the Greens in the polls forced the party to nominate one single chancellor candidate. Ultimately, only one person can hold the office of chancellor, the German constitution has no provision for collective leadership in the top government position. The undramatic decision-making process to nominate Baerbock is another indicator speaking for a stable leadership arrangement as a sound base to resolve contentious issues on.

As for the AfD, the party did not present leading electoral candidates in addition to its multimember leadership in 2013. In the 2017 elections, a party congress appointed Alexander Gauland and Alice Weidel, neither of whom was a party chair. The conflict behind this decision indicated that the party base turned away from the formal chair, Petry, who up to that time had been the most well-known among AfD politicians, foreshadowing her subsequent departure. Given the short history of the AfD, we cannot predict whether the preference for denying party chairs a position as leading electoral candidates will become the norm or if it was related to specific conditions concerning Petry. As a matter of fact, the AfD seems to cultivate an attitude of constraining the leaders who appear too ambitious, as has already happened with Lucke, and keeping the two roles separated certainly may be an effective strategy.

As for M5S, in the 2013 election the situation was unusual in that Grillo appeared as the iconic spokesperson of the movement and the undisputable communicator in chief. It should be stressed that Italy has a peculiar electoral law, requiring the explicit nomination of the parties' or coalitions' 'political head'. Consequently, the M5S nominated Beppe Grillo even though he was not a candidate for parliament. Actually, it is worth noting that neither Grillo nor Casaleggio were ever candidates for the party or interested in pursuing a 'political' career within the institutions. In a subsequent phase, in a more traditional fashion, Luigi Di Maio incarnated the roles of political chief and the electoral guide even if his name was not included with the electoral symbol on the ballot[1] and he was surrounded by other partners who were involved in the propaganda campaign, as shown in Chapter 6.

Finally, with regard to the dynamics existing between premiership and party leadership, not much can be said about the German cases, since neither of the two parties has headed a federal cabinet until now. In contrast, the analysis of the two Conte cabinets in Italy may certainly be informative (Valbruzzi, 2018). Indeed, in Chapter 6, we have seen how the presence of an external actor of the party collective leadership may trigger an organizational change of the leadership structure. Conte's surge to a high level of popularity, coinciding with a party electoral setback,

---

[1] In Italy, it is quite common, even if not mandatory, that the party or the coalition symbol contains the name of the leader.

may have contributed to challenge the influence of the political leader, Di Maio. As described in Chapter 6, the opening of this crisis went beyond the *persona* of Di Maio. In fact, he has not been simply replaced, but this led to a re-definition of the organizational arrangement toward a (more or less temporary) expansion of the multimember leadership.

A further issue that we have discussed in Chapter 3 is the importance of personal bonds among leaders, either in encouraging the formation of collective leadership or in maintaining it. Could it be argued that committed, durable and somehow affective associations among leaders give rise to more efficient and fruitful collective leadership? The analysis of the M5S offered us the opportunity to observe the case of a "united career" at work (Alvarez & Svejenova, 2005). The meeting between Beppe Grillo and Gianroberto Casaleggio, the famous comedian and the entrepreneur with a penchant for the new technologies, initiated a durable association and a successful and fulfilling endeavor, cemented by their high complementarity. Up to Casaleggio's illness and his subsequent death, the dual leadership ruling the M5S worked well. As observed above, each leader effectively performed different leadership functions within the movement. What followed after the turnover of this first leadership duo resulted in a more flawed arrangement. First of all, the new leadership structure was more articulated, featuring a shift from a dyad to a multimember team in which the emergence of different viewpoints could not be avoided. Grillo continued to play the role of founding father, but he stepped down from a more active involvement in the party leadership, leaving room for other 'faces' of the movement. None of the other members of the leadership team, however, first of all the new 'capo politico' (political leader) Luigi Di Maio and the direct replacement of Casaleggio, his son Davide, enjoyed the same degree of legitimacy as the two founders. So, tensions exploded, especially when the party entered a regressive phase, characterized by repeated electoral setbacks.

A strong bond such as that of Grillo and Casaleggio could not be found in the history of the other two political parties. The different duos of German Green leaders have experienced more or less harmonious relationships, but they always started out as individuals who were vying for a position, who then developed a working relationship. In contrast, as already stressed, the case of AfD was characterized more by competition and internal struggle. On the other hand, it demonstrates that collective leadership may tolerate a certain degree of conflict if other incentives sustain it. If adhesion to the model has never been jeopardized, however, the single duos or teams are exposed to dissolution, as seen with the departure of Lucke in 2015 and Petry in 2017.

In conclusion, it would be a mistake to assume that collective leadership means collaborative in any case. It could be argued that a well-established and peaceful relationship among leaders may be more productive or efficient (but of course more empirical research would be needed to support this statement); but surely the coexistence of competitive players alone does not prevent the development and the survival of dual or multimember leadership.

7.2 Country-Specificities in the Analysis of Cases of Collective Leadership

As we have seen in the previous section, while the Italian M5S was built on a complementary relationship between its two founders, the two German cases demonstrate a link between intraparty factionalism and collective leadership. Collective leadership was necessary for managing the heterogeneity of the parties at the time of their founding. In the Green party, early factionalism reflected not only policy disagreement but also a disagreement between those seeking pragmatic engagement in the existing institutional setting and those seeking to depart from the established style of politics. Having multiple leaders as advocates for the different tendencies helped to build an actual party organization and moderate conflicts. In the AfD, collective leadership created space for different policy priorities, while also paying respect to the different organizations from which the party had emerged. This pluralistic appeal broadened the parties' appeal, but also created conflict within leadership. The chairs represented particular group interests instead of working together to integrate the party, reinforcing rather than moderating conflicts. This in turn affected the preferences of the party base in selecting party leaders, where considerations about a potential complementarity were ignored.

For the German Greens, collective leadership reflected a broader commitment to "alternative politics" (Poguntke, 1993) that spoke to expectations of the party's base, but ultimately impeded an effective role as a new challenger in the party system. As part of a comprehensive and gradual reform process, which moved the party closer in structure to its competitors and elevated policy goals over organizational innovation, the multimember leadership was reduced to a dual leadership and other constraints eliminated. Simultaneously, actors in the party established routines to employ the unique set-up in a productive and gainful way. The last and current phase of the party history, after the participation in the federal government, saw a high stability of leadership and multiple examples of a successful complementarity and division of labor.

The AfD has not experienced a similar process yet (of course the party is significantly younger than the Greens). While at first glance the evolution of the AfD so far exhibits similar characteristics (i.e., positioning itself as a radical outsider aiming to disrupt and change the existing order), the euro-skeptic platform is mixed with populist elements (Decker, 2016). This introduces an anti-pluralist spirit, as the AfD claims to represent the homogeneous people against the allegedly corrupt elites (Mudde & Rovira Kaltwasser, 2017), opening the floodgates for nationalist and xenophobic positions. Parties with similar positions typically turn to a strong leader figure as these positions align with authoritarian and strongman perceptions of politics (Heinisch & Mazzoleni, 2016). In adopting collective leadership, therefore, the AfD is an outlier among populist movements. Admittedly, the collective leadership has functioned merely briefly in the foundational phase and subsequently became engulfed in intraparty struggles. With the deep internal divisions it is difficult to imagine the chairs jointly pursuing a successful integration strategy either way, but in addition the party picked individuals as leaders who had no aspirations or capabilities to take on such an endeavor. The AfD has experienced a process of escalation and increasing infighting in the executive committee. In its seventh year, the party is time and time again in danger of a split. Continuous defections by prominent party members or parliamentarians as well as splits of party groups on subnational level substantiate this risk.

Despite difficulties with collective leadership both parties managed to reach the lifespan threshold of representation (and the Greens of executive power). This raises the question whether, notwithstanding negative effects because of low unity, opting for a single leader at time of foundation might have prevented this trajectory. It is at least doubtful if a single chairperson would have been able to manage the existing high levels of conflict and dissent. Therefore, it could be a good strategy to include failed cases of collective leadership into future analyses to assess at what point an ineffective team becomes truly damaging to a party's evolution and establishment.

A shared characteristic of all three cases is their reluctance to conform to an established party organizational model. The German Greens evolved from social movements. In setting up their party they attempted to balance the tension between egalitarian demands of activists and the necessities of some form of hierarchical party organization. The M5S originated from Grillo's blog and first organized itself through local meet-up groups. In addition, the party strongly relies on populist, anti-establishment ideas. The other Italian parties are described as detached from ordinary people and part of a cartel, which the M5S wishes to distance itself from. They share this notion with the AfD which employs a similar populist rhetoric, labeling their competitors as *Altparteien* (old parties). The AfD was not based on a movement but did bring together multiple distinct groups that overlapped in their criticism of the EU (Bebnowksi, 2015). Both the M5S and AfD omitted any references to a "party" in choosing their names. In this sense, collective leadership was an additional symbol used to draw a distinction between them and traditional parties led by a single leader. For the Greens and M5S it is even doubtful whether at the time of foundation there was an explicit goal of becoming a full-fledged party at all. This was an extensive debate in the Green party. Grillo and Casaleggio shared a strong rejection of traditional Italian politics and wanted to exert pressure on the established parties. Organizing activists and sympathizers with online tools was not necessarily considered as a natural first step toward the formation of a new political party. The links to movements and the rejection of established parties fundamentally undermined the authority of party leadership. The origin in a movement or as a merger of existing organizations explains the decision to implement collective leadership, but also has an impact on effectiveness and complementarity.

All three cases share the use of novel means for determining party policy. In the 1980s the Greens did so through statutes and rules of procedure, while the M5S did so by following the so-called pirate parties in the adoption of new online technologies (Bieber & Leggewie, 2014; Bolleyer et al., 2015). The Internet and social media enable low-threshold methods of online deliberation and collaboration. Just as with the Greens in the 1980s, party leaders of the pirate parties again were reduced to a role of spokespersons for the positions generated by techniques of "liquid democracy" (Blum & Zuber, 2016). However, in the M5S there was tension between methods of online deliberation and the accentuated role of the co-founder Grillo. Independent of the outcome of the former, Grillo would often have the final say. In this respect, the AfD is an interesting mix. The populist rhetoric bolstered direct democratic demands, putting more weight on decision-making in referenda and less on debates and deliberation within a party organization. Nevertheless, it initially followed the Greens' example in organizing party congresses open to all members, clearly extending the realm of participation. The integration of social media on the other hand was top-down. The party understood the potential of online platforms to disseminate populist and provocative content, reaching and mobilizing a wide audience (Serrano et al., 2019).

At least in theory, the technological advances allow party members to engage more directly in deliberation and decision-making and therefore reduce the number of tasks delegated to party leadership. However, the short-lived existence of the various pirate parties demonstrates limits to this technocratic understanding of party organizations as a mere shell for policy processes that supposedly can be updated with digital technologies. Because the three parties we analyzed differ in age and strategy, we cannot draw general conclusions, but we could hypothesize that the embrace of digital activism increases the likelihood of collective leadership. At the same time the implementation of novel technologies affects how (collective) leadership can be exercised.

All of our cases reveal that the various life stages of a party affect the set-up and functioning of collective leadership models. First and foremost, the existence of a parliamentary group potentially challenges the party chairs and the party in central office. While this tension is often resolved by merging offices of party and group leader, this was not the case in our sample. The Green party's statutes initially prohibited any accumulation of offices. Even after some relaxation of these rules, the explicit prohibition on merging leadership positions of party and group remained. In the AfD the leadership team of Meuthen and Gauland implemented this union, as Gauland already was head of the group in the parliament. Yet, this was done to resolve the inability of a party congress to decide between two candidates and Gauland mainly focused his work and ambitions on the group. For the AfD this format remained a transitional phenomenon. In the M5S Grillo and Casaleggio refrained from entering parliament or running as a leading candidate in the elections. It fell to the second generation of leaders to become actively involved in parliament and government.

An even bigger challenge is posed by the exercise of executive power. In parliamentary systems the positions in government adhere to the essence of single leadership. The prime minister is the head of government and sets the priorities for his or her cabinet. She or he is the most visible and prominent representative of the executive (Müller 2020; O'Malley, 2007). In a coalition government this office is typically claimed by the largest party, but also the ministers or undersecretaries are influential positions (Blondel, 1991; Blondel & Müller-Rommel, 1993; Müller & Strøm, 2003). Especially for smaller parties, joining a government coalition elevates party elites into accentuated positions. If the prime minister defines the overall direction of a government, ministers exert extensive influence on the policy areas they are responsible for (Andeweg, 2020; Laver et al., 1996; Martin & Vanberg, 2014). The original operating mode of cabinet government as it emerged in the United Kingdom in the first half of the nineteenth century resembled the idea of collective leadership: "Then the cabinet discussed and decided the important issues collectively. The prime minister was first among equals (*primus inter pares*), not the boss of the other ministers" (Müller, 2020: 142). However, this operating mode evolved into a form of prime ministerial government, where collective deliberation and effective decision-making in and by the cabinet have been replaced by monocratic decision-making by the prime minister (Crossmann, 1972).[2] Depending on the specific institutional layout of a political system, there are other operating modes but all typically imply some element of hierarchy (Elgie, 1997; Helms, 2005; Müller, 2020; Sartori, 1994).

The hierarchical relationship within contemporary governments and the tension between the overall responsibility of the prime minister and the ministers' portfolio responsibilities clash with the ideas of collective leadership presented by political parties. This exerts pressure on the parties. As shown in one of our case studies (Chapter 4), when the most prominent Green politician Joschka Fischer became foreign minister in the federal government his influence over the party grew significantly. He pushed for a new party leadership conducive to the pragmatic strategy of the Green party in government. Independent of Fischer's individual

---

[2] The debate on the so-called presidentialization thesis for parliamentary regimes (Dowding, 2013; Poguntke & Webb, 2005; Webb & Poguntke, 2013), especially in the United Kingdom, is still open and the evidence on the increasing role of prime minister is far from conclusive.

strategies the reforms stabilized the party leadership and the autonomy that was won remained with the party chairs even after the end of government participation. A second example concerns the currently effective and successful Green party leadership of Baerbock and Habeck. In the run-up to the next national elections 2021 the party came under pressure to pick one of the two chairs to be the top candidate, according to traditional party practice. The argument was that the electorate might want to know who the party sees as viable for the most powerful office in the executive. External constraints pushed the Greens to downplay and adapt their collective leadership model.

If we consider the basic characteristics of a political system as the environment for political parties adopting collective leadership, the constitutional design of the political institutions at a national level is not the only aspect that exerts influence on parties. Our case studies illustrated that the federal or multi-level structure of a state plays a role in the party organization as well. This is in no way exclusive for parties with dual or multimember leadership and impacts all parties. Research on political parties in democratic systems demonstrates that the complex organizations, with their mix of voluntary activists and professional career politicians, usually mirror the levels of the political system and feature power centers on different levels (Korte et al., 2018: 32–35). Looking at the US parties, Eldersveld accordingly labeled them as stratarchies (Eldersveld, 1964). The autonomy of regional branches of political parties as multi-level organizations is apparent if we look at the policy positions of the regional branches. Typically we find quite a significant degree of variety within the overall policy consensus defined by the platform of the national party. Of course this is a result of the different policy fields that subnational entities are responsible for, but also holds true for aggregated policy positions in a two-dimensional policy space (for Germany, see Bräuninger & Debus, 2012).Stecker (2015) finds that this significantly affects the content and extent of legislative behavior at the state level in Germany particularly when combined with the status of a party (i.e., in government or the opposition party). Federalism also influences the coalition strategies of a party which have to be aligned and coordinated across the different levels (Albala & Reniu, 2018). Downs (1998) concluded that parties can use the states as laboratories and to build up trust between party actors. In this sense, federalism adds another constraint for party leaders, that makes the steering of a multi-layered political party even more challenging.

Our case studies illustrated that the Greens used the federal structure in Germany to assemble the party from local, to regional, to national level, according to their grassroots ideology. As a consequence, the rank and file still harbors an anti-elite skepticism against their own party leadership, that acts as a check on the authority of the leadership (Switek, 2015: 135ff.). Another element specific for the Greens is the unique position of the prime minister in Baden-Württemberg, Winfried Kretschmann, the only Green politician in such a position. He has a high degree of visibility and often takes the national spotlight. His prominence and high popularity make him a challenger for the national chairpersons, who have to integrate or take his positions into account for their strategies. For the AfD we saw that the there is a stark difference between the West and East German branches. On the one hand, the federal structure keeps stakeholders with diverging priorities in the same national party but, on the other hand, this transports conflicts into the already fraught collective leadership, further intensifying the already pronounced toxicity.

Ultimately, our cases indicate that the relevance of federalism is not that different to parties with single leadership. For our three cases and two countries there is barely any variance on this dimension. However, going forward it would be interesting to compare instances of collective leadership in federal systems with those in stronger unitarian settings.

Finally, beyond the Greens and the AfD Germany as a whole seems to be an interesting case as two more parties feature a dual leadership: the Left party since its merger with the WASG in 2007 and the SPD since a statute reform in 2019. Why is Germany such a laboratory for collective leadership in political parties? The emergence of coalition governments and consensual politics is only one element of the post-war style of German politics. After the catastrophe of fascism and Nazi-rule, the basic law (constitution) of the West German republic included provisions to create a stable and well-fortified democracy (Fulbrook, 2019). The constitutional court can ban extremist parties, the chancellor can only be removed by a constructive vote of no-confidence, and the federal power-sharing system gives states a check on national power. In addition, there was a centripetal tendency of the party system, by elite agreement and reinforced by voting behavior. For a long period the party system consisted of two dominant catch-all parties and a smaller liberal party. This was expedited by an electoral threshold which was implemented to prevent a fragmentation of the party system. The Greens were the first party to upset this equilibrium. The Greens and later the Left and the

AfD as the only new parties joining the party system all featured a collective leadership. Even if electoral systems with proportional representation lower the hurdles for new parties, the electoral threshold could be another reason why new contestants opted for collective leadership. The multiple groups that formed the Green party, like those which formed the AfD, would have been too marginal to surpass the five percent threshold by themselves. Only through joining forces was this feasible, and the collective leadership was one way to respect the background of the various groups. This was different with the Left party, which had a strong base in Eastern Germany but struggled to gain representation in the West German states. In this sense, the merger with the SPD splinter WASG was meant to extend the voter base and stabilize the party in regions where it had underperformed. On the one hand an electoral threshold might make collective leadership more likely, as it offers an incentive for otherwise disconnected groups to come together to gain parliamentary representation. On the other hand, the case of the Left demonstrates a pattern that collective leadership is a way to visibly represent different regions at the top of the party to reconcile different geographical strongholds.

One last insight from the German case, based on the decision of the SPD to adopt collective leadership in 2019, could be the prevalence of these models on the left side of the party spectrum. We learned that the right-populist AfD is an outlier in this respect, and the Greens, the Left and the SPD are all part of the left party spectrum. These parties share a criticism of established power structures and elites. Egalitarianism is an integral part of their progressive agenda and helps explain their inclination to reject a strong single leader figure in favor of multiple positions at the top. Furthermore, the case of the Greens and their gender quota demonstrates the ability of these models to allow for inclusion of underrepresented groups.

7.3 Heuristic Hypotheses for Future Comparative Inquiry on Collective Leadership

As we have spelled out in Chapter 1, the empirical analyses included in the second part of the book have mainly followed an exploratory approach. Therefore, the aim of our three case studies is to generate new and further fine-grained hypotheses on the working and development of forms of collective leadership in contemporary political parties. As we know, this is a sort of *terra incognita* for party politics, an uncharted territory where the opportunity to rely on grounded theoretical guidance is rather limited.

In the previous sections we have seen that some of the analytical and theoretical propositions that we have elaborated for the analysis of collective party leadership can be effectively used for understanding the formation as well as the evolution of plural leadership. In this section we are more interested in assessing the extent to which some of the findings from the case studies of the three selected parties can be extended to other countries or generate new research questions.

To begin with, it is important to reflect on the evolution over time between different types of collective leadership and, in particular, on the specific challenges that a party faces during its organizational development. In this respect, we may expect that multimember leadership is more suitable for the founding or launching stage of a party, whereas dual leadership may be better equipped to cope with the new challenges from entry into legislative or executive institutions. When party identity is still in the making, the existence of a chorus of voices reaching different audiences may be more effective than a monologue played by a soloist. However, with the passing of time and when crossing different party lifespan thresholds (e.g., getting political representation and executive power), a party needs greater control and coordination of its growing organization. As a result, a first research question that is worth exploring in the future relates to the potential temporary nature of multimember leadership, in contrast with the more stable or durable solution provided by dual leadership.

However, as shown in Chapter 6, the case of the M5S represents an exception to the generalization that we have just suggested. In fact, originally formed as a common enterprise between two co-leaders, over time the party adopted a multimember and more collegial form of leadership, in particular, when it decided to accept the challenge of government (in 2018). In this respect, the M5S followed the opposite trajectory of the Greens and the AfD.

How is it possible to account for these divergent trajectories? What hypothesis can be formulated accordingly? We know that, among other more contextual factors, the genesis of the party, and especially its original type of leadership, is a crucial factor accounting for the different organizational paths followed by the M5S. More specifically, we argue that a fundamental role is played by the special personal bond that united the two undisputed co-founders/leaders of the M5S and that allowed the party to stay united during the launch of the new political project.

Arguably, we expect that future research on collective party leadership invests more time on specifying the personal attributes, attitudes and skills of the team leaders. Furthermore, this analysis should focus not only on one single member of the collective leadership, detached from the others but, more importantly, on how the skills of one leader fit with the personal attitudes of the others. In other words, what makes a collective leadership structure effective may be the specific combination of qualities of each of the leaders that is involved. On this basis, it could be hypothesized that if a plural leadership relies on a strong personal bond between its members, characterized by a planned or spontaneous alignment in their respective skills and functions, the positive effects on the organization can be observed both in the initial and in the more institutionalized stages of the party.

As said, personal attributes and attitudes of the leaders may play a significant role in the performance of collective leaderships. Unfortunately, until recently, in most of the political science literature "[l]eaders were treated as interchangeable 'black boxes' that responded to external constraints and opportunities in a similar way" (Krcmaric et al., 2020: 135). As a result, little or no room is left for the biographical details or personal features of the leaders. Only recently, we have witnessed a modest growth in the number of studies aimed at the "unpacking of the black box to examine how individual-level attributes and experiences influence political outcomes" (135). Although the focus of this new strand of studies is still centered on the single, solo leader, the need to delve into the personal skills and attitudes of the leaders is equally relevant—or perhaps even more relevant—in the future analysis of collective party leadership.

The performance of a collective leadership, to a large degree, relies on the personality traits and the individual skills of each distinct leader. Collective leadership is not just the sheer sum of 'interchangeable black boxes'. The relationship that links one leader to another is inevitably conditioned by their personal attitudes. Consequently, in the future it would be essential to carry out a much more in-depth investigation as to whether, and to what degree, different types of collective leadership are more suitable for, or more conducive to, the formation of strong personal bonds between party leaders.

For instance, it is possible to hypothesize that a dual leadership results in better performance in a context characterized by a power-sharing arrangement where there is a strong personal bond between the co-leaders. In other words, dual leadership is effective when it turns into something similar to a single leadership. This can happen when the leadership roles in the party organization are perfectly aligned with specific tasks and functions. That is, when the dual leadership looks more like a duet than a duel, and the co-leaders are committed to follow the same script, then plural party leadership may become an asset for the party.

This inevitably brings up the question of how to build such a cooperative, committed, complementary dual leadership. In some cases, it is just a matter of fortunate circumstances that cannot be planned in advance but that can be, as the experience of the M5S clearly shows, maintained and turned into a structural, long-lasting arrangement. The initial meeting between Grillo and Casaleggio and, subsequently, their dual leadership are good instances of this type of 'planned fortunate circumstance'.

When circumstances are less fortunate, in the sense that there is no *ex ante* match between the attitudes and the skills of the co-leaders, then those circumstances should be artificially constructed by the party organization with an appropriate structure of incentives. One of these structures pertains to the process through which would-be leaders are recruited, selected and appointed. Until now, the literature in this research subfield has paid exclusive attention to the appointment of a single, almighty individual within the party organization. However, as we know, this is just a part of the story, because in many circumstances power may be distributed between different actors or in different units. Accordingly, a research question that deserves to be investigated in the future concerns the extent to which different methods of leadership selection condition the emergence, persistence and performance of a given collective leadership.

For instance, when the dual leadership is the result of a selection in which the candidates compete in tandem or as a ticket, rather than as single individuals, we can expect that the chance of finding compatible or more cooperative leaders is higher. Similarly, the probability of effective cooperation increases if the term of office for the pair of co-leaders has the same duration. There are circumstances in which co-leaders are elected individually and their stay in office is out of synchronization. Consequently, the likelihood to form a ticket or build a 'united career' over time is rather remote. Other forms of collaboration or cooperation between the co-leaders may be implemented in the party statute, with a specific distribution of tasks and functions between them.

Here, an aspect that has hitherto received little attention concerns the communication function within the party. In a context of collective leadership, who is in charge of the electoral campaign? Who is the public 'face' of the party? Both in Germany and Italy, before the election the political parties present their candidate for the office of prime minister, but how does this arrangement alter the distribution of power in the leadership structure? And, above all, how do other parties in Western Europe, which adopt forms of collective leadership, deal with these sensitive situations? There is, indeed, an inherent tension between the monocratic nature of the executive offices and the existence of a collective leadership. This represents a real predicament for those parties which do not rely on a solo leader. Understanding how political parties with collective leadership solve this organizational dilemma represents a question to be placed on the research agenda. In general terms, it could be hypothesized that when parties are called, either formally or informally, to indicate a top (electoral) candidate, the tensions within the collective leadership increase and may jeopardize the survival of the overall leadership structure that is in charge at that time.

If we turn to the complementarity in leadership roles, we can formulate two further hypotheses to be explored in the future. The first concerns the distinction between power sharing and position sharing as distinct arrangements for the distribution of tasks within a party. In particular, we can expect that the former exhibits a more flexible nature than the latter and, as a consequence, it may be more conducive to situations in which effective complementarity and cooperation between co-leaders prevail. Indeed, at least in the short run power-sharing solutions are expected to better accommodate the personal skills of each leader and favor a more effective distribution of tasks between the leading figures.

However, as the case study of the M5S has demonstrated, these specific situations, where the distribution of leadership roles operates mainly on an informal basis, have a downside, which is represented by the inherent instability of the leadership structure. To put it differently, the performance of collective leadership depends heavily on the personal bond that unites the co-leaders, and this connection can be accommodated more easily in organizational contexts characterized by a power-sharing arrangement in which the division of labor is left to informal bargaining between the leaders. In turn, this informal bargaining requires a strong commitment on shared, whole-organization goals, a sense of mutual trust between the leaders and well-grounded beliefs about the capacity of each member within the leadership body.

As a result, we can speculate that the occurrence of power-sharing arrangements and multimember leadership is more likely in the early stages of the party organization, that is, when a political party is not yet institutionalized, there is no formal division between the different 'faces' or strata of the organization and there is no conflict between distinct goals (i.e., vote, office, policy) pursued by party actors. In this respect, effective power-sharing arrangements can be interpreted as a more temporary solution whose performance is inevitably related to the destiny of the co-leaders. Once a member of the collective leading body steps down or loses confidence in his/her partner's capacity, the advantages of a power-sharing solution may turn into potential disadvantages. Summing up, power-sharing arrangements may be more flexible and successful but their positive effects are short-lived. By contrast, position-sharing solutions are less prone to favor effective collective leadership, but they appear to be more stable over time.

The second hypothesis on the complementarity of different co-leaders deals with the specificities of the mechanisms of position sharing within political parties. As we have stated above, this arrangement for the division of labor in a party is more rigid than power-sharing solutions. In some circumstances, this rigidity can be (and has been) circumvented by informal practices, such as the ones put in place by the Greens during the 1990s and the early 2000s when "the emergence of informal leadership structures" (Detterbeck & Rohlfing, 2014: 79) went hand in hand with formal collective leaderships.

Nevertheless, the rigidity of position-sharing arrangements cannot be completely avoided. In particular, the parties that have adopted this mechanism for the distribution of leadership tasks have chosen two criteria for making co-leaders complementary with each other. The German Greens, as other ecologist parties throughout Western Europe, have incorporated the gender criterion for the composition of the leadership structure. Therefore, the co-leaders must be complementary in terms of gender (i.e., one man and one woman). The implications of this choice in terms of the leadership practices, however, need to be thoroughly investigated. There is a debate about the existence of a female style of leadership, that is, if women leaders behave differently to men (Stevens, 2007, Chapter 6). It should be noted that the dynamics within a couple or a small group of leaders may diverge from what characterizes individual leadership.

For instance, the division of labor is likely to emphasize complementary attitudes and behaviors among co-leaders, but would they adhere to stereotypes, with female partners being more collaborative and compassionate than their male counterparts? More empirical work is required to investigate the gender factor in political leadership and a focus on plural leadership would highlight another valuable facet.

In contrast, the AfD has adopted, albeit informally, an ideological criterion that, to some degree, overlaps with a geographical criterion. Accordingly, the dual leadership of AfD must strike a balance between the two main ideological wings existing in the parties and the geographical distribution of their respective support (one stronger in West Germany, the other in East Germany). Thus, the complementarity in terms of ideological/geographical features is not based on a shared vision of the future of the party. Quite the opposite, it is based on a pattern of constant competition between the co-leaders, rather than cooperation.

Therefore, a heuristic hypothesis that can be developed for future research on this topic is whether position-sharing arrangements in which the criteria for complementarity between co-leaders are indicated in advance by the party (either formally or informally) hinder or advance the emergence of collective leadership having a strong complementarity in terms of skills, attitudes and other personal features. In some circumstances, such as those observed in the Greens under the dual leadership of Baerbock and Habeck, it is possible to observe a sufficient degree of 'personal' or behavioral complementarity even in a context characterized by position-sharing solutions. But these episodes look more like exceptions to the general rule outlined above.

7.4 Directions for Future Research

The final section of this concluding chapter is dedicated to propose possible lines of research that may be developed from the hypotheses generated by our analysis. First of all, we believe that our theoretical framework may be fruitfully applied to other similar cases. The empirical chapters in this volume provide systematic investigation of three parties, two in Germany and one in Italy. As a consequence, we are aware that our arguments are limited in national terms and some of them are clearly case-specific. Thus, the study of other political parties, also those beyond

Western Europe, might be a valuable addition and offer further confirmation of the importance of analyzing collective leadership with the goal of improving and refining the conceptualization of the phenomenon.

We are convinced, however, that research could go beyond the collection of more case studies and rather face the higher challenge of a proper comparative design that is able to encompass all forms of party leadership. Starting from the assumption that we cannot consider the phenomenon of leadership as only being an individual configuration, but that we also need to include forms of plural leadership, we believe that each national party system may present a variety of types and needs to be assessed with the aim of identifying and distinguishing such different arrangements. Therefore, by combining a shared theoretical framework and comparative perspective, a cross-national mapping of party leadership and its forms could be obtained. Such an enterprise is not only commendable for expanding our knowledge about plural leadership; for instance, by giving an assessment of its overall occurrence in a number of countries and better highlighting possible patterns of its diffusion in terms of regions, ideological linings and organizational characteristics. In fact, we believe that attempting at mapping individual and collective leadership together may also extend our knowledge of individual leadership as well by unveiling nuances and distinctions that could lead to a richer and more meaningful categorization of the phenomenon of party leadership.

Of course, this endeavor implies a further effort of definition and an elaboration of crucial dimensions as well as the collaboration of a group of country experts. A lesson we have learned from our explorations in this book is that all cases of plural leadership in action can be correctly interpreted and classified only with the help of an extensive knowledge of the history and characteristics of the party in consideration. In other words, a superficial overview of a broad population of cases can be misleading for the main reason that our three case studies helped to disclose, which is that formal arrangements do not always correspond to substantive mechanisms of power sharing. As we have seen, a formal individual leadership may cohabit with a de facto partnership. Or formal position sharing may be inserted in a wider network of power sharing, and so on.

Another point that should be taken into account in planning research on these topics is that in the history of a party there may be comings and goings. For example, some parties experience a collective leadership in an initial phase, but, then, an individual leader succeeds in prevailing and concentrating power in his/her hands. Or powerful dual leadership can be replaced by an individual leadership as soon as that specific couple of leaders has bowed out. In other words, collective leadership is not always a constant trait. But also temporary and possibly exceptional cases are worthy of reflection, at least they may highlight the reasons why collective leadership ends, and consequently offer insight into what mechanisms may increase the chances of stability over time.

On the other hand, long-term experiences also produce an evolutionary path over time. The evolutionary trajectories demonstrated the establishment of routines. While there was always pressure to change rules that were internally and externally disputed, the actors have built over time routines in dealing with collective leadership and in crafting power-sharing agreements.

Reflections on short-term experiences direct attention to leadership couples and tandems. As anticipated in the introduction, our preference for focusing on cases that could plot an evolutionary trajectory of collective leadership over time suggested that we looked at cases of collective leadership that have proved to pass the test of the turnover of leaders. Thus we left out of the selection of case studies several instances of duos formed by presidents, premiers and formal party leaders with their deputies, vices or other senior colleagues. Nonetheless, we consider many of such duos as extremely interesting cases and as a potentially excellent test for studying the impact of specific variables, such as personal bonds or mentor/protegee relationships. Qualitative analyses of some selected experiences in a comparative framework could allow for deeper exploration of the psychological aspects of the practice of sharing power and, in general, for better detailing its underlying mechanism. A fecund research approach may be that employed by Strangio et al. (2015), which explored the relationship between a prime minister and another powerful minister in the time-limited context of a policy reform. Other key episodes can be identified and analyzed, for instance, the role of duos or teams in the founding stage of parties and movements. If limiting the focus to a phase or a specific endeavor may be appropriate, reconstructions of life-time "united careers" over time may also be of interest. In sum, the study of instances of co-leadership is open to the employment of several, alternative research strategies. Overall, it is a fertile and hitherto underexplored field that may enrich our knowledge about party organizational structure.

Our final observation concerns the possible expansion of research in the direction of European political parties. Until now we have considered national parties as our unit of analysis. It should be observed, however, that several European parties, such as the Greens (EGP), the Liberal (ALDE) and the Left (EL), have already introduced plural candidacies for the role of *Spitzenkandidaten* (Switek & Weissenbach, 2020; Wolfs et al., 2020). The European context should be even more receptive to collective leadership than the national context, since European parties bring together members from different countries and, therefore, must represent a variety of regions and sociodemographic variables. By giving voters a team of individuals as candidates, instead of just one, this may help identification mechanisms and encourage voters to feel closer to an election that, despite the 2019 increase, still suffers from a low turnout compared to national elections.

References

Albala, A., & Reniu, J. M. (2018). *Coalition politics and federalism*. Springer.
Alvarez, J. L., & Svejenova, S. (2005). *Sharing executive power: Roles and relationships at the top*. Cambridge University Press.
Andeweg, R. B. (2020). Parties and executives in parliamentary systems: From party government to party governance. In R. B. Andeweg, R. Elgie, L. Helms, J. Kaarbo, & F. Müller-Rommel (Eds.), *The Oxford handbook of political executives* (pp. 460–480). Oxford University Press.
Bebnowski, D. (2015). *Die Alternative für Deutschland*. Springer Fachmedien Wiesbaden.
Bieber, C., & Leggewie, C. (Eds.). (2012). *Unter Piraten: Erkundungen in einer neuen politischen Arena*. Transcript.
Blondel, J. (1991). Cabinet government and cabinet ministers. In J. Blondel, & J. -L. Thiébault (Eds.), *Profession of government minister in Western Europe* (pp. 5–18). Palgrave Macmillan.
Blondel, J., & Müller-Rommel, F. (Eds.). (1993). *Governing together: The extent and limits of joint decision-making in Western European cabinets*. Palgrave Macmillan.
Blum, C., & Zuber, C. I. (2016). Liquid democracy: Potentials, problems, and perspectives. *Journal of Political Philosophy, 24*(2), 162–182.
Bolleyer, N., Little, C., & von Nostitz, F.-C. (2015). Implementing democratic equality in political parties: Organisational consequences in the Swedish and the German pirate party. *Scandinavian Political Studies, 38*(2), 158–178.
Bräuninger, T., & Debus, M. (2012). *Parteienwettbewerb in den deutschen Bundesländern*. VS Verlag für Sozialwissenschaften.
Crossman, R. (1972). *Inside view: Three lectures on Prime ministerial government*. Jonathan Cape.

Decker, F. (2016). The "Alternative for Germany:" Factors behind its emergence and profile of a new right-wing populist Party. *German Politics and Society, 34*(2), 1–16.
Detterbeck, B., & Rohlfing, I. (2014). Party leader selection in Germany. In J.-B. Pilet, & W. Cross (Eds.), *The selection of political party leaders in parliamentary democracies. A comparative study* (pp. 77–92). Routledge.
Dowding, K. (2013). The Prime Ministerialisation of the British Prime Minister. *Parliamentary Affairs, 66*(3), 617–635.
Downs, W. M. (1998). *Coalition government, subnational style: Multiparty politics in Europe's regional parliaments*. Ohio State University Press.
Eldersveld, S. (1964). *Political parties: A behavioural analysis*. Rand McNally.
Elgie, R. (1997). Models of executive politics: A framework for the study of executive power relations in parliamentary and semi–presidential regimes. *Political Studies, 45*(2), 217–231.
Fulbrook, M. (2019). *A concise history of Germany* (3rd edn.). Cambridge University Press.
Heinisch, R., & Mazzoleni, O. (2016). Comparing populist organizations. In R. Heinisch & O. Mazzoleni (Eds.), *Understanding populist party organisation* (pp. 221–246). Palgrave Macmillan.
Helms, L. (2005). *Presidents, prime ministers and chancellors: Executive leadership in Western democracies*. Palgrave.
Helms, L. (2020). *Spitzenkandidaten* beyond Westminster: Comparing chancellor candidates in Germany and Austria. *Parliamentary Affairs, 73*(4), 808–830.
Korte, K.-R., Michels, D., Schoofs, J., Switek, N., & Weissenbach, K. (2018). *Parteiendemokratie in Bewegung: Organisations—und Entscheidungsmuster der deutschen Parteien im Vergleich* (1. Auflage). Nomos.
Krcmaric, D., Nelson, S. C., & Roberts, A. (2020). Studying leaders and elites: The personal biography approach. *Annual Review of Political Science, 23*(1), 133–151.
Laver, M., & Shepsle, K. A. (Eds.). (1996). *Making and breaking governments: Cabinets and legislatures in parliamentary democracies*. Cambridge University Press.
Leithwood, K., Mascall, B., Strauss, T., Sacks, R., Memon, N., & Yashkina, A. (2006). Distributing leadership to make schools smarter. In K. Leithwood, B. Mascall, & T. Strauss (Eds.), *Distributed leadership according to the evidence* (pp. 223–251). Routledge.
Martin, L. W., & Vanberg, G. (2014). Parties and policymaking in multiparty governments: The legislative median, ministerial autonomy, and the coalition compromise. *American Journal of Political Science, 58*(4), 979–999.
Mudde, C., & Rovira Kaltwasser, R. C. (2017). *Populism: A very short introduction*. Oxford University Press.

Müller, W. C. (2020). Governments and bureaucracies. In D. Caramani (Ed.), *Comparative politics* (5th ed., pp. 139–158). Oxford University Press.
Müller, W. C., & Strøm, K. (2003). *Coalition governments in Western Europe*. Oxford University Press.
O'Malley, E. (2007). The power of prime ministers: Results of an expert survey. *International Political Science Review, 28*(1), 7–27.
Poguntke, T. (1993). *Alternative politics: The German Green Party*. Edinburgh University Press.
Poguntke, T., & Webb, P. (Eds.). (2005). *The presidentialization of politics. A comparative study of modern democracies*. Oxford University Press.
Rucht, D. (2012). Leadership in social and political movements: A comparative exploration. In L. Helms (Ed.), *Comparative political leadership* (pp. 99–118). Palgrave Macmillan.
Sartori, G. (1994). *Comparative constitutional engineering: An inquiry into structures, incentives and outcomes*. New York University Press.
Serrano, J. C. M., Shahrezaye, M., Papakyriakopoulos, O., & Hegelich, S. (2019). The rise of Germany's AfD: A social media analysis. In *Proceedings of the 10th international conference on social media and society* (pp. 214–223). Presented at the SMSociety '19: International conference on social media and society. ACM.
Strangio, P., 't Hart, P., & Walter, J. (2015). Leadership of reforming governments: The role of political tandems. In D. Alexander, & J. M. Lewis (eds.), *Making public policy decisions: Expertise, skills, and experience* (pp. 166–184). Routledge.
Stecker, C. (2015). Parties on the Chain of Federalism: Position-Taking and Multi-level Party Competition in Germany. *West European Politics, 38*(6), 1305–1326.
Stevens, A. (2007). *Women, Power and Politics*. Palgrave Macmillan.
Switek, N. (2015). *Bündnis 90/Die Grünen. Koalitionsentscheidungen in den Ländern*. Nomos.
Switek, N., & Weissenbach, K. (2020). An ever-closer party? The institutionalization of the European Green Party after the 2019 European election. In M. Kaeding, M. Müller, & J. Schmälter (Eds.), *Die Europawahl 2019* (pp. 63–77). Springer Fachmedien Wiesbaden.
Valbruzzi, M. (2018). When populists meet technocrats. The Italian innovation in government formation. *Journal of Modern Italian Studies, 23*(4), 460–480.
Webb, P., & Poguntke, T. (2013). The Presidentialisation of Politics Thesis Defended. *Parliamentary Affairs, 66*(3), 646–654.
Wolfs, W., Put, G.-J., & Van Hecke, S. (2020). The second time around: Status quo and reform of the Europarties' selection procedures for Spitzenkandidaten in 2019. In M. Kaeding, M. Müller, & J. Schmälter (Eds.), *Die Europawahl 2019* (pp. 157–168). Springer Fachmedien Wiesbaden.

Author Index

A
Adam, K., 107, 109, 113, 114, 116, 117, 119, 121
Albala, A., 195
Aldrich, H., 41
Alvarez, J.L., 6, 10, 16, 19, 20, 26, 41, 47, 48, 53, 54, 163, 189
Amann, M., 110, 119, 122, 128
Anderson, S., 23
Andeweg, R.B., 194
Aquino, C., 41
Arzheimer, K., 104, 106, 124

B
Baerbock, A., 68, 70, 78, 79, 81, 91, 92, 96, 184, 187, 195, 203
Bailo, F., 134, 145
Bale, T., 45
Balmas, M., 3
Barber, J.D., 52
Barbieri, G., 167
Bardi, L., 141

Barisione, M., 2
Bebnowksi, D., 103, 116, 192
Becchi, P., 148
Beckmann, L., 70, 81
Beer, A., 70, 81
Bellanova, T., 40
Beller, D.C., 3, 34, 83
Belloni, F.P., 3, 34, 83
Benington, J., 24
Bennett, W.L., 135
Bennis, W., 21
Bentivegna, S., 167
Berbuir, N., 106
Bérègovoy, P., 42
Berlusconi, S., 1, 137
Berstein, C., 43
Bertsou, E., 140
Beste, R., 77
Bhutto, B., 41
Biancalana, C., 136
Bianchi, V., 167
Bickerton, C.J., 137
Bieber, C., 192

© The Editor(s) (if applicable) and The Author(s), under exclusive license to Springer Nature Switzerland AG 2021
D. Campus et al., *Collective Leadership and Divided Power in West European Parties*, Palgrave Studies in Political Leadership, https://doi.org/10.1007/978-3-030-75255-2

Biondo, N., 148
Biorcio, R., 134, 137, 147, 156
Birthler, M., 70, 72, 81
Bischof, D., 150
Bittner, A., 2
Blair, T., 9, 22, 45, 48, 54, 55
Blais, A., 34, 83
Blondel, J., 1, 4, 25, 49, 194
Blum, C., 192
Bobba, G., 137, 149
Böhmer, A., 110, 120
Bolden, R., 23
Boll, B., 84
Bolleyer, N., 136, 173, 192
Bordignon, F., 137, 139, 149, 151, 152, 156, 158, 163, 165, 167
Bosco, A., 48, 56
Boucek, F., 3, 34
Brandt, W., 39, 64
Bräuninger, T., 195
Brost, M., 110
Brown, A., 4
Brown, G., 9, 22, 48, 55
Bukow, S., 74, 78, 82
Burchell, J., 37, 63, 71, 79, 84
Burgmann, D., 70, 81
Bütikofer, R., 70, 81, 88, 90, 94, 96
Bynander, F., 34

C
Calise, M., 137
Campus, D., 38, 41, 122
Cancelleri, G., 153
Canestrari, M., 148
Cannella, B., 17, 128
Caramani, D., 140
Carey, J.M., 5
Carinelli, P., 153
Carlin, D., 43
Carter, N., 41
Carty, K.R., 138

Caruso, L., 137
Casaleggio, D., 154, 160, 165, 167–170
Casaleggio, G., 11, 46, 134, 138, 140, 143, 146, 149, 151, 153, 163, 167
Catalfo, N., 153
Ceccanti, S., 139
Ceccarini, L., 137, 139, 149, 151, 152, 156, 158, 163, 165, 167
Cerasa, C., 40
Ceri, P., 141
Ceron, A., 3, 34
Chamorro, V., 41
Chase, J., 119
Chiapponi, F., 140
Chrupalla, T., 113, 114, 126, 127
Clinton, B., 21
Clinton Rodham, H., 43
Coca, C., 48
Conger, J., 15, 16
Conte, G., 40, 139, 156–158, 161, 169, 188
Conti, M., 40
Corbetta, P., 134, 137, 139, 156
Cosenza, G., 162
Crimi, V., 153, 158
Cross, W.P., 1, 2, 34, 83
Crozier, M., 153
Cué, C., 46
Curreri, S., 139
Curtice, J., 2
Curtis, P., 49
Cyert, R.M., 18

D
D'Alema, M., 51
Damus, R., 70, 81
Day, C., 16
Dean, J., 46
Debus, M., 195

AUTHOR INDEX 211

Decker, F., 106, 109, 115, 118, 122, 191
De Gasperi, A., 35
Della Porta, D., 134, 138, 143, 146, 151
Denis, J-L., 17
De Rosa, R., 136, 149
Deseriis, M., 137
Detterbeck, K., 34, 65, 202
de Voogt, A., 16, 20
De Vries, C.E., 139
Diamanti, I., 51, 137
Di Battista, A., 152, 156, 165, 167, 169
Dilling, M., 116, 124
Di Maggio, M., 140
Di Maio, L., 152–155, 157, 158, 165, 167–169, 188, 189
Ditfurth, J., 70
Dolezal, M., 37
Donovan, T., 115
Dowding, K., 194
Downs, W.M., 195
Draghi, M., 156, 169
Duverger, M., 3, 19, 29, 34, 40, 135, 149

E
Egle, C., 74
Eldersveld, S., 195
Eleonor d'Aquitaine, 41
Elgie, R., 5, 194
Ennser-Jedenastik, L., 34
Errejòn, I., 36, 46
Esken, S., 39
Etheredge, L., 52
Etzioni, A., 10, 26, 27, 30

F
Faas, T., 77
Falter, J.W., 71, 72, 85

Farrell, M., 47
Faucher, F., 38
Ferdinand d'Aragon, 41
Fillon, F., 187
Finkelstein, S., 17, 18
Fischer, A., 66, 74, 88
Fischer, J., 66, 74, 86, 88, 89, 93, 183, 187, 194
Fittipaldi, R., 36
Foley, M., 55
Forkmann, D., 74
Fraccaro, R., 153
Frankland, E.G., 75, 79, 84, 116, 120, 126
Franzmann, S.F., 103, 106, 117
Fücks, R., 70, 81
Fulbrook, M., 196

G
Gaffney, J., 45, 46
Galbraith, J., 16
Gandhi, I., 41
Garzia, D., 2
Gauja, A., 39
Gauland, A., 111–114, 116, 119, 120, 124–127, 129, 188, 193
Gerbaudo, P., 134, 150, 154
Gerring, J., 7
Geywitz, K., 39
Goerres, A., 106
González, F., 9, 47, 48, 56
Gore, A., 21
Göring-Eckart, K., 67, 72, 91, 96
Greene, Z., 3
Grillo, B., 11, 46, 133, 134, 136–141, 143, 145–155, 157, 160–165, 167–169, 171–173, 185, 188, 189, 192, 193, 200
Gronn, P., 16, 19, 21, 26
Gross, M., 77
Gualmini, E., 137
Guerra, A., 9, 47, 48, 56

H

Habeck, R., 68, 70, 78, 79, 81, 91, 92, 96, 184, 187, 195, 203
Haber, M., 3
Halstenbach, A., 120
Hambauer, V., 117
Hambrick, D., 17, 18
Hammerbacher, R., 70, 81
Hansen, J., 45
Hansen, M.A., 111
Harmel, R., 3, 34, 162
Harris, A., 165
Hartley, J., 24
Hartlinski, M., 44
Haußleitner, A., 70
Hawke, B., 55
Heenan, D.A., 21
Heffernan, R., 54
Heinisch, R., 115, 191
Helms, L., 54, 187, 194
Henry II of England, 41
Heo, U., 3
Hermann, M., 52
Heyer, J., 96
Hine, D., 3, 34
Hobolt, S.B., 139
Höcke, B., 107, 108, 124, 127
Hockenos, P., 86
Hodgson, R., 19, 27
Hofreiter, A., 91, 95
Hollande, F., 42, 187
Hölscher, W., 71
Hommes, K., 16, 20
Hopkin, J., 138
Hopper, R.D., 68, 106, 141
Hurrelmann, A., 65, 73, 74, 78, 88

I

Iacoboni, J., 134, 148, 163, 168
Iglesias, P., 36, 42, 46
Ignazi, P., 141

Ilonszki, G., 36
Inglehart, R.F., 68, 133
Isabel of Castile, 41

J

Jahn, D., 74
Janda, K., 3
Jasiewicz, K., 44
Johnson, R., 15
Jospin, L., 42
Jun, U., 39, 40, 64, 106, 110, 114, 126
Jungjohann, A., 73
Jung, M., 87, 118

K

Kaczynski, J., 44, 45
Kaczynsky, L., 44
Kalbitz, A., 105, 127
Kaltwasser, R.C., 114, 191
Kantorowicz, E., 162
Karremans, J., 134
Katz, R.S., 1, 3, 24, 34
Kavanagh, D., 49
Keating, P., 55
Keller, T., 53
Kelly, P., 70, 81
Kemmerich, T., 108
Kenig, O., 3
Kennedy, J-F., 44
Kennedy, R., 44
Kerr, P., 55
Kettell, S., 55
King, A., 2, 4
Kioupkiolis, A., 36, 46
Kitschelt, H., 63, 69, 80, 83, 138
Klein, M., 71, 72, 85
Klingelhöfer, T., 77
Knabe, W., 70, 81
Knight, B., 39
Kocolowski, M., 15

Kohl, H., 54
Korolczuk, S., 74
Korte, K.R., 91, 195
Krcmaric, D., 199
Kretschmann, W., 67, 91, 95, 196
Krieger, V., 70, 81
Kuhn, F., 70, 75, 81, 88, 90, 93
Künast, R., 66, 70, 74, 75, 81, 88, 90, 93
Kurer, T., 150

L

Lafontaine, O., 42
Lahel, A., 45, 46
Lanfrey, D., 135
Langley, A., 17
Lanzone, M.E., 150
Lau, M., 105
Laver, M., 194
Lawler, E., 16
Lees, C., 73, 79, 106
Leggewie, C., 192
Leithwood, K., 23, 24, 84, 86, 90, 92, 164, 168, 170, 184
Lemke, S., 75, 77, 95
Lendvai, P., 47
Le Pen, M., 41, 54, 122
Liao, Z., 15
Lioy, A., 153
Lisi, M., 36, 46
Lobenstein, C., 104, 117
Lobo, M.C., 2
Loizeau, P-M., 43
Lombardi, R., 153
Lucke, B., 104, 106, 107, 109–117, 119–121, 123, 124, 128, 129, 186, 188, 190
Ludwig, A., 55

M

Maccaferri, M., 152, 153

Macron, E., 1
Mair, P., 3, 24, 34, 137
Malouines, M., 42
Mann, N., 70, 81
March, J., 18
Marcos, A., 46
Marcos, J., 46
Maren-Grisebach, M., 70, 81
Martini, F., 40
Martin, L.W., 194
Mascall, B., 23
Matonti, F., 42
Mays, A., 117
Mazzoleni, O., 64, 191
McDonnell, D., 137, 140
McIntyre, J., 45
Memon, N., 23
Mende, S., 65, 71, 82
Merkel, A., 11, 54, 103, 104, 107, 117, 119
Mershon, C., 51
Merten, H., 65
Meus, C., 42
Meuthen, J., 105, 107, 109, 112–114, 122, 124–127, 129, 184, 186, 193
Meyrowitz, J., 28
Michalik, R., 70, 81
Michels, R., 36
Middelhoff, P., 104, 106
Miles, S., 26, 52
Miliband, D., 45
Miliband, E., 45
Monedero, C, 36
Montero, I., 42
Moore, S., 23, 147
Morosini, M., 148
Mosca, L., 135, 137
Mudde, C., 104, 114, 137, 191
Müller, J.-W., 114
Müller, W.C., 194
Müller, W G., 51

Müller-Rommel, F., 194
Murray, R., 42
Musella, F., 1, 3
Musso, M., 152, 153

N
Nadolny, G., 117
Natale, P., 134, 147, 156
Navarria, G., 141
Neukirch, R., 96, 117
Neuner-Duttenhofer, C., 89
Niclauß, K., 78, 85
Niedermayer, O., 70, 111
Niendorf, T., 77
Nishida, M., 71, 82, 85, 86
Nizzoli, A., 165
Nye, J.S., 28

O
Ohr, D., 3
Olsen, J., 34, 111
O'Toole, J., 16, 26, 27
Özdemir, C., 67, 70, 75, 77, 81, 92, 94–96, 186

P
Padrò-Solanet, A., 48
Padzerski, G., 112, 125, 129
Panebianco, A., 18, 35, 36, 63, 80, 135, 153, 169
Paolucci, C., 138
Pasquino, G., 5, 35, 51, 139, 140
Passarelli, G., 136, 139
Patta, E., 40
Patton, D.F., 34, 64
Pearce, C., 15, 16
Pedersen, M.N., 69, 142
Pels, D., 28
Peron, E., 43
Peron, J.D., 43

Perrone, M., 140
Peter, S., 70, 81, 95
Petry, F., 105, 107–114, 116, 117, 119–122, 124, 125, 129, 184, 186, 188, 190
Pilet, J-B., 1, 2, 34, 37, 83
Pirro, A.L.P., 137
Poguntke, T., 37, 65, 69, 74, 80, 84, 190, 194
Porter, L., 18
Post, J., 53
Probst, L., 65, 71, 78, 79, 89
Prodi, R., 51
Pruysers, S., 1
Put, G-J., 206

R
Radcke, A., 70, 81, 88
Rahat, G., 3
Raschke, J., 65, 69, 71, 73, 74, 78, 82, 88
Reniu, J.M., 195
Renshon, S., 52
Renzi, M., 40
Richter, S., 75, 88, 90, 91, 94
Rihoux, B., 37, 38
Rohlfing, I., 34, 65, 202
Rokkan, S., 142
Rosato, E., 40
Rosell, F., 48
Rosenfelder, J., 114, 116
Röstel, G., 70, 81, 88
Roth, C., 81, 88, 89, 92, 94, 186
Rothe-Beinlich, A., 75
Royal, S., 42, 187
Rucht, D., 10, 24, 28, 29, 35, 37, 53, 69, 93, 143, 162, 163, 184
Rüdig, W., 95
Ruef, M., 41
Rühle, H., 70, 81
Ruiza, M., 56

AUTHOR INDEX

Ruocco, C., 152
Rupps, M., 64

S
Sacks, R., 23
Sager, K., 70, 81
Sally, D., 10, 50, 52
Salvini, M., 157
Santoro, C., 42
Sarrazin, T., 119
Sartori, G., 5, 25, 34, 139, 194
Sayn-Wittgenstein, D., 112, 125, 129
Schlesinger Jr., A., 44
Schlieben, M., 74
Schmidt, C., 81
Schmidt, H., 39, 64
Schmidt, R., 81
Schnoebelen, J., 43
Scholz, O., 39, 74
Schröder, G., 73
Schroth, Y., 87, 118
Schwanholz, J., 114
Seers, A., 53
Sendyka, P., 45
Sergi, V., 17
Serrano, J.C.M., 193
Sforza, F., 42
Shenhav, S., 3
Shepsle, K.A., 194
Shugart, M.S., 5
Sibilia, C., 152
Siegert, J., 72
Smith, D., 22
Spillane, J.P., 22, 118, 125
Spitz, M., 75
Stecker, C., 195
Steinberg, B., 52
Stevens, A., 202
Stevenson, W., 18
Strangio, P., 5, 20, 25, 26, 55, 205
Stratton, A., 45

Strauss, T., 23
Ströbele, C., 70, 81
Strøm, K., 51, 194
Sun, J., 23
Svåsand, L., 162
Svejenova, S., 6, 10, 16, 19, 20, 26, 41, 47, 48, 53, 54, 163, 189
Switek, N., 65, 71, 73–76, 79, 81, 83, 196, 206

T
Tan, A., 3
Tarchi, M., 137, 140
Taylor, J., 43
Terragni, M., 40
Thaa, W., 72
Theakston, K., 55
Thiébault, J-L., 1
Thompson, J.G., 18, 28
Tiefenbach, P., 83
Tilley, J., 139
Träger, H., 89, 96
Trampert, R., 70, 81
Trittin, J., 67, 70, 74, 81, 86–88, 91
Tronconi, F., 137, 140, 148–150, 153, 158, 171
Tye, L., 44
Tyrnauer, M., 163

U
Ulrich, B., 110
Unfried, P., 86, 91, 95

V
Vaccari, C., 135
Valbruzzi, M., 134, 139, 140, 158, 188
Vanberg, G., 194
Vassallo, S., 134
Veltri, F., 141

Verba, S., 10, 26, 27
Verhofstadt, G., 157, 168
Vignati, R., 139, 140, 148, 149, 152, 153, 162, 163
Villalba, B., 37
Visconti, B., 42
Vittori, D., 136, 138, 139, 148, 150, 151, 154, 155, 159, 168, 171
Vives, L., 26
Volmer, L., 70, 81
von Storch, B., 115

W

Wagenknecht, S., 42
Wall, I., 42
Walter, J., 5, 64
Walter-Borjans, N., 39
Watkins, M., 26, 52
Wawreille, M-C., 37
Webb, P., 54, 194
Wehner, H., 39, 64
Weidel, A., 111, 124, 126, 188
Weir, S., 44
Weiske, C., 70, 81
Weissenbach, K., 110, 120, 206
Weisskircher, M., 110
Wiesendahl, E., 91
Wilkerson, J., 53
Winter, D.G., 52
Wintour, P., 45
Wolf, A., 87, 118
Wolinetz, S.W., 135

Y

Yam, K., 15

Z

Zaleznik, A., 19
Zanatta, L., 44
Zariski, R., 35
Zhu, J., 15, 16
Zons, G., 103, 106, 109, 110, 115, 120, 127–129
Zuber, C.I., 192
Zulianello, M., 137, 139

SUBJECT INDEX

A

Alignments
  anarchic, 23, 83, 93
  planful, 23, 92, 93, 129, 164
  spontaneous, 23, 93, 130, 164, 184, 199
Alliance 90/The Greens (*Bündnis 90/Die Grünen*), 10, 63, 66, 70, 72, 85, 93, 181
Alternative for Germany (AfD, *Alternative für Deutschland*), 2, 7, 11, 38, 64, 103, 107, 181
Alternative politics, 190

C

Charismatic leader, 22, 103
Christian Democracy (DC, *Democrazia Cristiana*), 34
Coalition government, 11, 25, 66, 68, 73, 78, 79, 87, 187, 194, 196
Collective leadership/plural leadership
  and brothers, 45
  and friends, 10
  and institutional arrangements, 50
  and parents and child relationship, 41
  and spouses/partners, 41
  definition, 49
  paths to, 10, 33, 198
  sustenance of, 6, 10, 49, 51, 52, 54, 185
Communist Refoundation (*Rifondazione comunista*), 51
Constellations, 17, 19, 79, 121

D

Democratic Party (PD, *Partito Democratico*), 40, 139, 156
Direct democracy, 65, 105, 114, 128, 153, 162, 186
Distributed leadership, 16
Division of labor, 3, 6, 20, 22–26, 35, 39, 48, 127, 183–185, 187, 191, 201–203

Dominant coalition, 18, 35
Dual executive/dual authority structure, 5
Dual leadership, 2, 4–9, 11, 20, 21, 26, 27, 33, 34, 37, 38, 41, 42, 44, 45, 48, 50, 64, 80, 82, 85, 90, 97, 106, 109, 114, 121, 122, 125, 126, 148, 151, 152, 154, 155, 161, 163–165, 172, 173, 182, 189, 190, 196, 198–200, 203, 204. *See also* Collective leadership
Duos (dyads, couples, tandems), 1, 5, 6, 9, 17, 19, 22, 25, 44, 79, 184, 185, 190, 205

E
Election campaigns, 1, 77, 89, 187
Executive committee, 37, 39, 65, 67, 75, 77, 78, 83, 85, 89, 90, 96, 108, 110, 114, 116, 117, 119, 121, 122, 125–127, 186, 191

F
Factionalism, 71, 97, 127, 184, 185, 190
  party fractions, 35, 83, 186
Fidesz-Hungarian Civic Party (*Magyar Polgári PártFidesz*), 47

G
Gender parity and quotas, 66, 82
German Greens (*Die Grünen*), 7–9, 11, 37, 63, 65, 66, 71, 72, 77, 80, 82, 84, 85, 90, 97, 114, 182, 183, 185, 187, 190, 192, 202
Grass Roots Ideology, 82, 84, 114, 196
Green parties (ecologist/environmental parties), 37, 38, 63, 82, 133, 134, 138, 202

I
Individual leadership, 1, 3, 9, 12, 19, 28, 36, 38, 50, 202, 204, 205
  and effects on voting, 125
  and model of party governance, 1
Intraparty politics, 6
Italy Alive (IV, *Italia Viva*), 40

L
Law and Justice (PiS, *Prawo i Sprawiedliwość*), 44
Lead electoral candidates, 187
Leaders' complementarity
  cognitive complementarity, 26
  expertise complementarity, 26
  role complementarity, 26, 173
  task complementarity, 26
Leadership
  capital, 79, 85, 88, 90, 122, 129
  functions, 10, 23, 24, 26, 27, 29, 35, 38, 50, 53, 90, 93, 130, 164, 183, 184, 189
  expressive, 10, 26, 27, 29
  instrumental, 10, 26, 29
  profiles, 162
  the motivator, 29
  the organizer, 29
  the president, 29
  the strategist, 29
  selection, 2, 39, 105, 200
League (*Lega*), 139, 143, 156, 157
Left Democrats (DS, *Democratici di sinistra*), 51
Left, The (*Die Linke*), 74, 77, 95, 196, 206

M
Misalignments

spontaneous, 23, 86, 92, 93, 130, 168, 184
Motivation, 52, 114, 121
Movement party, 84, 139, 142, 143
Multimember leadership, 6, 7, 10, 20–22, 30, 33, 41, 46, 50, 51, 69, 72, 81, 83, 84, 109, 114, 120, 154–156, 160, 161, 172, 173, 182, 183, 186, 188–190, 195, 198, 202

N
National Front (FN, *Front National*), 41
National Rally (RN, *Rassemblement National*), 41

O
Olive Tree (*Ulivo*), 51
Organizational reform, 66, 68, 71, 72, 75, 79, 80, 85, 92, 120

P
Party
  in central office, 24, 159, 183, 193
  in public office, 24, 40, 64, 70, 71, 77, 79, 82, 89, 111, 113, 126, 149, 151, 155, 156, 165, 170
  on the ground, 24, 40, 65, 70, 74, 75, 89, 91, 96, 109, 113, 116, 117, 122, 126, 138, 150, 186
Party congress/assembly, 40, 65, 66, 72, 75, 77, 78, 82–84, 91, 92, 105, 107–112, 115, 120, 121, 124, 125, 159, 170, 188, 193
Party Lifespan
  authorization, 70, 113
  declaration, 113
  executive power, 70, 74, 198
  representation, 70, 113, 191, 198
PDS. *See* Left, The (*Die Linke*)

Personalization, 1, 3, 4, 79, 89, 139
Political entrepreneur, 41, 119, 136, 138, 146
Populism, 114, 137
Position sharing, 20, 22, 50, 84, 86, 204
Power sharing, 20–22, 25, 42, 86, 126, 204
Power, soft, 28
Professionalization, 68, 73, 75, 78, 84, 88–90, 110, 121

S
Separation of office and mandate, 63, 83
Shared leadership, 15, 16, 20, 21, 26, 53, 64
Social Democratic Party of Germany (SPD, *Sozialdemokratische Partei Deutschlands*), 64, 69, 73, 79, 90
Spanish Socialist Workers Party (PSOE, *Partido Socialista Obrero Español*), 9, 47, 48, 56
Strategic leadership, 17, 141
Subnational level, 64, 74, 127, 191

T
Territorial diffusion, 36, 63, 135
Top management team, 17
Trade Unions, 18

U
UK Labour, 9, 18
United career, 53, 54, 56, 163, 172, 189, 200, 205

W
WASG. *See* Left, The (*Die Linke*)
We can (*Podemos*), 86, 92, 169, 200–202